IMAGES
of America

Columbia County Georgia

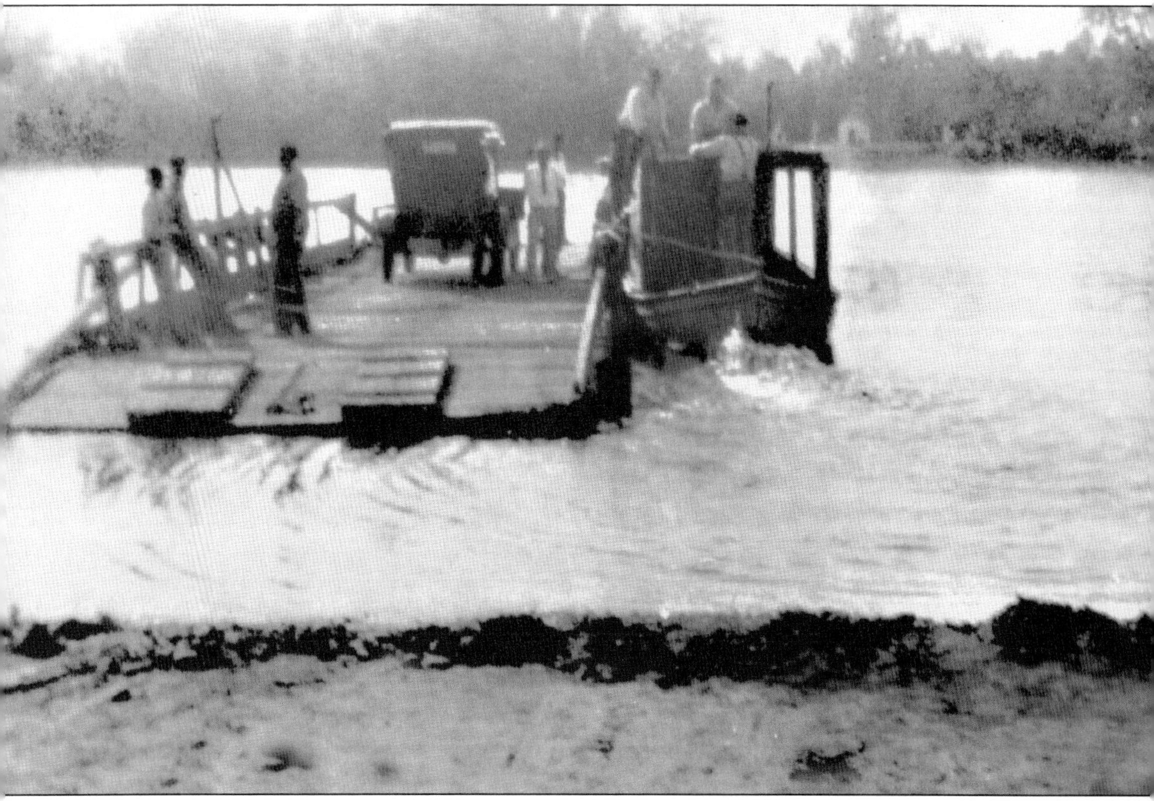

Old Fury's Ferry crosses the Savannah River, c. 1920. Note the Petersburg motorboat that was used for power on one side. (Courtesy of Bradley Myers.)

IMAGES
of America

COLUMBIA COUNTY
GEORGIA

William C. Blackard, Thomas Huckabee,
and Gerald J. Smith, Ph.D.

ARCADIA
PUBLISHING

ISBN 978-0-7385-0628-9

Published by Arcadia Publishing
Charleston, South Carolina

Printed in the United States of America

Library of Congress Catalog Card Number: 00-107276

For all general information contact Arcadia Publishing at:
Telephone 843-853-2070
Fax 843-853-0044
E-mail sales@arcadiapublishing.com
For customer service and orders:
Toll-Free 1-888-313-2665

Visit us on the Internet at www.arcadiapublishing.com

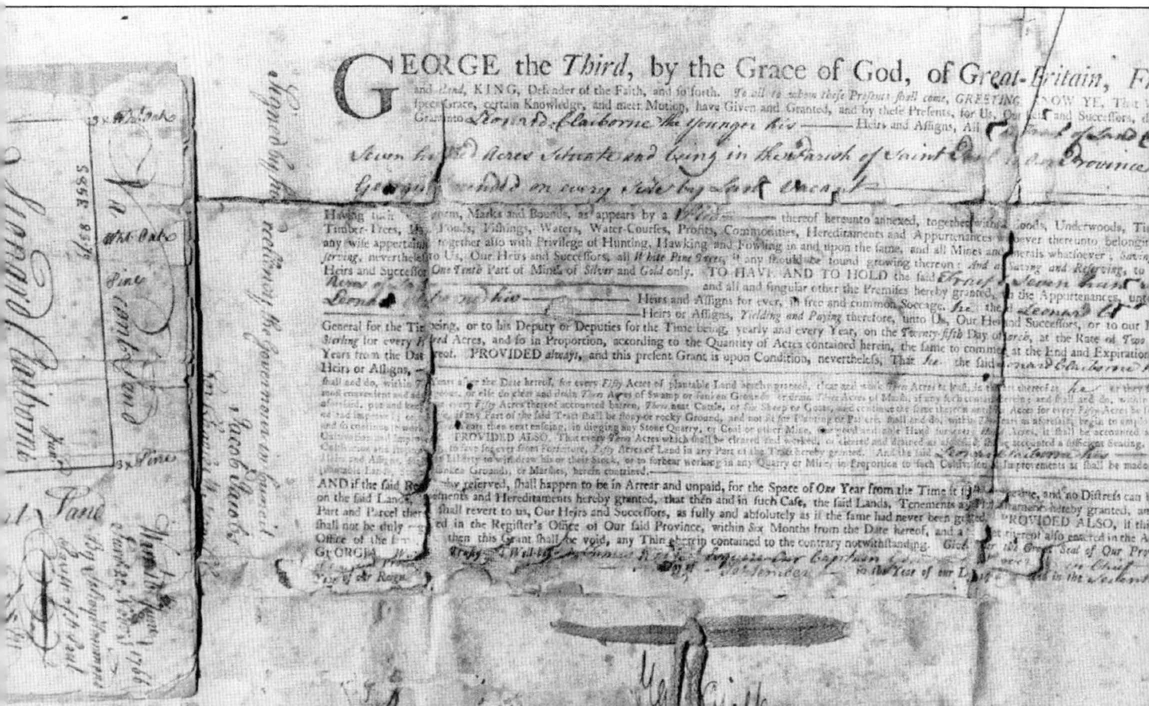
GEORGE the *Third*, by the Grace of God, of Great-Britain, F

Shown here is the land grant by King George III that can be found today in the Robert Lane home. (Courtesy of Lallie Dozier Benkoski.)

Contents

ACKNOWLEDGMENTS

The authors would like to thank the following people for their contributions to this project:

Jean Blackard
G.L. Polatty
Lallie D. Benkoski
Dan Marshall
Thomas Holley
Carla Grimaud
Mary Sanders
Edna Ruth Paschal
Jake Pollard
Bill Jackson
Carole Davis
Darwin Morris
Pat Blanchard
Edith Hardin Reese
Barbara Seaborn
Elizabeth L. Johnson
Lewis Bartles
Helen Ghann
Berma Gibson
Lane Morris
Elma Jean Lazenby
Jimmy Wallace
Billy Snellings
Francis Tracy
Robert Tankersly
Bradley Myers

INTRODUCTION

Columbia County was originally a part of Richmond County that comprised the old St. Paul's Parish of colonial Georgia. Richmond County had its county seat in Augusta, the largest municipality. Citizens in the upper part of the county had to travel 30 or 40 miles for county government functions. Led by William Few Jr., a delegation petitioned the state government to break up the old parish into two counties. The petition was granted and the new county became a reality in 1790. Named for Christopher Columbus, Columbia County was born. Appling eventually became the county seat.

Rich in prehistory, Columbia County boasts Stallings Island in the Savannah River where early Native Americans made the first pottery in North America. Kiokee Creek, a major tributary that drains the central portion of the county, was also inhabited by prehistoric man known for a distinctive projectile point that has been named by archaeologists "Kiokee Creek Stemmed." As the centuries passed, the Euchee, Creek, and Appalachee Indians settled in the area. When the first Europeans arrived, the Indians, despite a few raids on such settlements as Quaker Springs, for the most part proved friendly and helpful. The Euchees finally moved westward toward the Chattahoochee River but left their name for posterity in the county in such things as Euchee Creek and Euchee Old Fields (near Grovetown).

The Revolutionary War reached the county, not only with the forming of militia units, but also with a significant skirmish at Middleton's Ferry on the Savannah River. At the close of the war, several of the county's leaders became integral in the founding of the new republic. William Few Jr., for instance, was one of the signers of the Constitution.

In the antebellum period, the county saw several large plantations where cotton was king and slavery the major instrument in producing it. The Civil War caused three companies of Confederate infantry to be raised in the county, all of which served well in the conflict. Local militia units again were organized.

The Reconstruction period went badly for the county, which saw an economic depression that lasted well into the 20th century. Prosperity finally came, however, with the establishment of nearby Fort Gordon Military Reservation and the Savannah River Site, both of which brought the construction of homes and subdivisions for the hundreds of new residents. An excellent public education system under the leadership of John Pierce Blanchard and a host of competent teachers replaced the old field schools and became one of the best in the state, attracting young families to the area. New businesses brought in employees, retired military families moved in, and Clark's Hill Reservoir—with its recreational opportunities—proved a lodestone. The African-American population remained a stable factor as it had in the 19th century. The county grew from 1950 onward until the number of residents topped out in the 2000 census at over 100,000, a sharp contrast to the 10,000 in 1883. Today, Columbia County is among the fastest-growing counties in the state outside the Atlanta metropolitan area.

The images presented in this book were selected to illustrate the many facets of life in this fascinating county. At least four ambrotypes of the Civil War period are showcased here, as well as a 1930s photo of the excavation at Stallings Island, representing the area's prehistory. Several pictures of farms, plantations, churches, towns, stores, schools, and important early figures are included.

Readers will enjoy the variety of images as they travel back in time to see Columbia County through the decades. Nostalgia, that gift from God that makes the hustle of modern life and its impermanence somewhat more bearable and less tedious, will brighten the reader's perspective and perhaps give him an anchor of hope by which he can secure his future. The authors have labored to this effect. Realizing that the "good old days" were not as good as often thought, we trust that the good will be remembered and the bad forgotten—at least for a moment.

One

PEOPLE THROUGHOUT THE YEARS

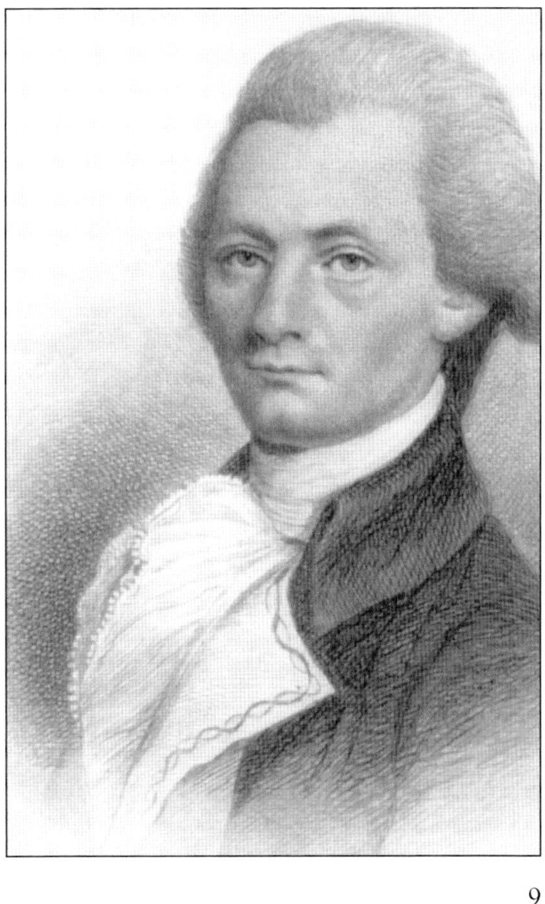

William Few Jr. (1748–1828) founded Columbia County in 1790. A veteran of the American Revolution, he served in the state and national congresses. Most significantly, he helped to frame and signed the Constitution. (Courtesy of G.J. Smith.)

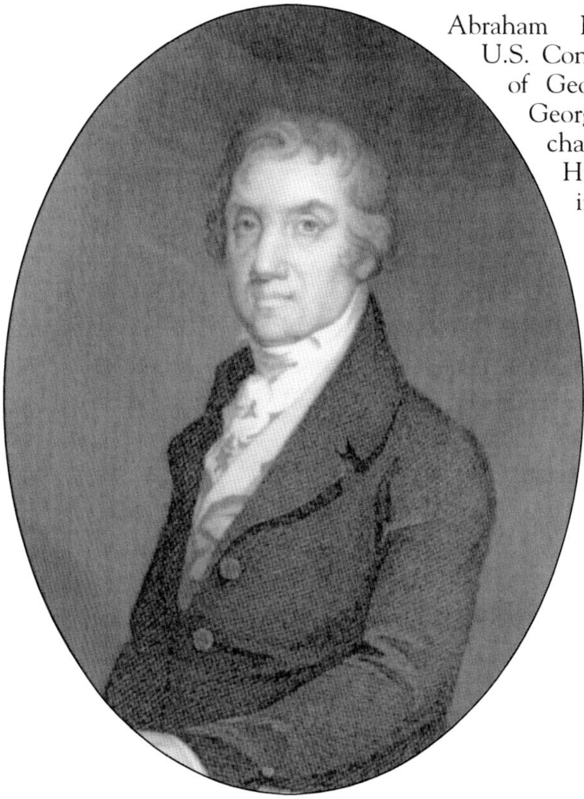

Abraham Baldwin (1754–1807) signed the U.S. Constitution and founded the University of Georgia. A Yale graduate and one of Georgia's most able men, he served as a chaplain in the American Revolution. His name is remembered in the state in Baldwin County (Milledgeville) and Abraham Baldwin Agricultural University. (Courtesy of G.J. Smith.)

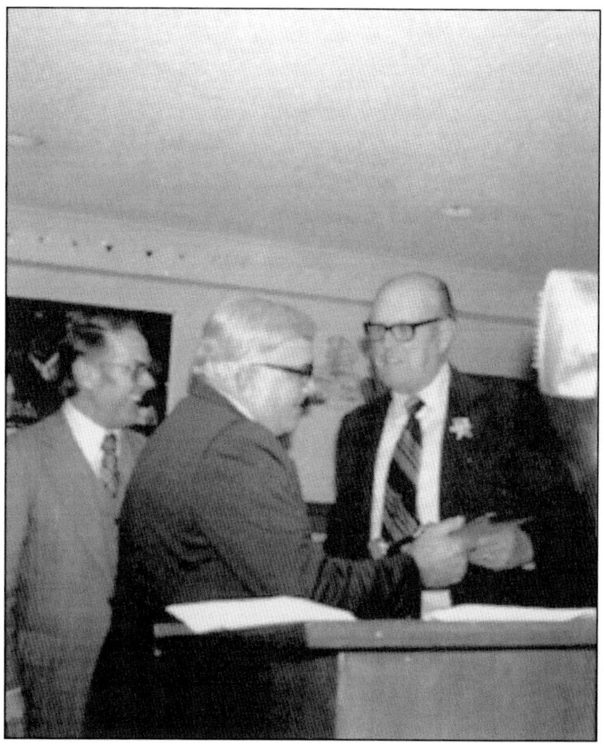

In this 1960s photograph, Lynn Norris (center), chairman of the County Commissioners, hands a plaque to Sheriff Edward Tankersly in appreciation of his 28 years of law enforcement service in Columbia County. (Courtesy of Robert Tankersly.)

Thomas Edward Watson (1856–1925) was known as the "Agrarian Rebel" and a leader of the Populist Party at the beginning of the 1900s. He lectured and wrote widely on behalf of the nation's farmers and championed the rural lifestyle and values. (Courtesy of G.J. Smith.)

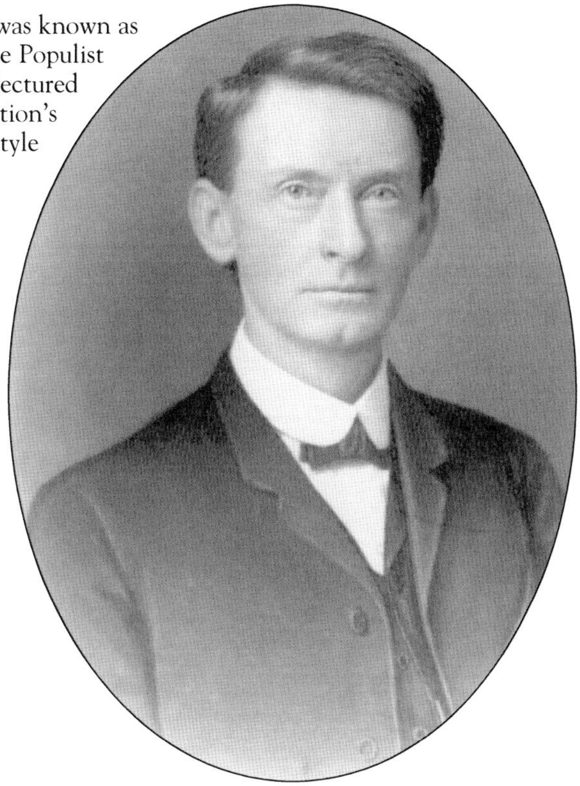

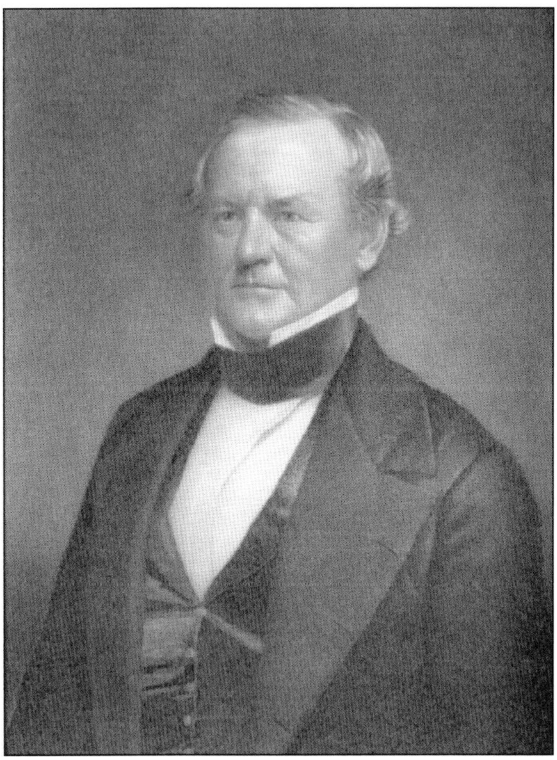

George Walker Crawford (1798–1872) was governor of Georgia from 1843 to 1847. His two terms as the state's leader were very successful. He also served as secretary of war under President Zachary Taylor and president of the Georgia Secession Convention in 1861. (Courtesy of G.J. Smith.)

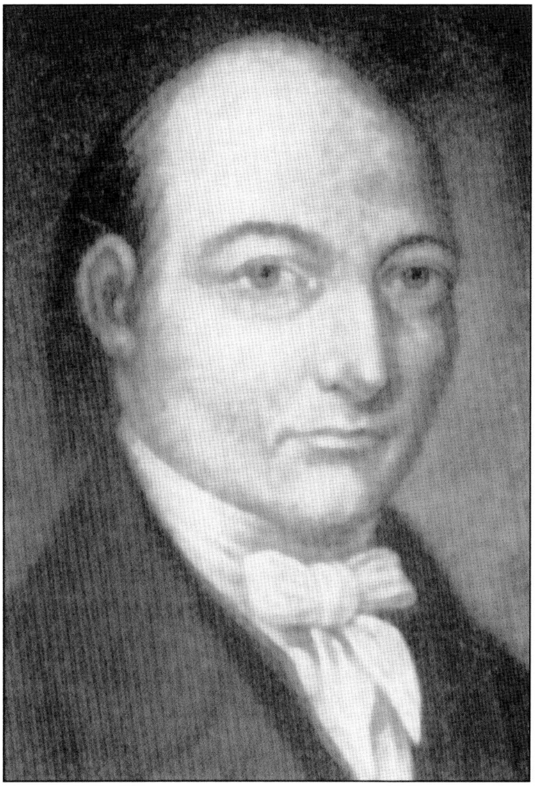

Jesse Mercer, the founder of Mercer University, was an eminent Baptist minister, editor of the *Christian Index*, and publisher of *Mercer's Cluster*, an early hymnbook that went through four editions. His work and esteemed place in Georgia Baptist history will likely stand the passage of time. (Courtesy of G.J. Smith.)

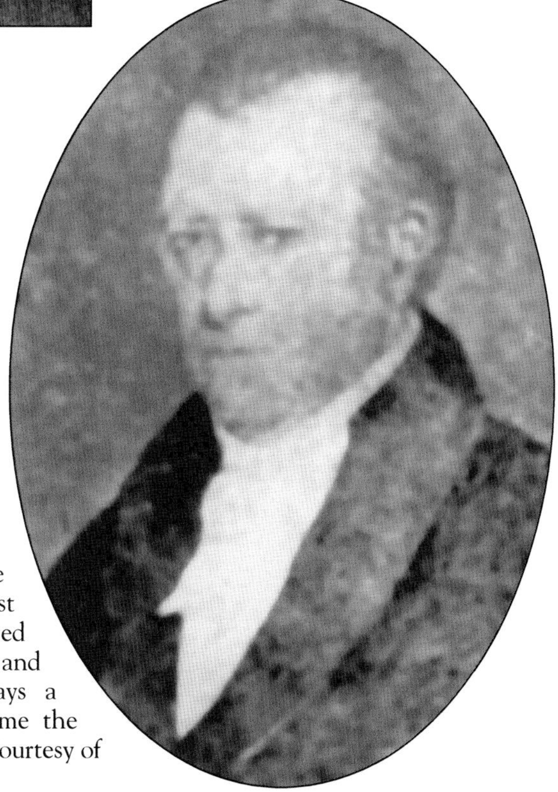

Moses Waddel came to the county in the 1790s to preach to a Presbyterian congregation near Appling. He there established Carmel Academy, the first classical school in the area. He later moved the school within the limits of Appling and renamed it Columbia Academy. Always a leader in education, Waddel later became the president of the University of Georgia. (Courtesy of G.J. Smith.)

Reverend Juriah Harris, the pastor of Kiokee Baptist Church, was one of the best pulpiteers in the South. Always ardent in his ministry, he ventured out, even as an old man, into all kinds of weather—rain or shine, hot or cold—to spread the Word and minister to his flock. His name will always be mentioned when the finest Georgia Baptist ministers are listed. (Courtesy of Lallie Dozier Benkoski.)

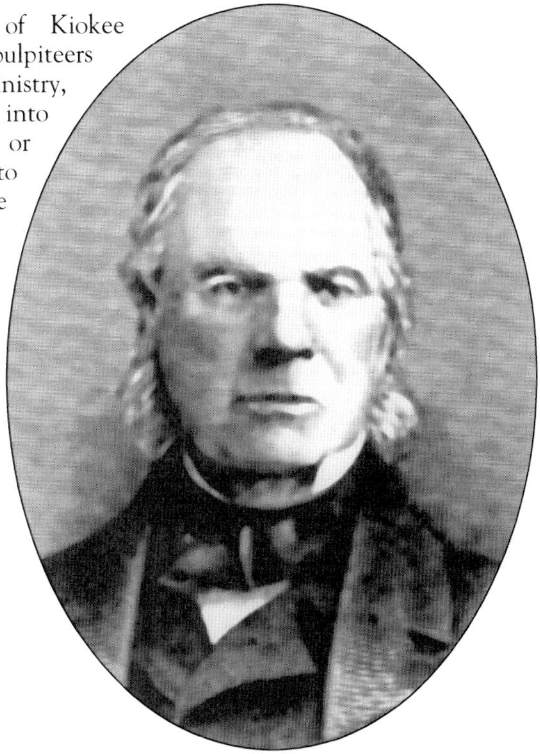

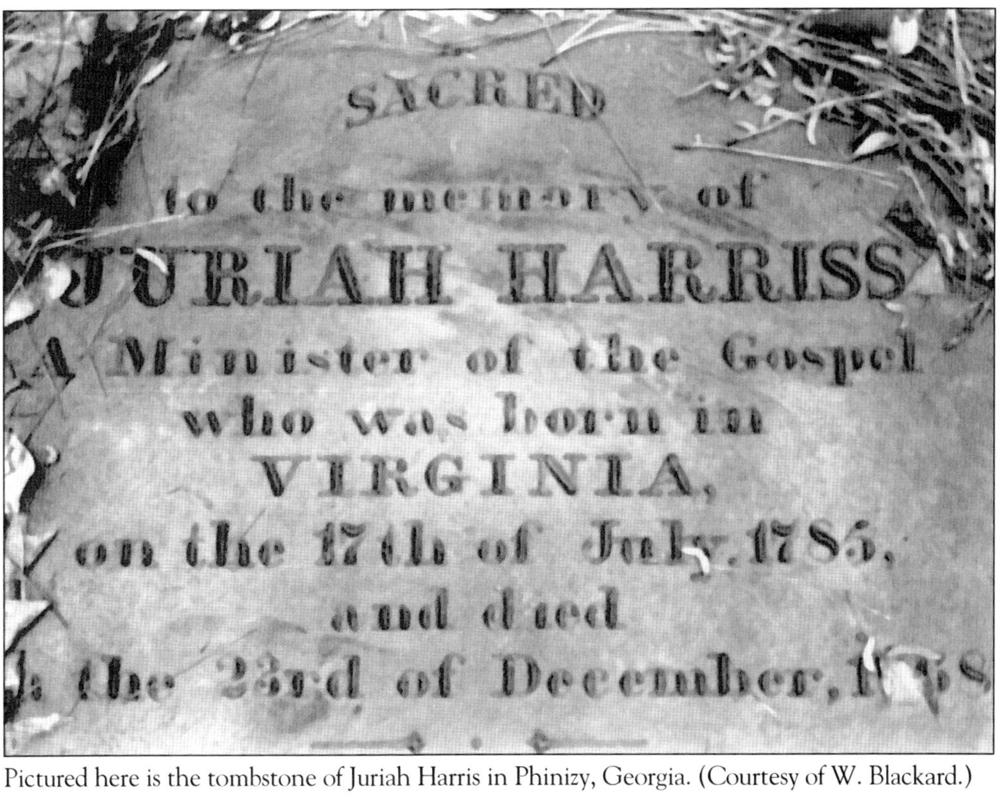

Pictured here is the tombstone of Juriah Harris in Phinizy, Georgia. (Courtesy of W. Blackard.)

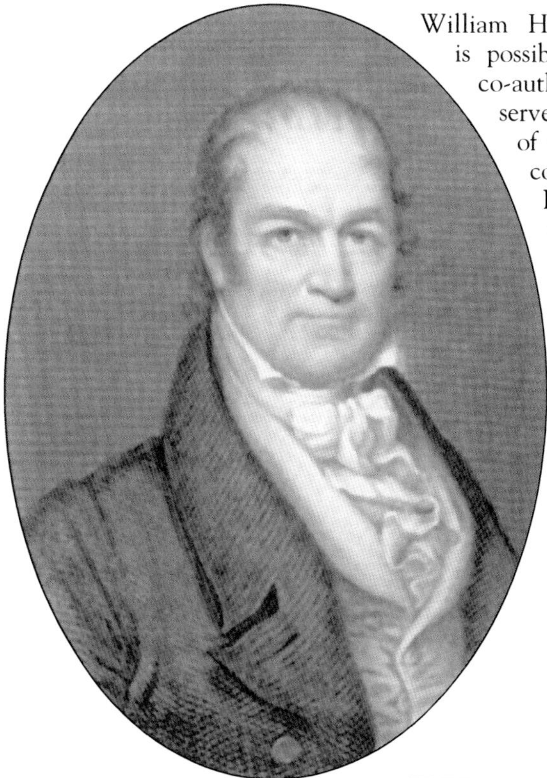

William Harris Crawford, a lawyer and senator, is possibly the greatest man from Georgia. He co-authored the famous Monroe Doctrine, served as secretary of the treasury and secretary of war, and represented the nation in the court of Napoleon Bonaparte. The famous French emperor stated that Crawford was one of the ablest men in diplomacy that he had ever met. The towns of Crawford and Crawfordville, Georgia are named for William Harris Crawford, as is Crawford County, Georgia. (Courtesy of G.J. Smith.)

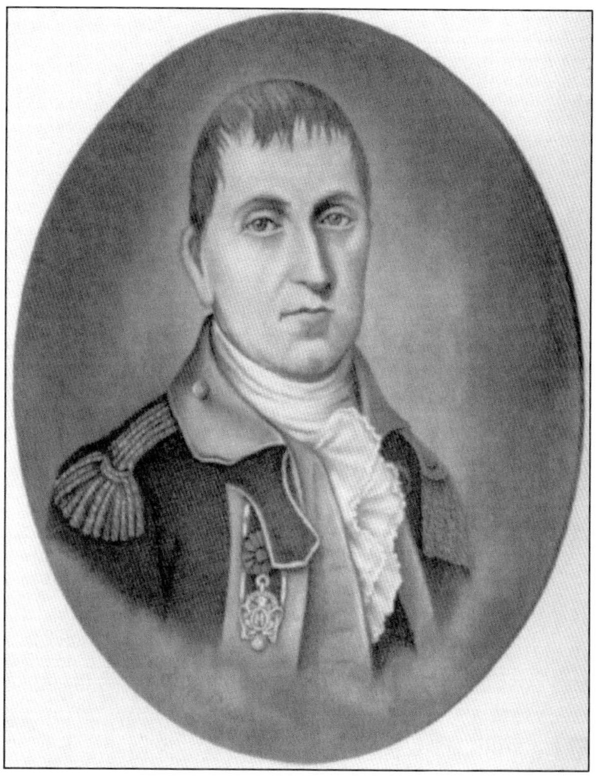

Pictured here is Thomas Glascock, a brigadier general in the Continental Army. General George Washington spoke very highly of Glascock's leadership abilities. A famous Georgian, Glascock is remembered in the names of Glascock County, Georgia. (Courtesy of G.J. Smith.)

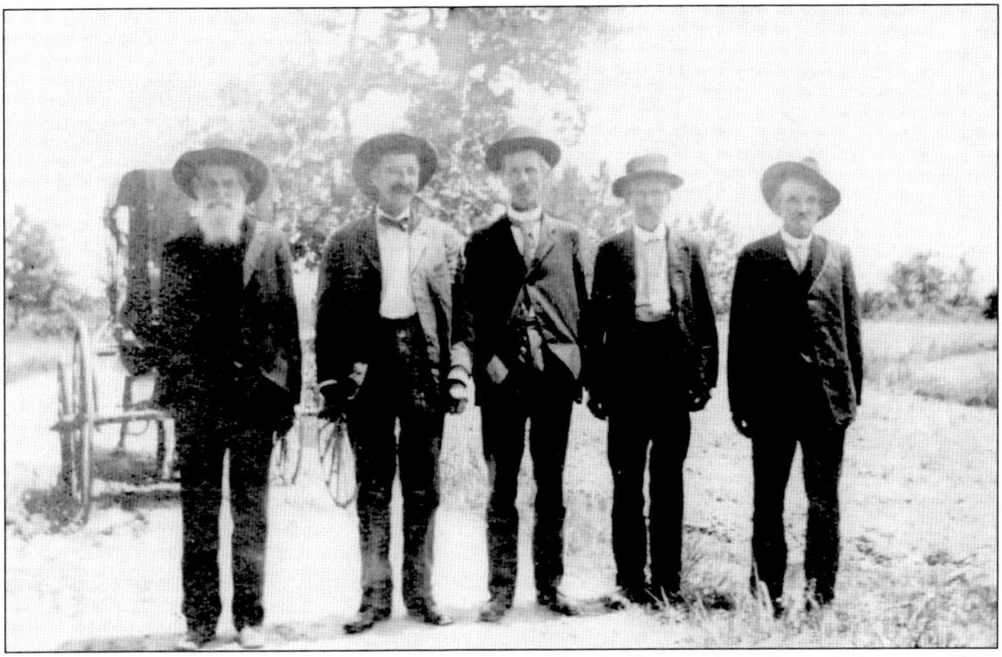

Five county citizens are pictured with a buggy in the background in this 1900 image. The identity of the men is unknown. (Courtesy of Edna Ruth Paschal.)

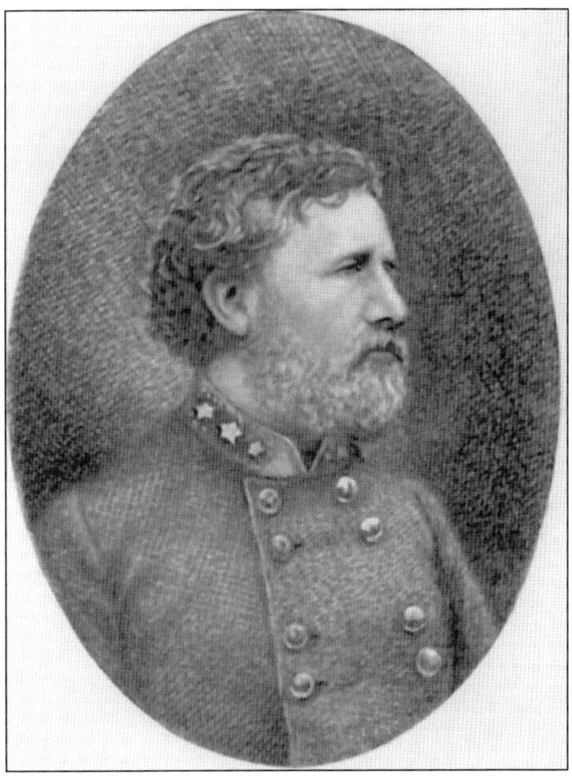

Henry Lewis Benning was born in Columbia County on April 2, 1814. He became a lawyer, a solicitor general, a representative in the Georgia Congress, a judge, and a general. He attained the rank of major general in the Army of Northern Virginia, acquiring the nickname "The Rock" for his steadfastness in battle. He died on July 8, 1875. (Courtesy of G.J. Smith.)

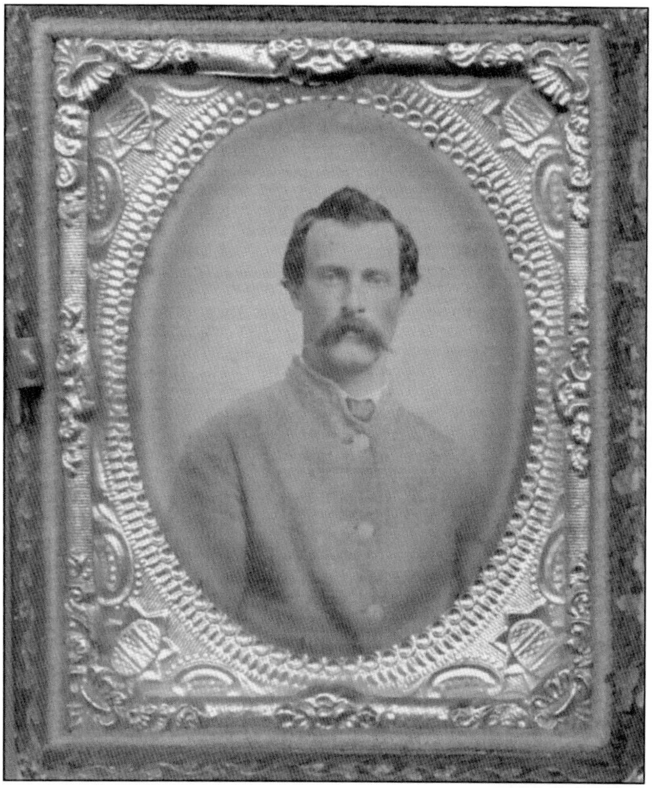

Pictured here is Private Jabez Pleiades Marshall of the Oglethorpe Artillery and 1st Georgia Regiment. He later transferred to the 63rd Georgia Regiment, Colonel G.A. Gordon's Brigade, Army of Tennessee. (Courtesy of Dan Marshall.)

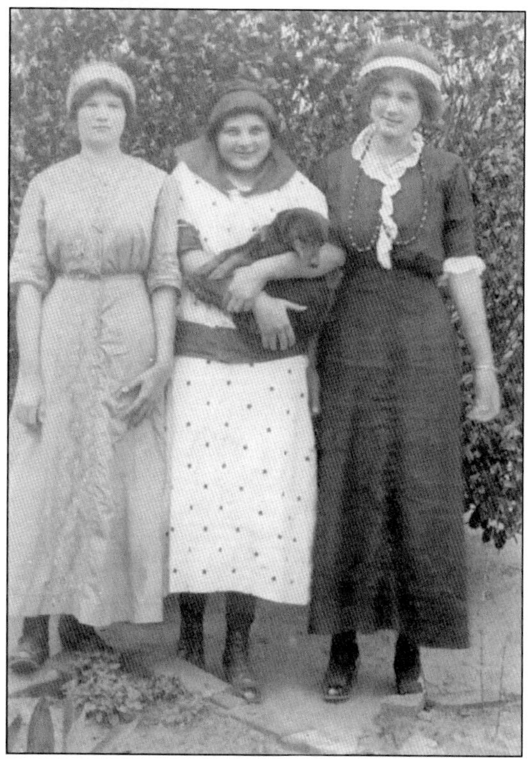

Shown are Annie Percival, Willie Pearson, and Clara Percival Whitaker. The little dog is unnamed, but no less loved. (Courtesy of Judy Sanderlin.)

Margaret Percival Pearson is the subject of this c. 1900 photograph. (Courtesy of Judy Pearson.)

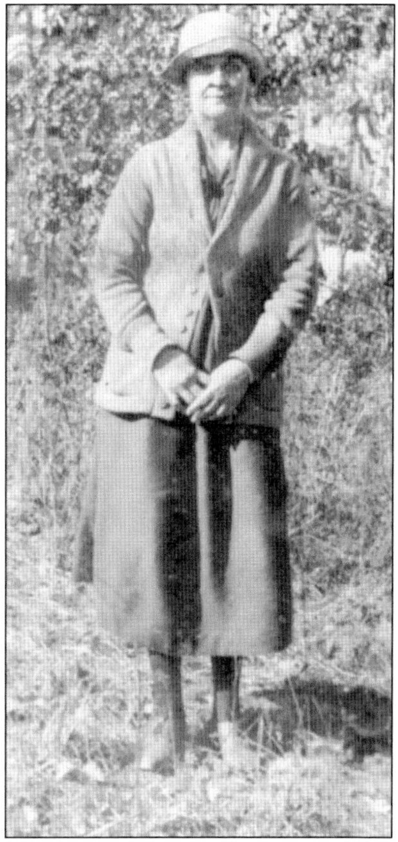

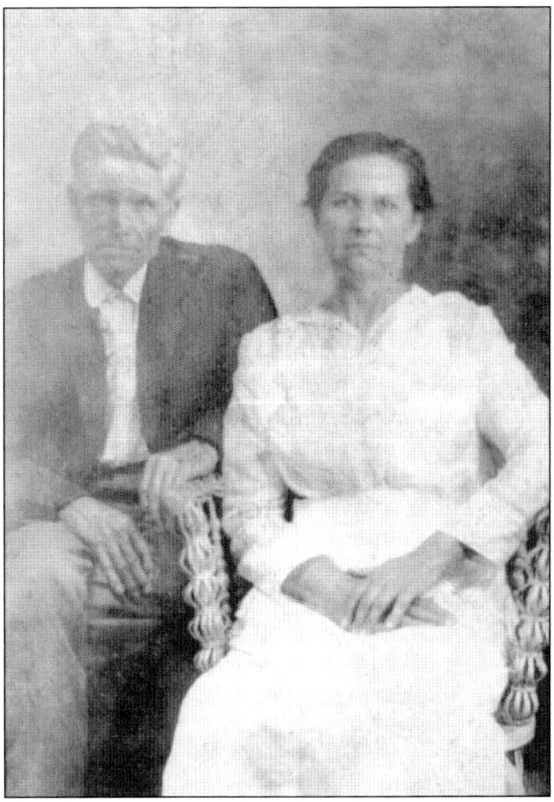

John Wesley Pearson and Margaret Percival Pearson pose for a formal portrait. (Courtesy of Judy Sanderlin.)

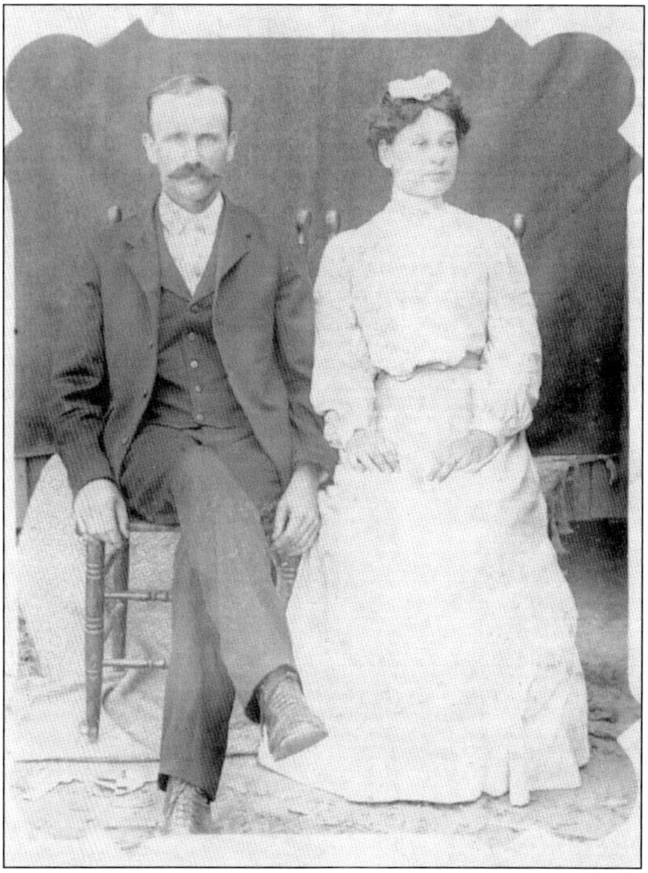

An unidentified couple is shown here. This photograph was obviously taken in a studio; note the cloth backdrop and the chairs. The couple is obviously "posing" as directed by the photographer. (Courtesy of Judy Sanderlin.)

A family gathers for a photograph at "The Oaks." They are, from left to right (standing) Robert Hugh Lamkin, J. Walton Davenport, and Robert Walton Lamkin Sr.; (seated) Martha Davenport, Ethel Lamkin Davenport, "Daisy" Elizabeth Lamkin, Elizabeth Benton Lamkin, and Walton Lamkin Jr. (front). (Courtesy of Elizabeth L. Johnson.)

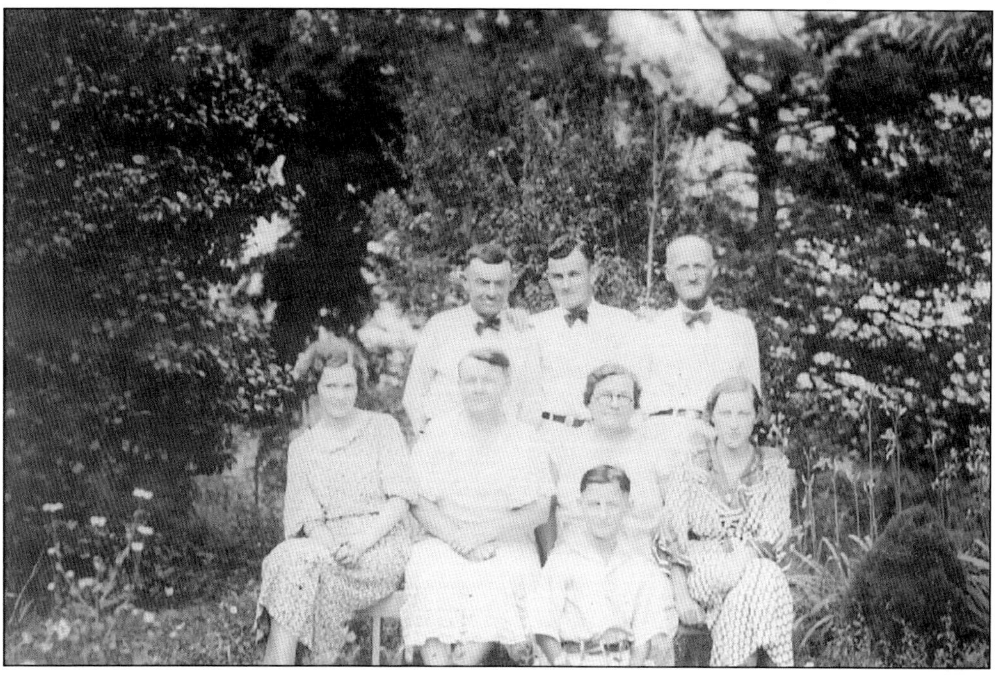

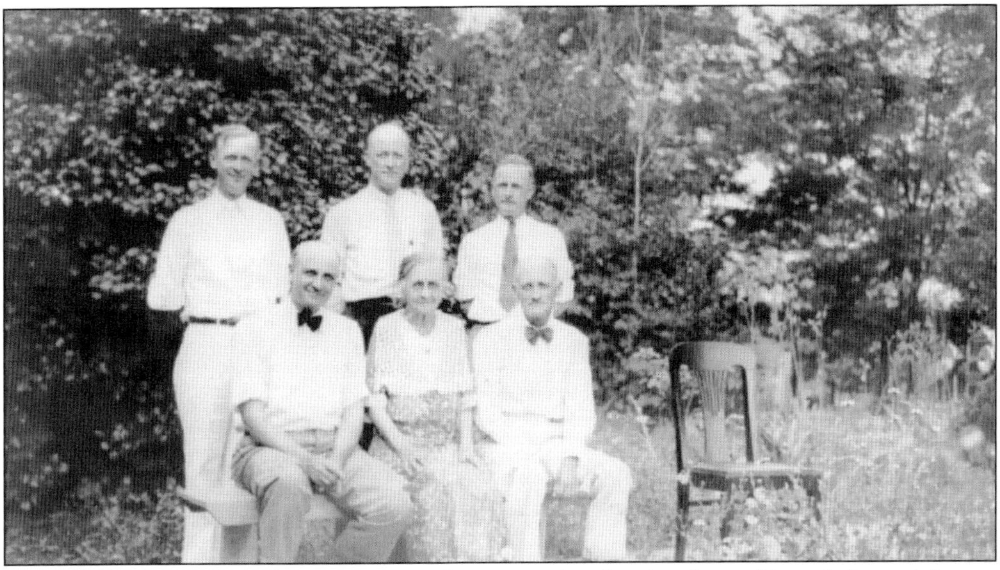

Ella Walton Lamkin and her sons are shown in this family photo. From left to right are (standing) Griffith B. "Dip" Lamkin, Frances Eve Lamkin, and Jacob Phinizy Lamkin; (seated) James Alexander Lamkin, Ella Gertrude Walton Lamkin, and Robert Walton Lamkin Sr. (Courtesy of Elizabeth L. Johnson.)

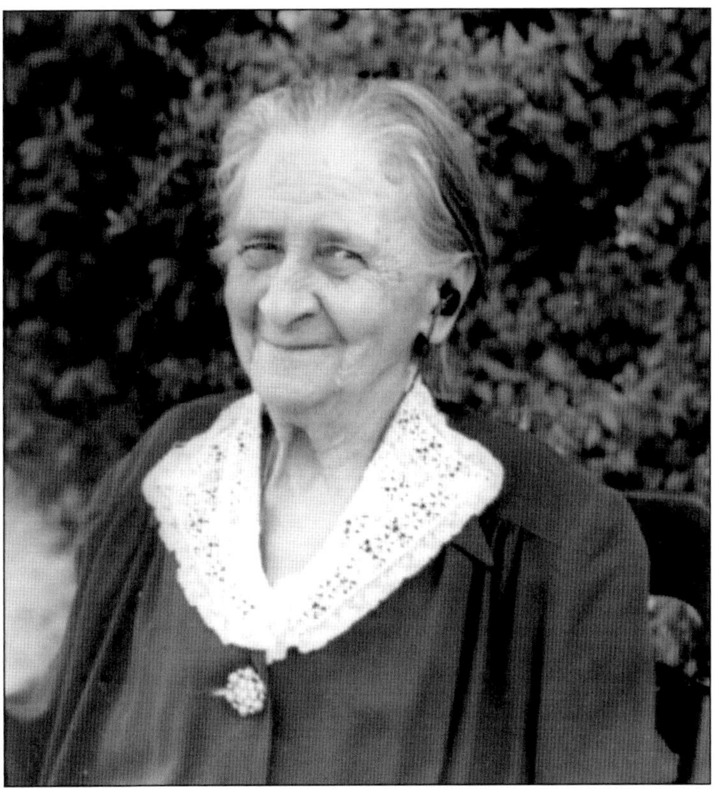

Pictured is Ella Gertrude Walton Lamkin. "Her children rise up and call her blessed; her husband also, and he praiseth her. Many daughters have done virtuously, but thou excellest them all" [Psalms 31:28]. (Courtesy of Elizabeth L. Johnson.)

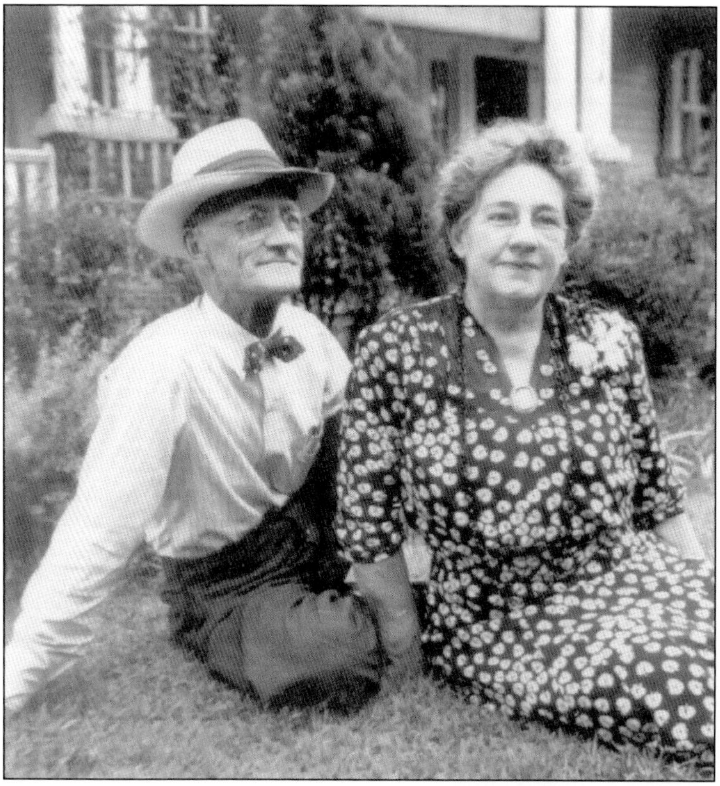

Robert Walton Lamkin Sr. and his wife, "Daisy" Elizabeth Lamkin, pose for this casual photo. "Grow old along with me/ The best is yet to be" [from "Rabbi Ben Ezra" by Robert Browning]. (Courtesy of Elizabeth L. Johnson.)

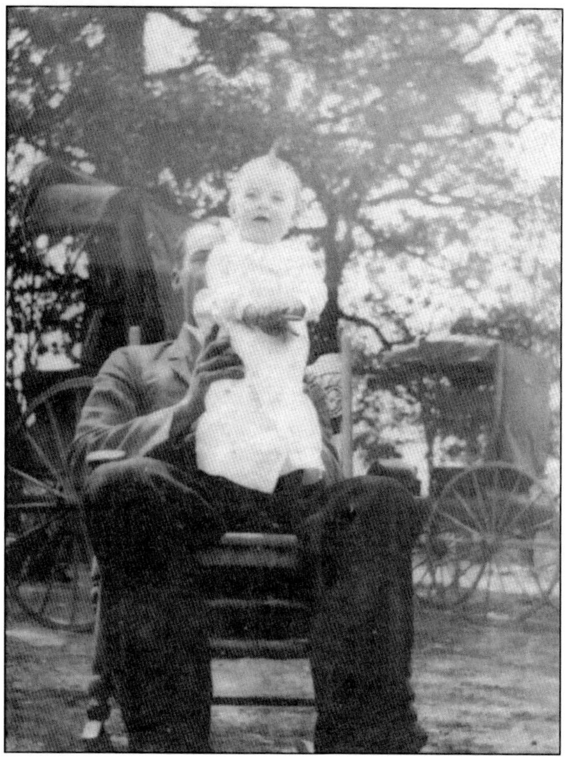

Held here by his father, Joseph Hartwell Marshall was just one year old in 1881, when this photograph was taken. Note the buggies in the background. The days of the "horseless carriage" had not yet arrived! (Courtesy of Daniel Marshall.)

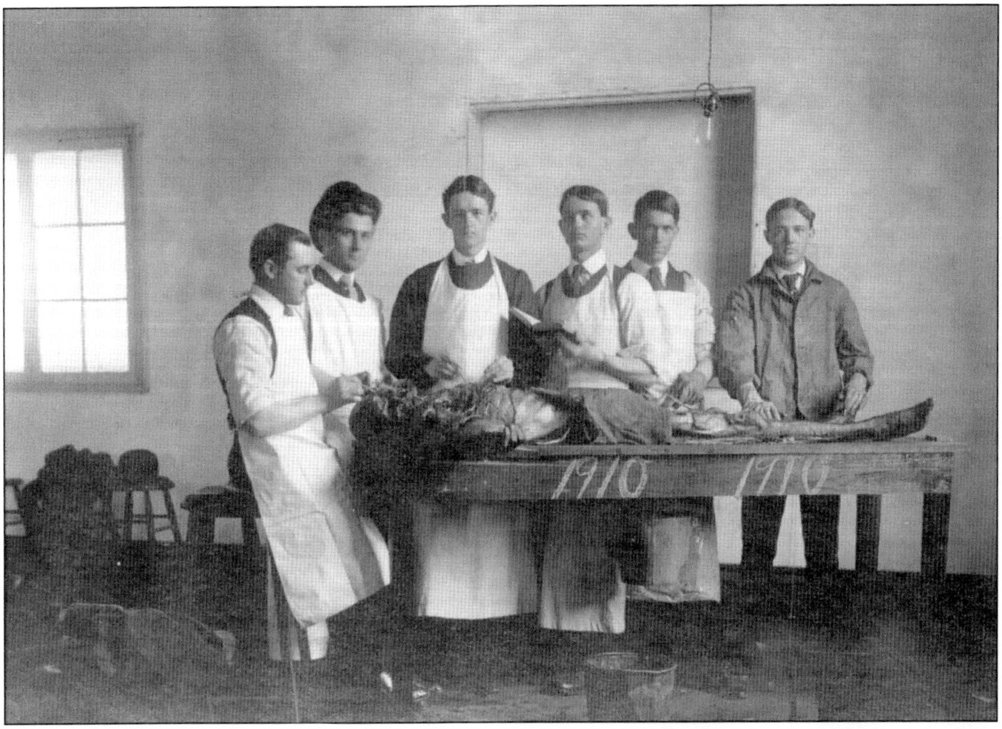

Shown is the Augusta Medical College of the University of Georgia in 1900. Second from the left is medical student Pierce Gordon Blanchard. (Courtesy of Carole Davis.)

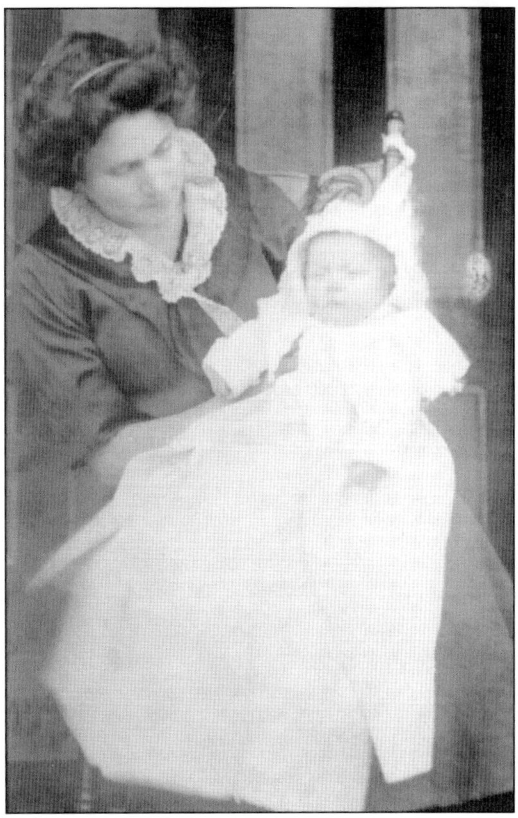

Pictured is Moralle Ramsey Blanchard and her daughter Clara in 1913. Look at the magnificent dress the baby has on! (Courtesy of Carole Davis.)

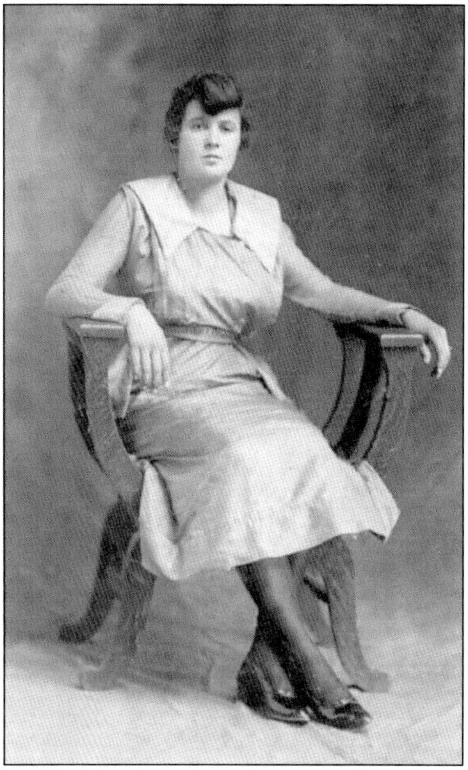

Pictured here is a 16-year-old Ila Yelton Bartles, c. 1916. Ila posed for this picture in a studio with a curtain backdrop. (Courtesy of Jean Blackard.)

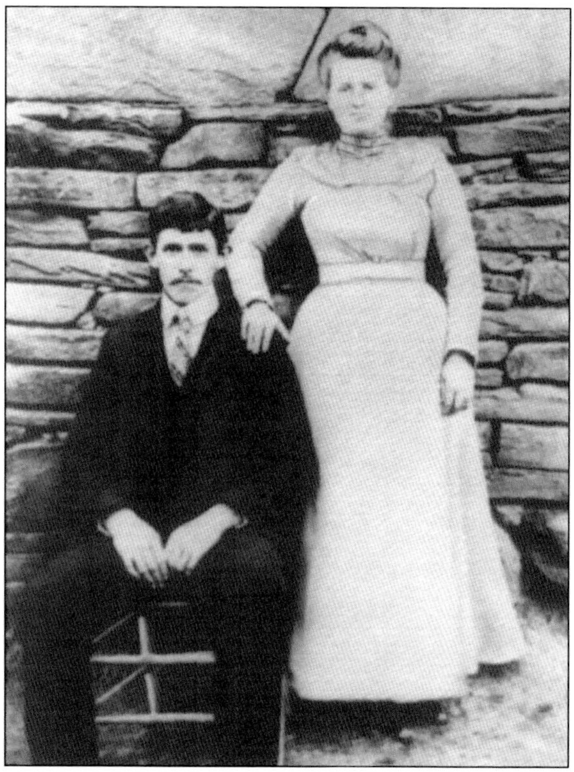

Edgar and Lilly Yelton are pictured in front of a very unique studio backdrop, c. 1890. (Courtesy of Jean Blackard.)

Millard and Sarah Bartles pose in front of yet another unique studio backdrop for this portrait made around 1925. (Courtesy of Jean Blackard.)

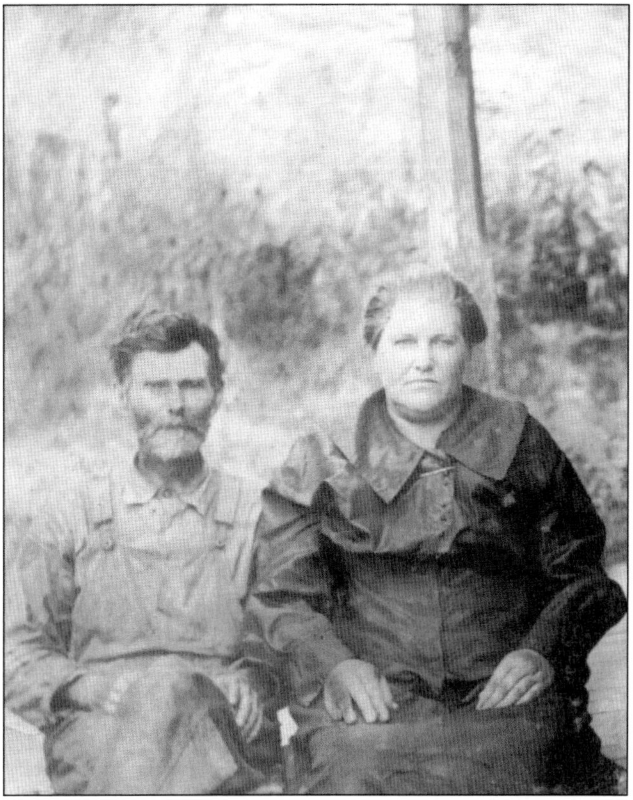

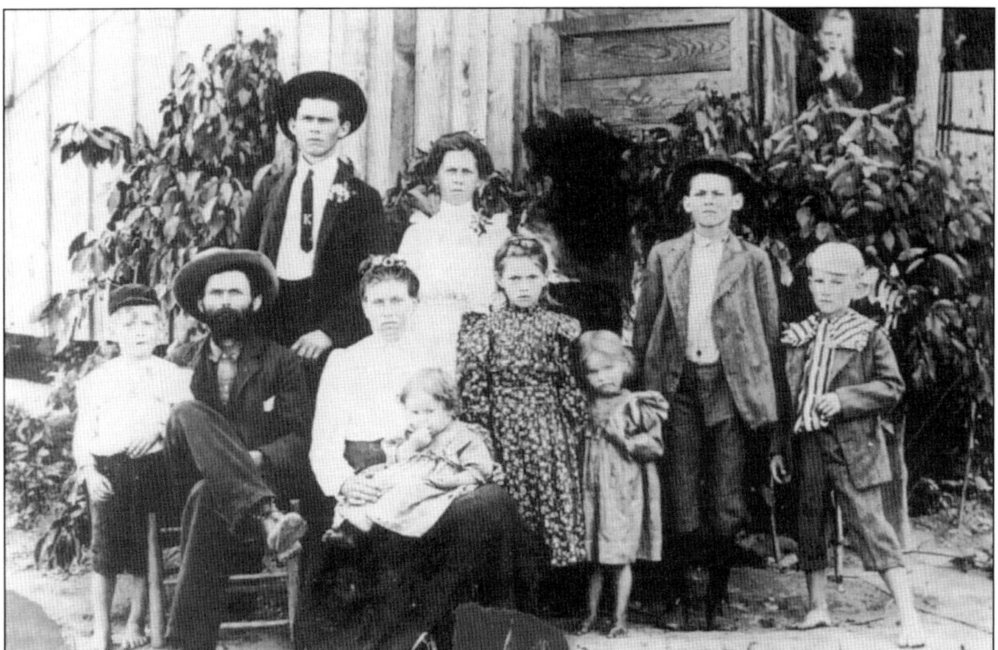

M.V. Bartles and his wife, Sarah Keeter Bartles, are shown here with their children, c. 1898. (Courtesy of Jean Blanchard.)

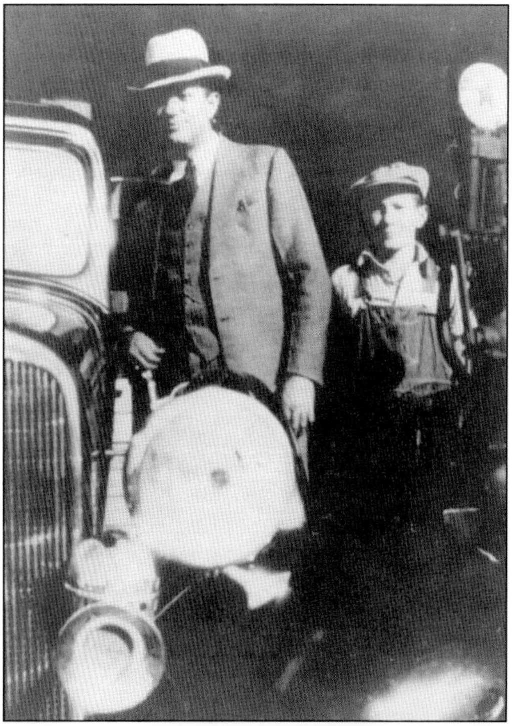

Dr. Pierce Gordon Blanchard and young John Pierce Blanchard appear in front of Wallace's Store in Phinizy, Georgia in 1933. Note the vintage automobile and the "crank" gasoline pump. Gas was just pennies a gallon then. Haven't times changed! (Courtesy of Pat Blanchard.)

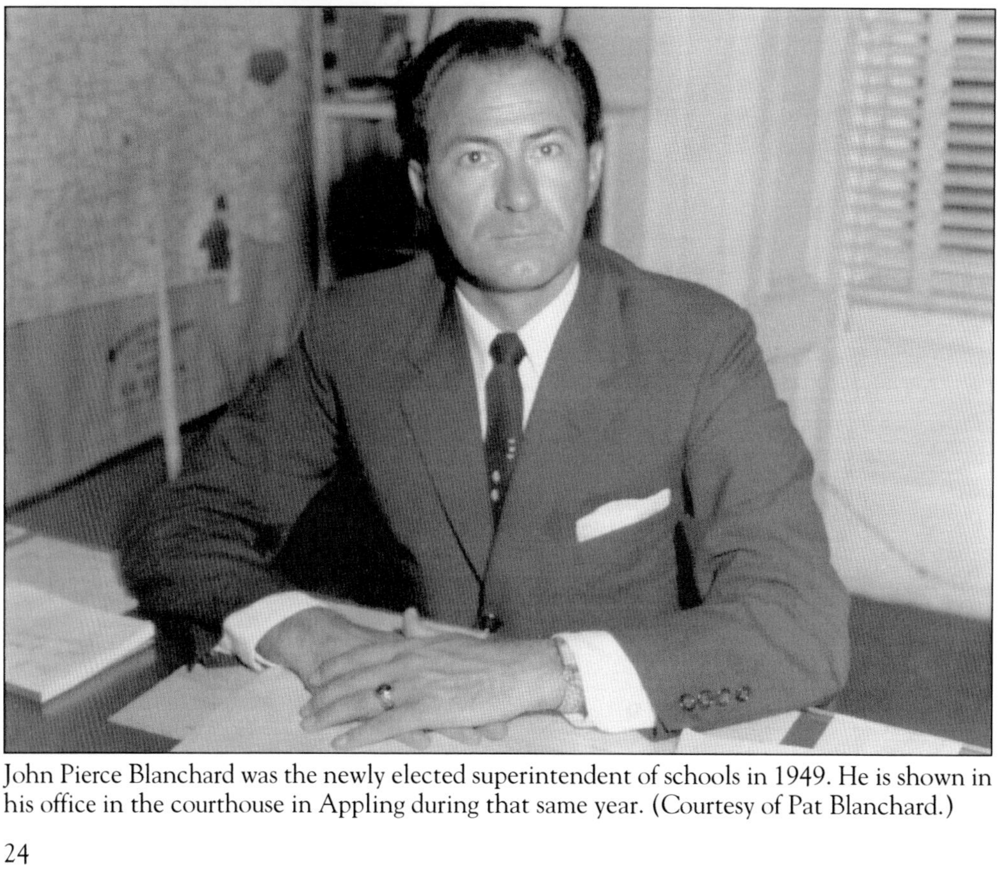

John Pierce Blanchard was the newly elected superintendent of schools in 1949. He is shown in his office in the courthouse in Appling during that same year. (Courtesy of Pat Blanchard.)

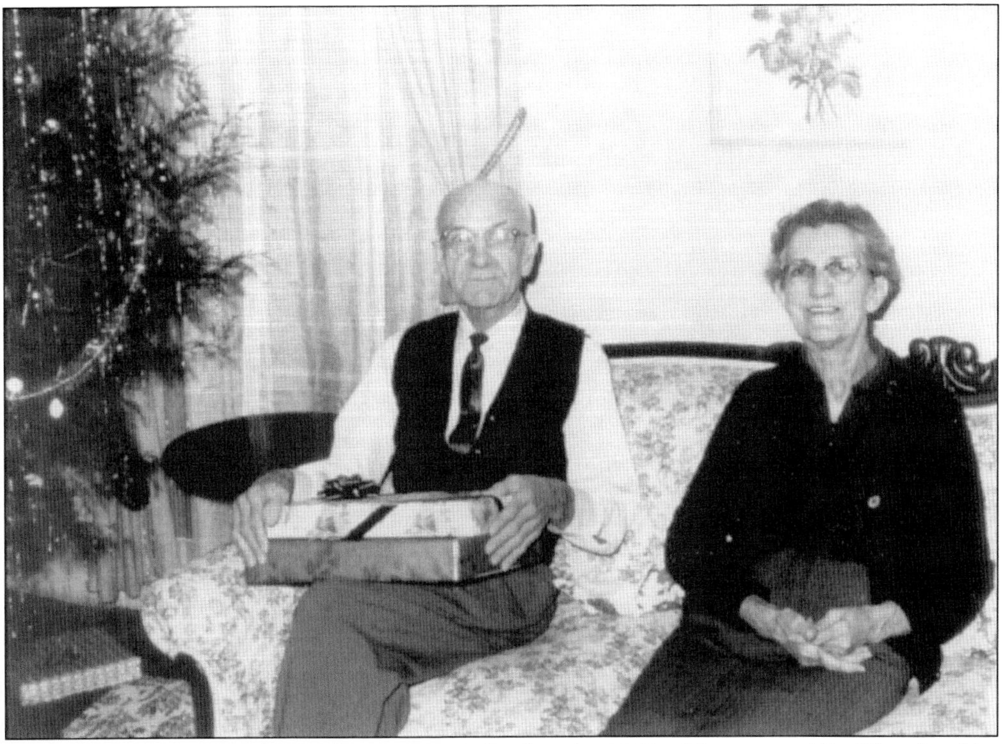

Shown here are G.B. "Jake" and Mattie K. Pollard in the 1960s. (Courtesy of Pat Blanchard.)

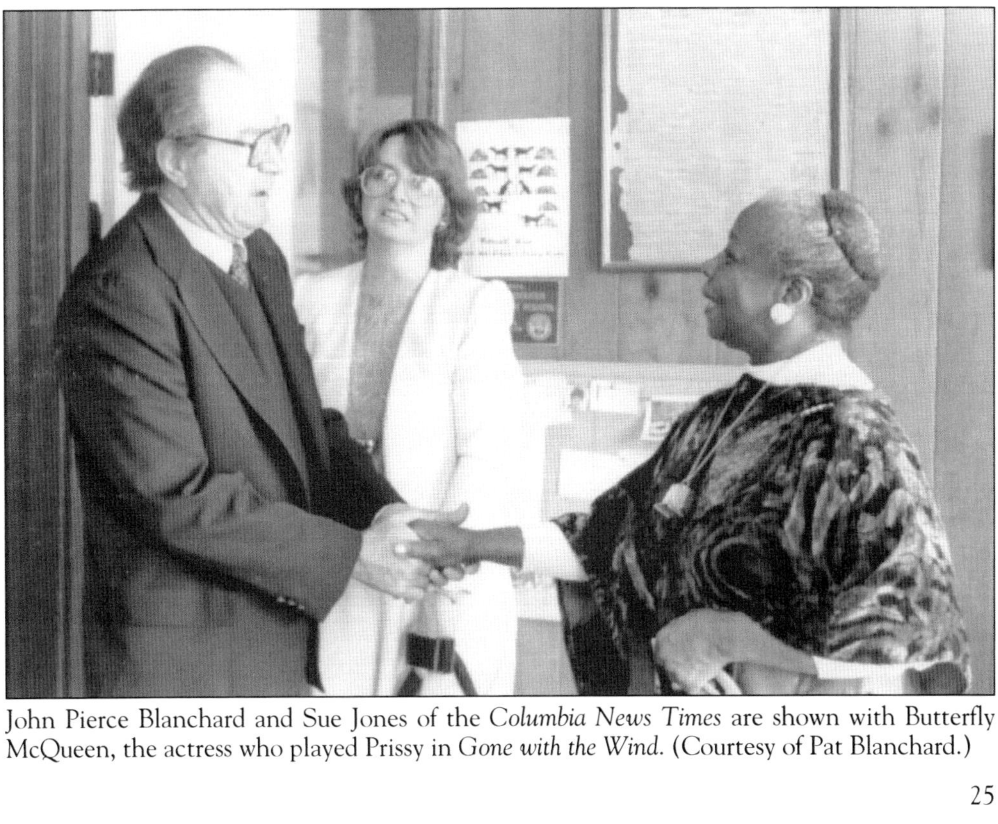

John Pierce Blanchard and Sue Jones of the *Columbia News Times* are shown with Butterfly McQueen, the actress who played Prissy in *Gone with the Wind.* (Courtesy of Pat Blanchard.)

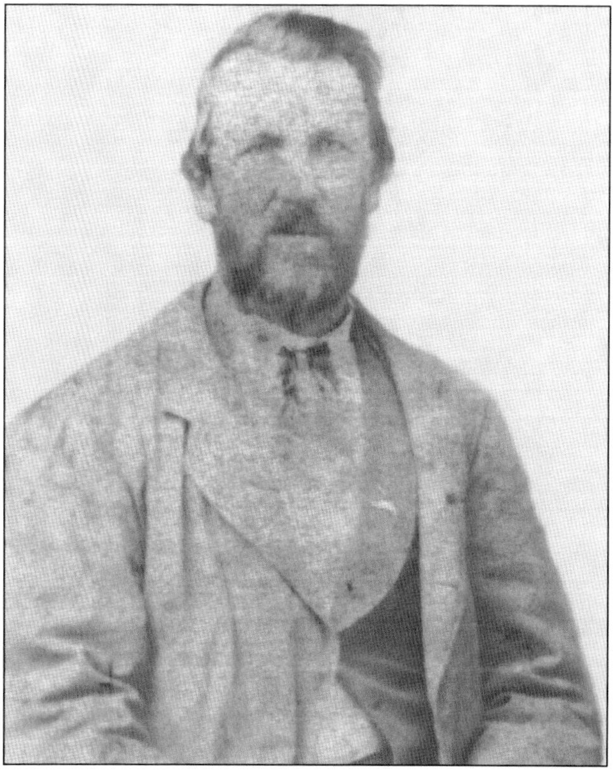

This photograph of Noah Stone was taken in 1862. He was a quartermaster sergeant in the Thomson Guards, 10th Georgia Regiment, in which he served from 1862 to 1865. (Courtesy of Thomas Holley.)

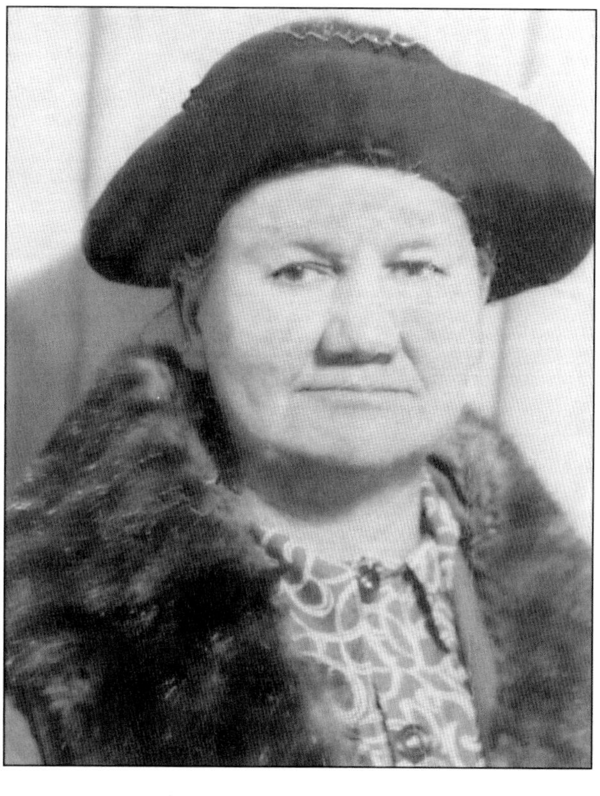

Shown here is Esther Prather, the wife of John Prather who served in the Thomson Guards, 10th Georgia Regiment, in the Civil War. (Courtesy of Thomas Holley.)

Pictured here is Captain John Stovall, 10th Georgia Regiment, in 1861. He was captured on April 6, 1865 and held as a prisoner of war at Johnson's Island, Ohio. He was released in June 1865. (Courtesy of Thomas Holley.)

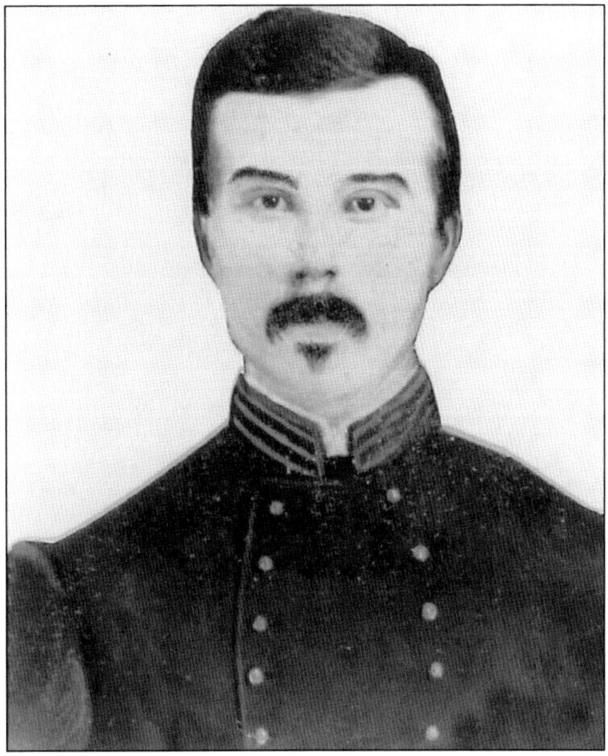

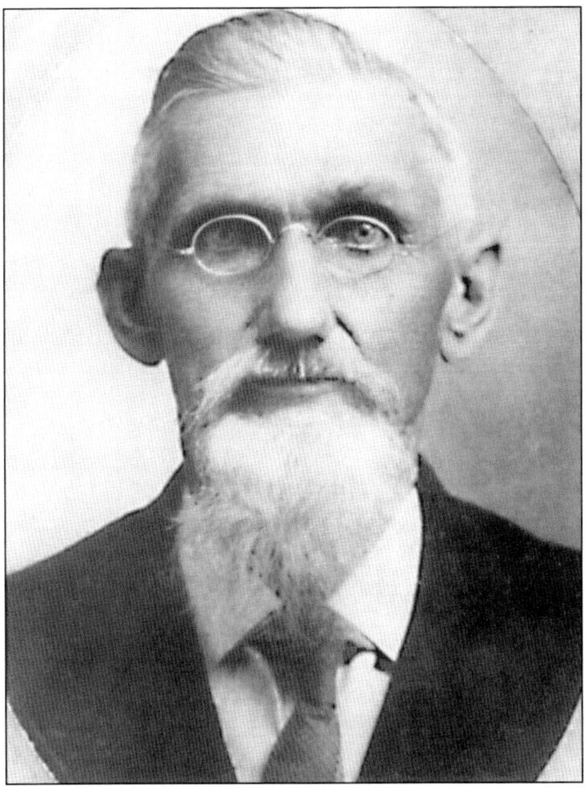

William Thomas Wilson served in the 10th Georgia Regiment from 1861 to 1865. This distinguished gentleman's photograph was taken much later in his life. (Courtesy of Thomas Holley.)

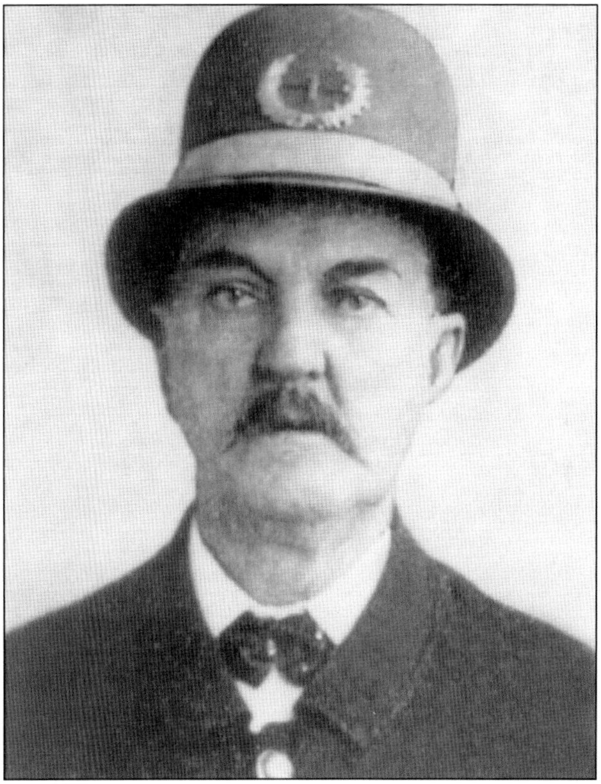

Simeon Dawson Morris was a private in the Thomson Guards, 10th Georgia Regiment from 1861 to 1865. Following the Civil War, Morris worked as a policeman in Augusta, Georgia. This photograph was taken *c.* 1890. (Courtesy of Thomas Holley.)

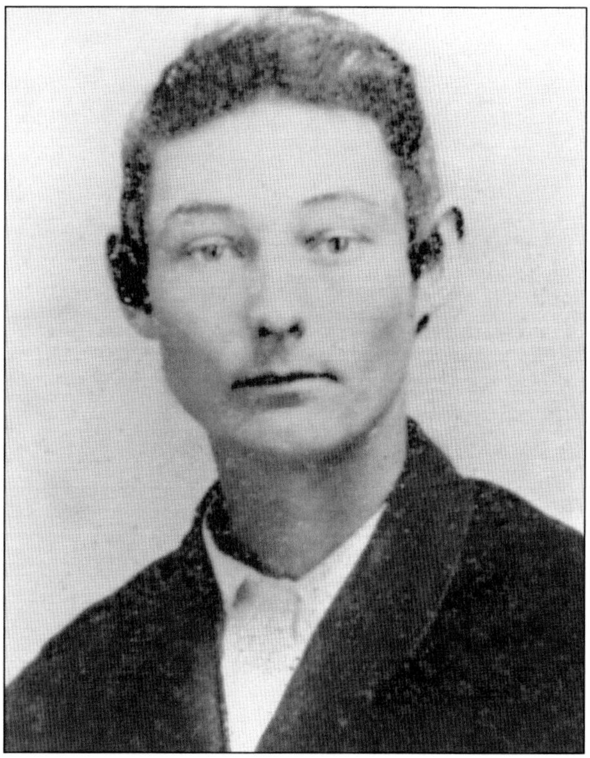

John Jordan served in the 10th Georgia Regiment from 1861 to 1862. The photo was taken in 1861. (Courtesy of Thomas Holley.)

Shown here is Captain William Johnston, who served in the Thomson Guards, 10th Georgia Regiment from 1861 to 1863. After the battle of Sharpsburg, Maryland on September 17, 1862, Johnston wrote home to his wife: "Ruthless! Bloody War! the saddest of all evils—No grave historian has ever written, nor weeping poet sung its dreadful ills. 'Tis writ in tears and blood." (Courtesy of Thomas Holley.)

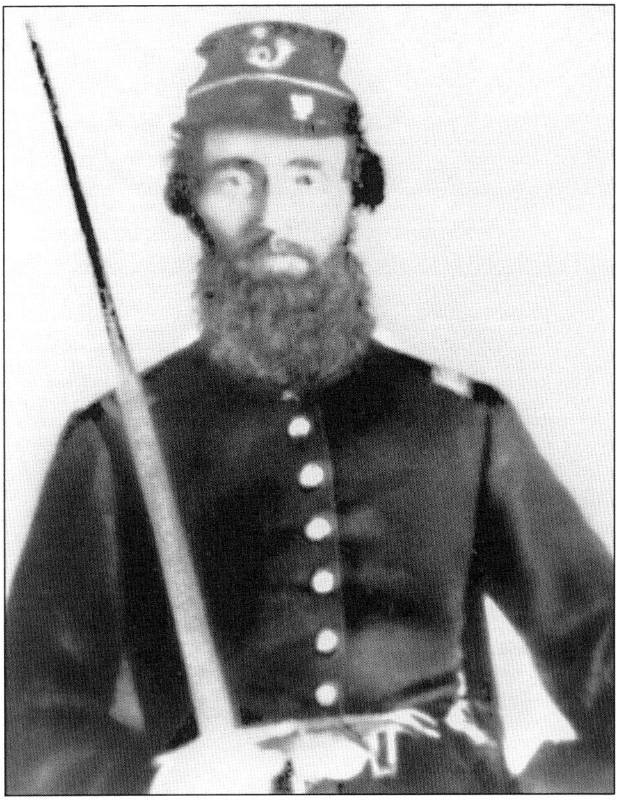

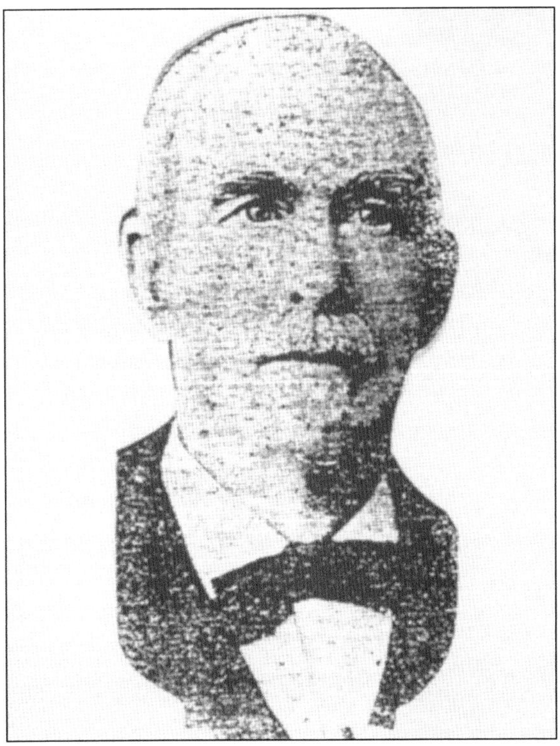

Reverend Doctor Thomas Cleveland, a private in Thomson Guards, 10th Georgia Regiment, was later a noted Presbyterian minister. (Courtesy of Thomas Holley.)

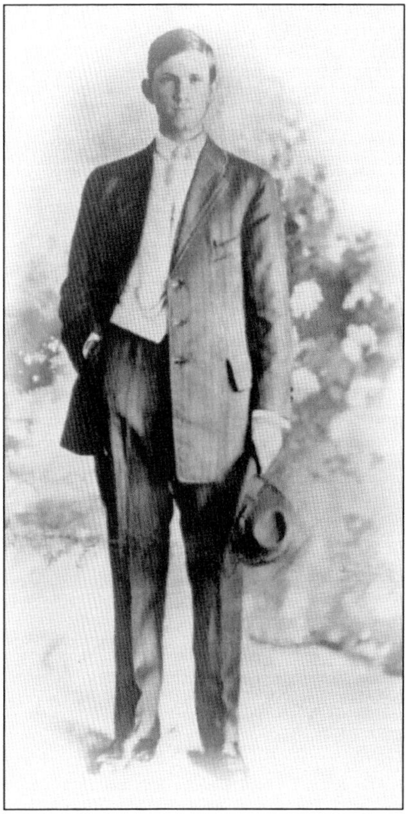

Dr. Pierce Gordon Blanchard was a medical student, c. 1910. Dr. Blanchard was the "country doctor" of Columbia County for many years, ministering to the sick, the infirm, and the dying. He was, perhaps, the dearest earthly friend that many families ever had. (Courtesy of Pat Blanchard.)

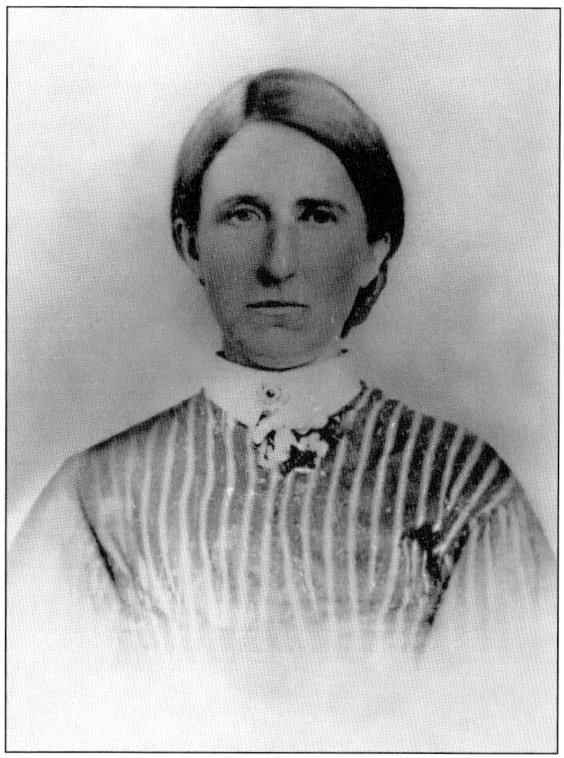

Zana Belle Holly was married to William Jasper Holly of the Thomson Guards. (Courtesy of Thomas Holley.)

Shown in this c. 1890 photograph is Jeremiah Blanchard, a member of the Thomson Guards, Company F, 10th Georgia Regiment from 1861 to 1865. (Courtesy of Thomas Holley.)

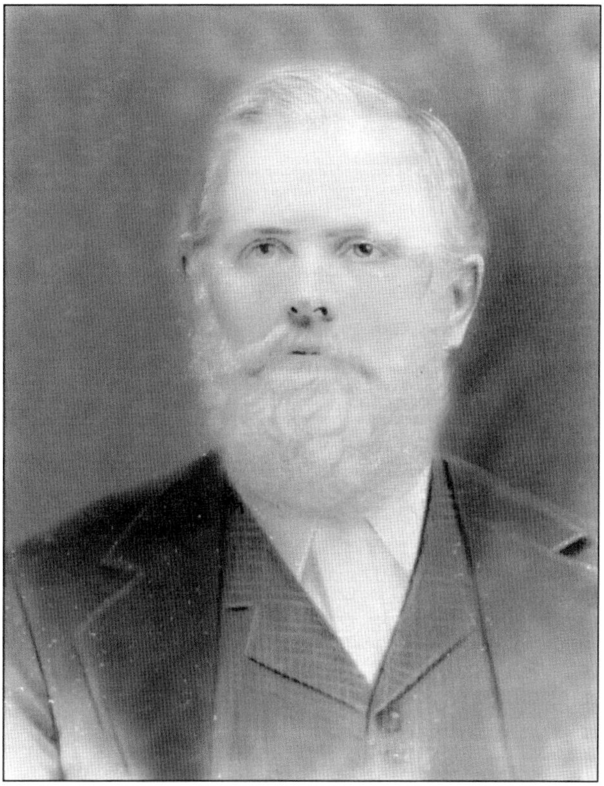

James Harris and Nannie Elizabeth Blanchard were married in 1863, when this photo was taken. A private in the Thomson Guards, James had been badly wounded in the battle of Sharpsburg on September 17, 1862, rendering his right arm badly impaired. (Courtesy of Thomas Holley.)

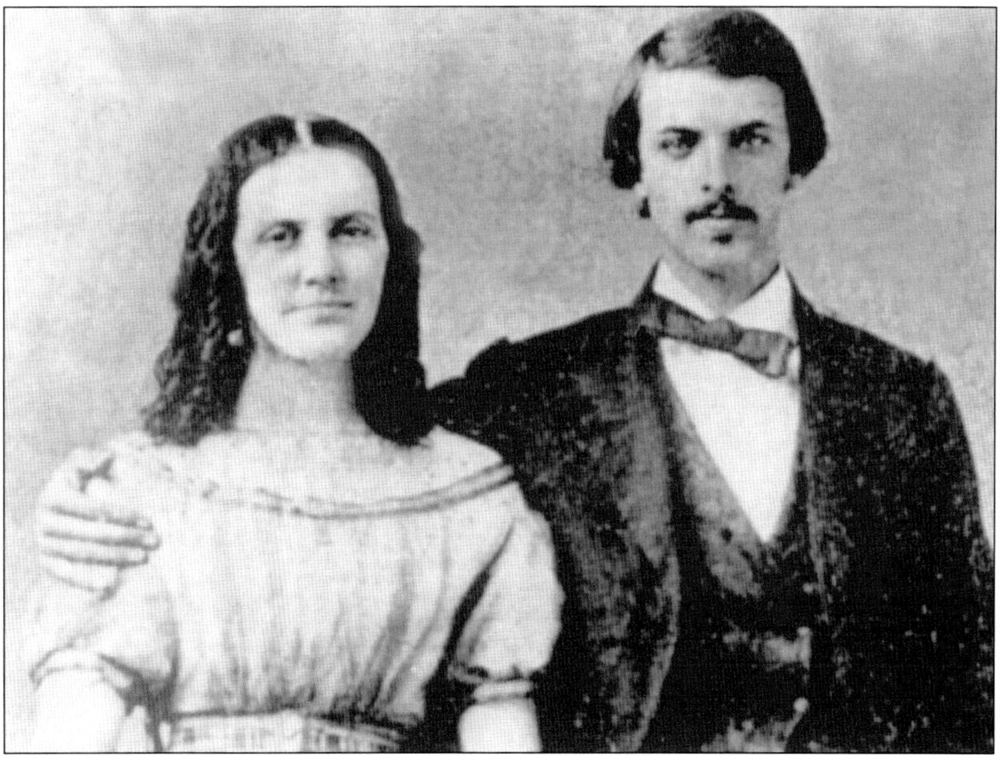

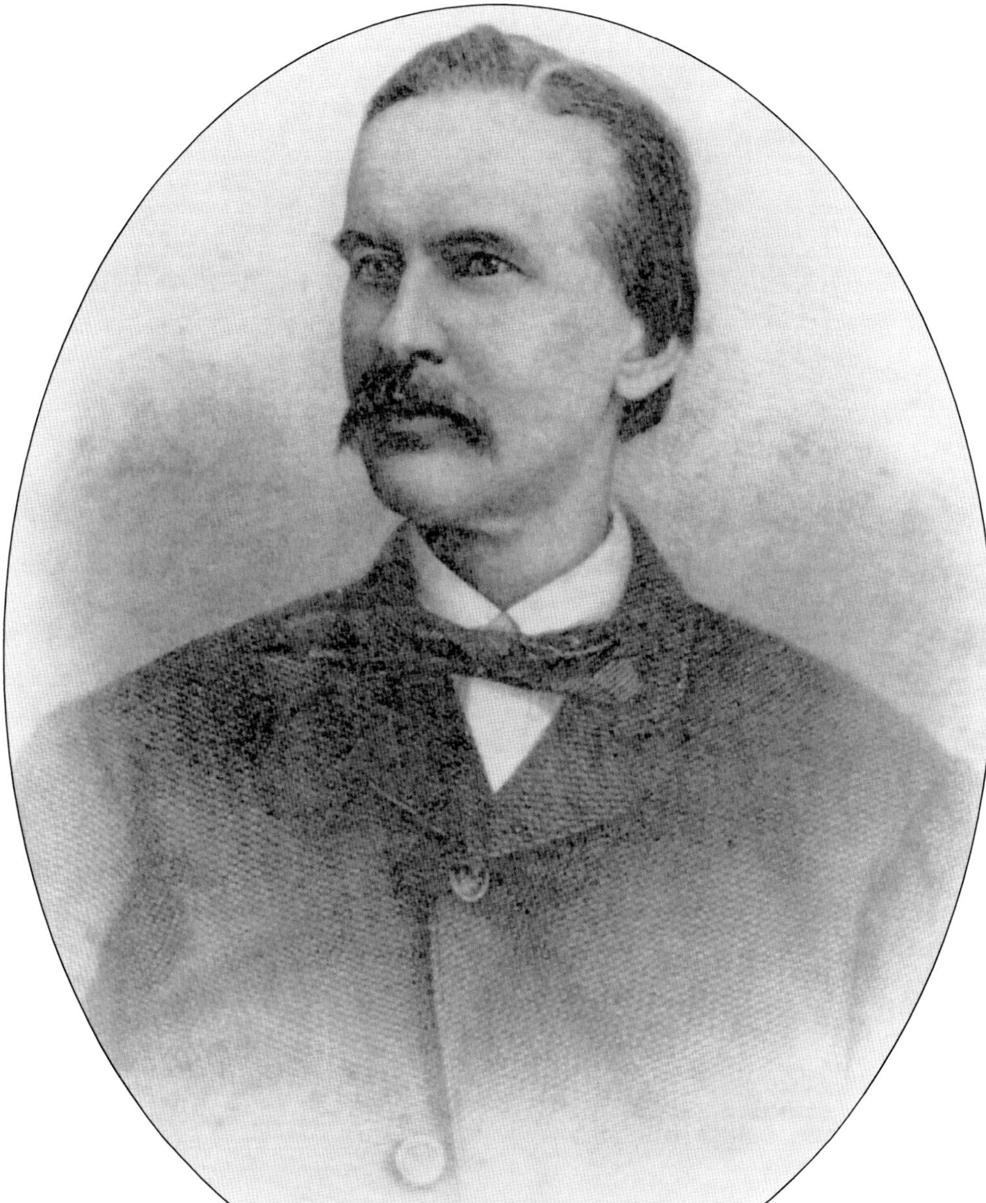

Paul Hamilton Hayne, a great Southern "man of letters" after 1870, lived near Grovetown, Georgia. Born in 1830, he came to Grovetown after the Civil War and lived by publishing his poetry. He died in Grovetown in 1886. This image shows Hayne in a carte de visite. (Courtesy of G.J. Smith.)

Mary Elizabeth Clanton was eight months old when this studio photograph was taken in June 1900. "Mommy's little baby but Daddy's little girl!" (Courtesy of G.L. Polatty.)

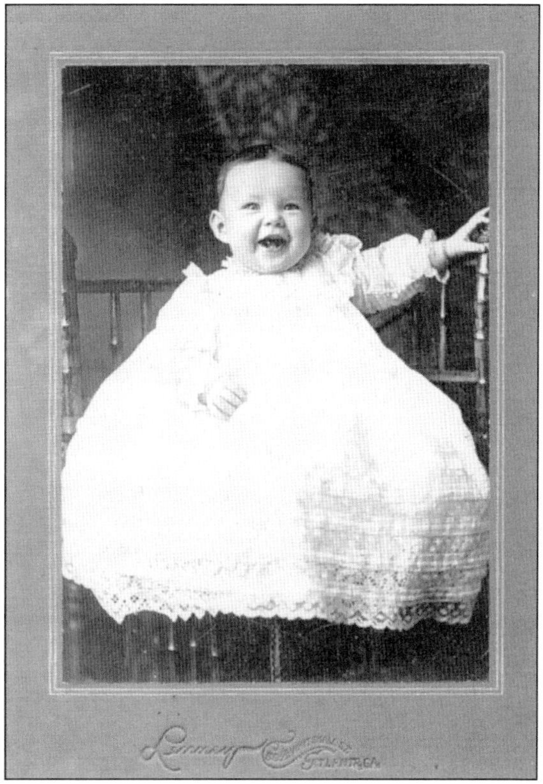

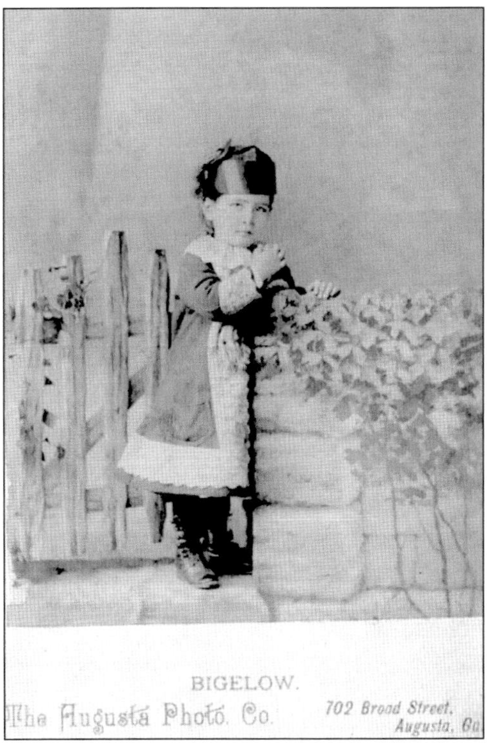

Turner Clanton Lamkin, pictured in 1889, died in April 1902. This lovely portrait was made in the studio of the Augusta Photo Co., located at 102 Broad Street in Augusta, Georgia. (Courtesy of G.L. Polatty.)

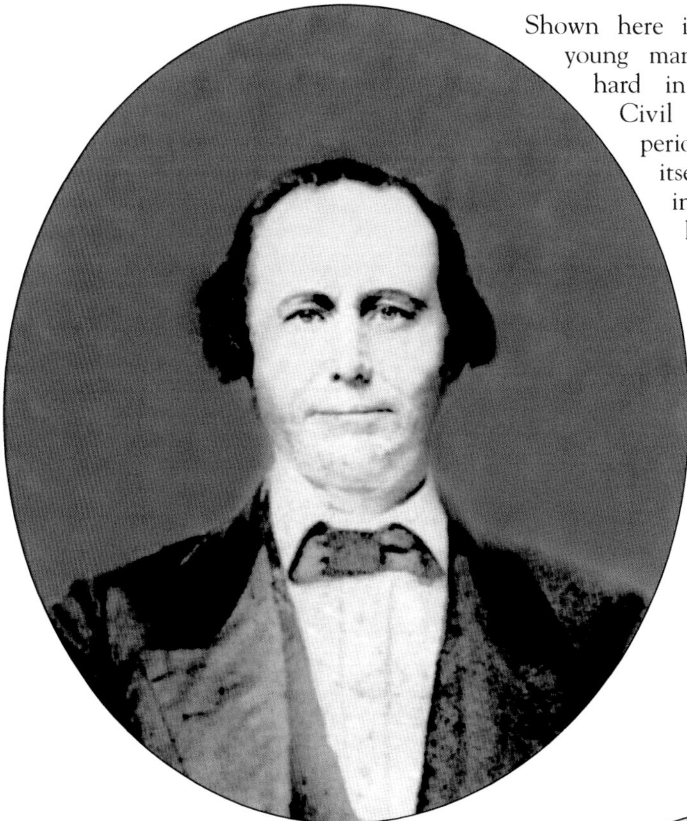

Shown here is Jesse Sims Walton as a young man in the 1850s. Life was hard in Mr. Walton's day. The Civil War, Reconstruction woes, periodic droughts, and aging itself—all have taken a toll in these before (to the left) and after (below) shots. Note the lips in each image—they reveal much. (Courtesy of G.L. Polatty.)

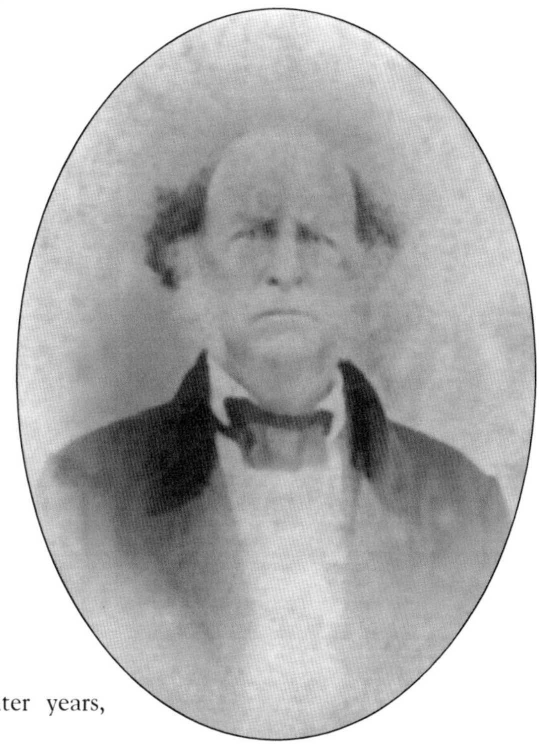

Jesse Sims Walton is shown here in later years, c. 1900. (Courtesy of G.L. Polatty.)

Robert Walton was 11 years old in this c. 1900 photograph. (Courtesy of G.L. Polatty.)

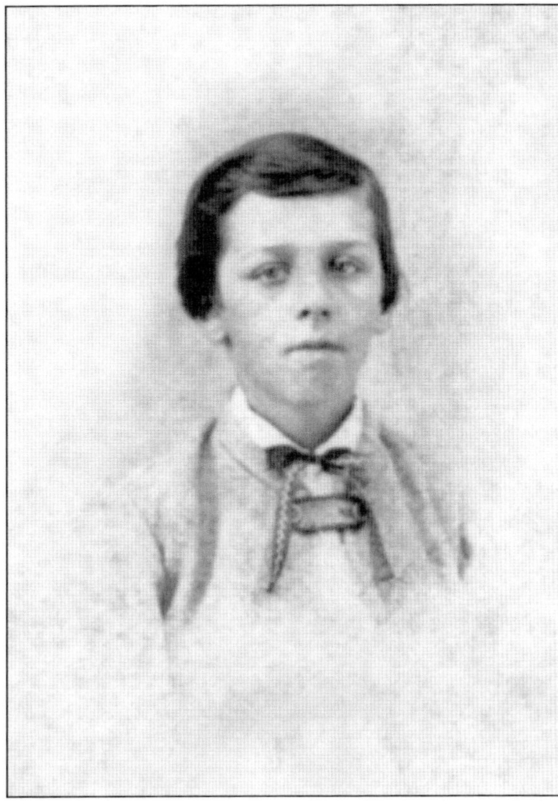

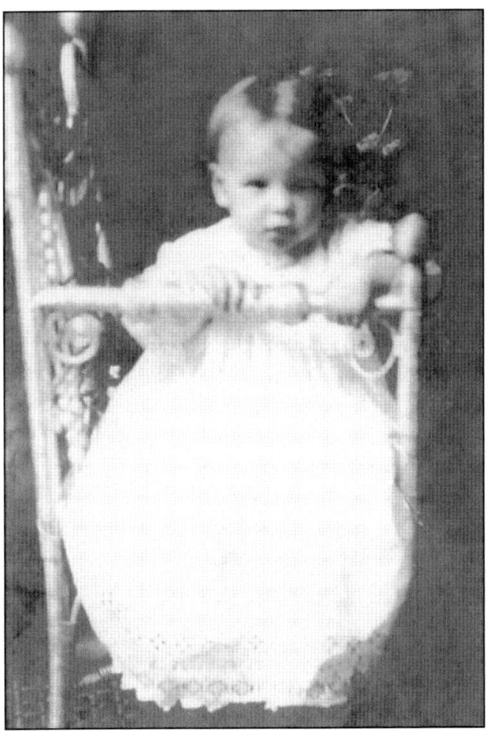

Shown here is Rosalie Fullbright in 1906. Note the "high chair" and the flower bouquet. "What is that funny man doing behind that box on three legs?" (Courtesy of Berma Ansley Gibson.)

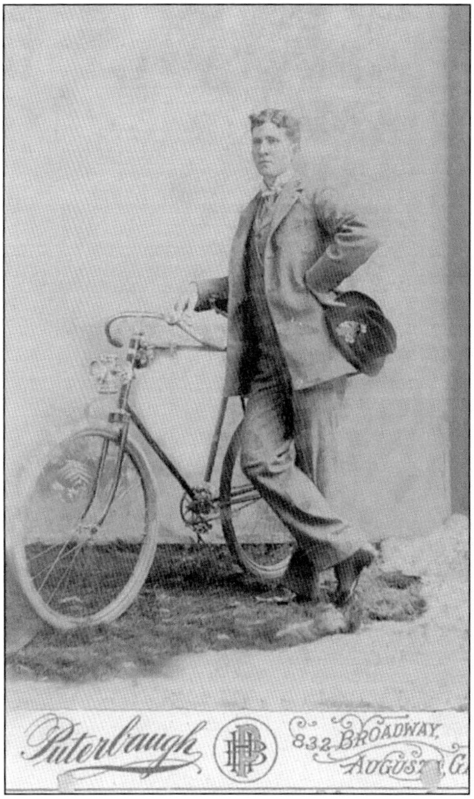

M. Walton is pictured here with a vintage bicycle, c. 1900, in a professional portrait. The backdrop and rug are studio props. (Courtesy of G.L. Polatty.)

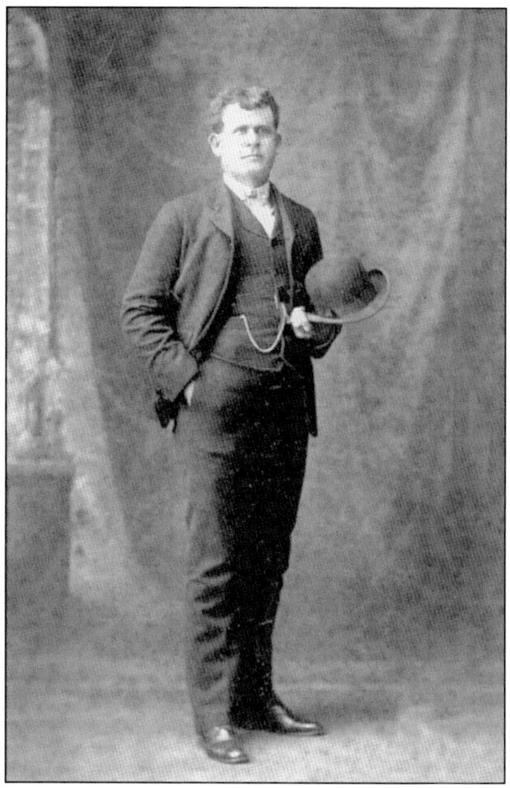

In another studio photograph with a backdrop and props is L.D. Walton, c. 1900. Note the classic style pose of the subject and that wonderful hat! (Courtesy of G.L. Polatty.)

Here is an 1850 ambrotype of Polly Jones Walton. The lady's jewelry has been gold tinted, a common practice used to accent a photograph. The beautiful case holding the photo, typical of the day, provides a unique border around the cherished image. (Courtesy of G.L. Polatty.)

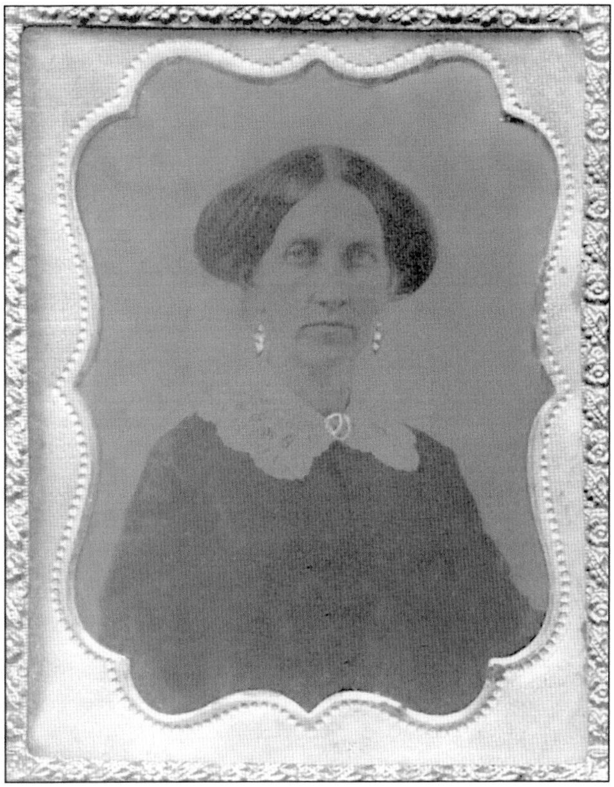

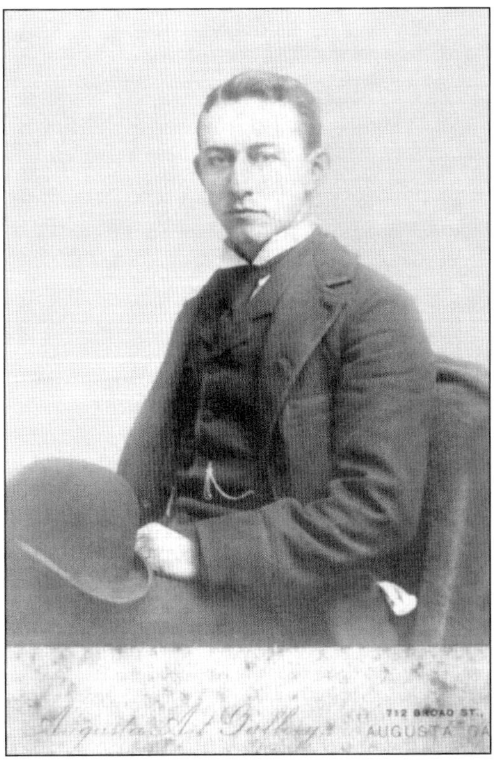

This is William Walton, c. 1900. Life awaits the dashing youth in all its fullness and potential. (Courtesy of G.L. Polatty.)

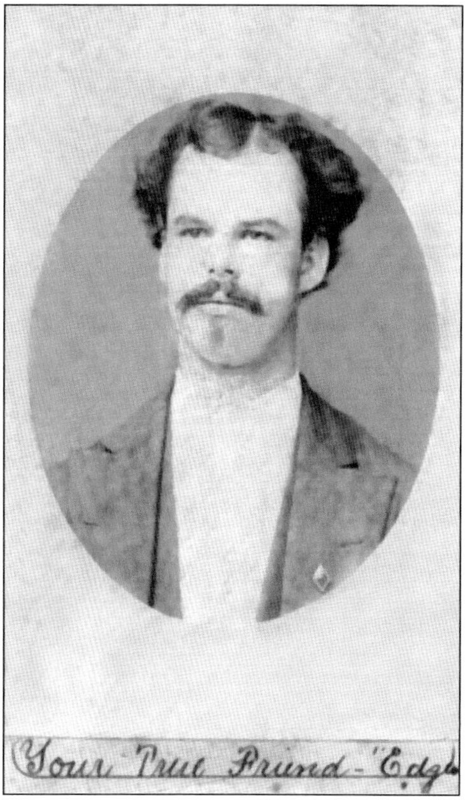

This photograph shows Edgar Smith, c. 1890. This style of photo was the calling, or business card of the day, and was called a carte de visite, or c.d.v. The subject would autograph his or her card and present it as we do our business cards today. (Courtesy of G.L. Polatty.)

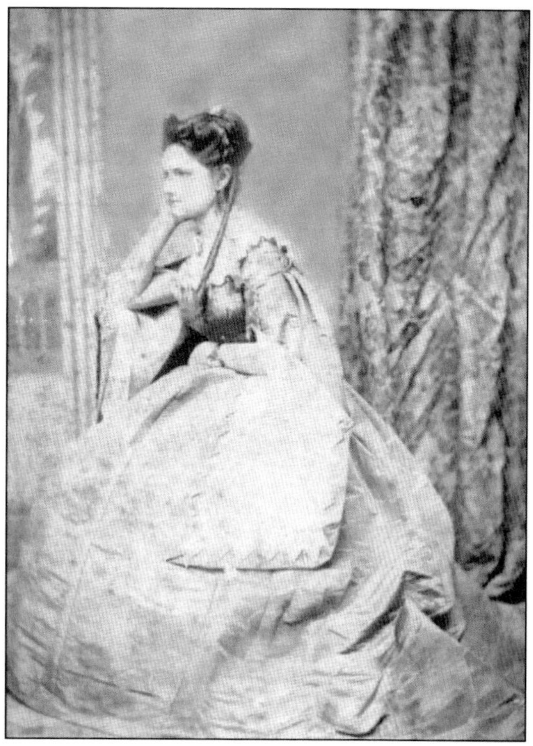

In this magnificent picture, Mary Elizabeth "Lizzie" Lamkin Eve poses with some outstanding studio props, c. 1860. Note the hair style and that wonderful dress! (Courtesy of G.L. Polatty.)

This is an early 1900s photograph of Jabez Sanford Hardin. He was the superintendent of schools in Columbia County for many years in the early half of the 20th century. (Courtesy of Edith Hardin Reese.)

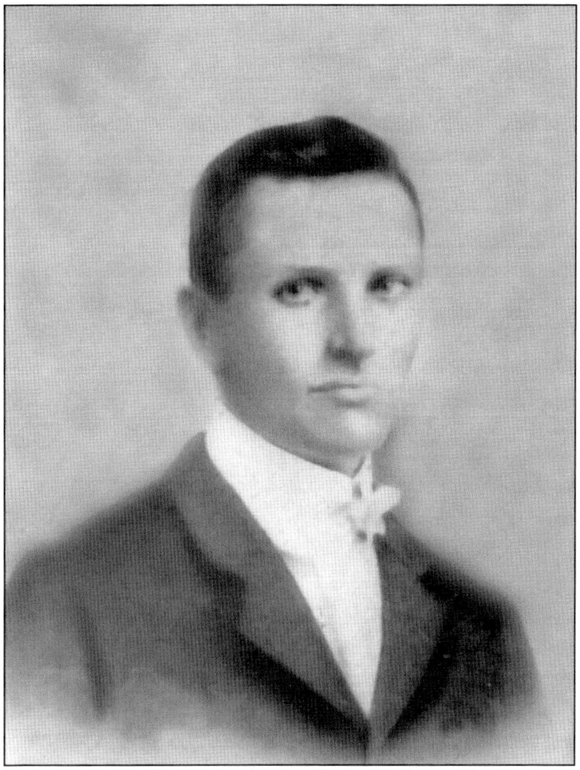

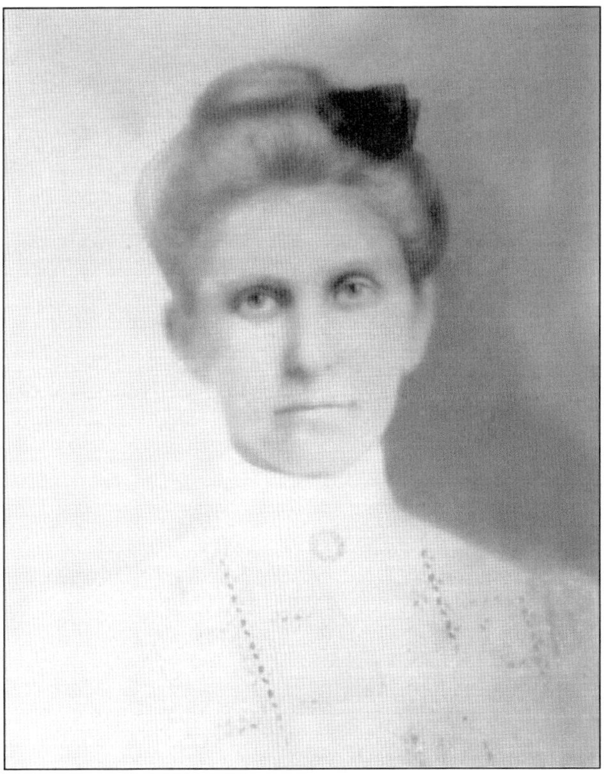

Effie Mae Cliatt Hardin was the wife of J. Hardin. (Courtesy of Edith Hardin Reese.)

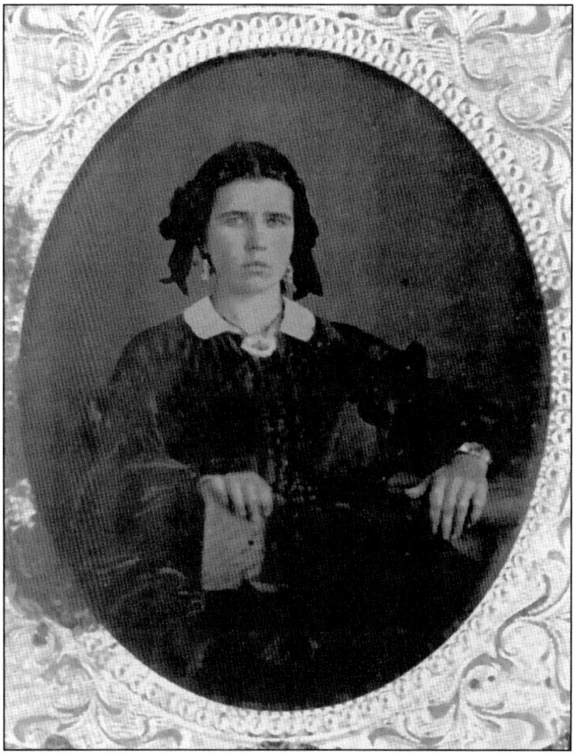

Mary Bryant Snellings, seen in this beautiful tinted ambrotype, was married to James S. Snellings. (Courtesy of Billy Snellings.)

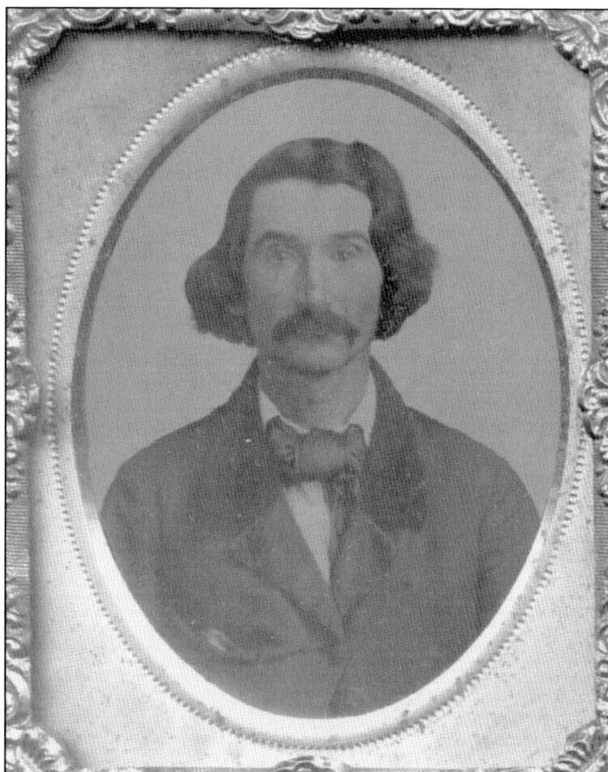

This 1862 ambrotype shows James S. Snellings, a Confederate soldier at Fort Moultrie from 1862 to 1864. The fort guarded the harbor of Charleston, South Carolina during the Civil War. (Courtesy of Billy Snellings.)

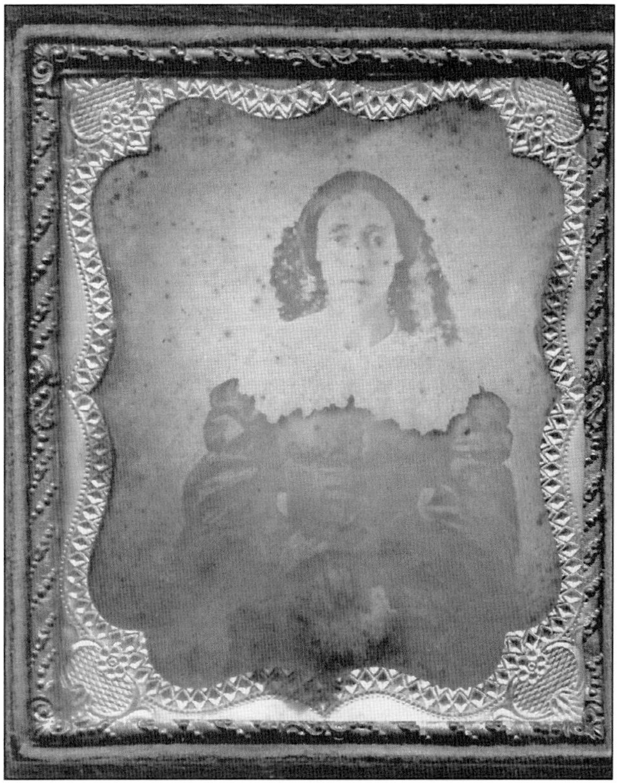

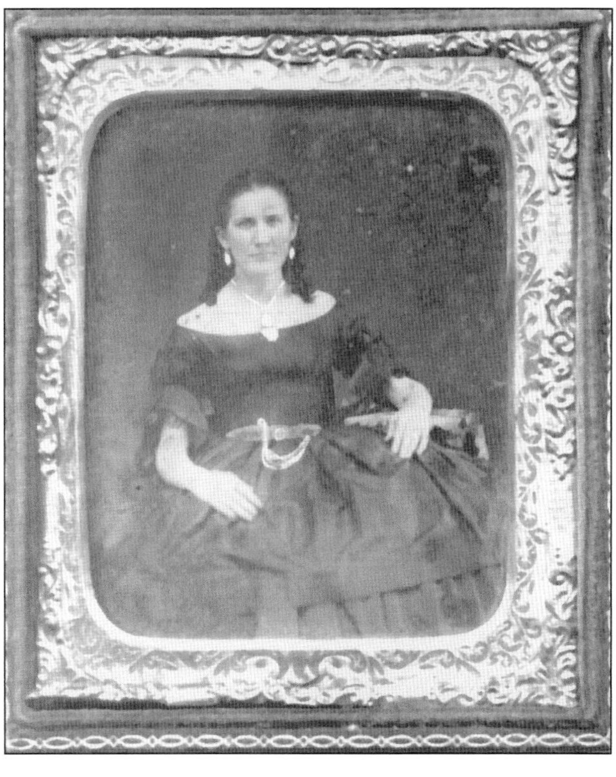

These ambrotypes, typical of the antebellum South, depict two unidentified ladies.

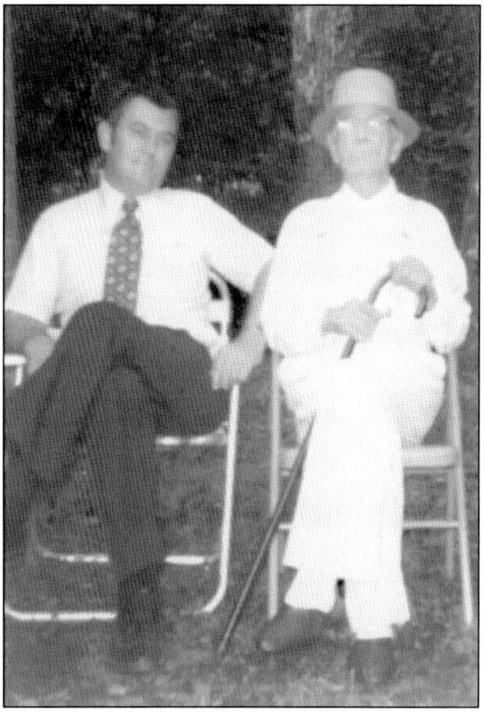

Reverend Harold Eubanks (left) is shown with Mr. J.S. Hardin. Reverend Eubanks, now deceased, was pastor of Damascus Baptist Church in Leah, Georgia, one of the oldest churches in the county. (Courtesy of Edith Hardin Reese.)

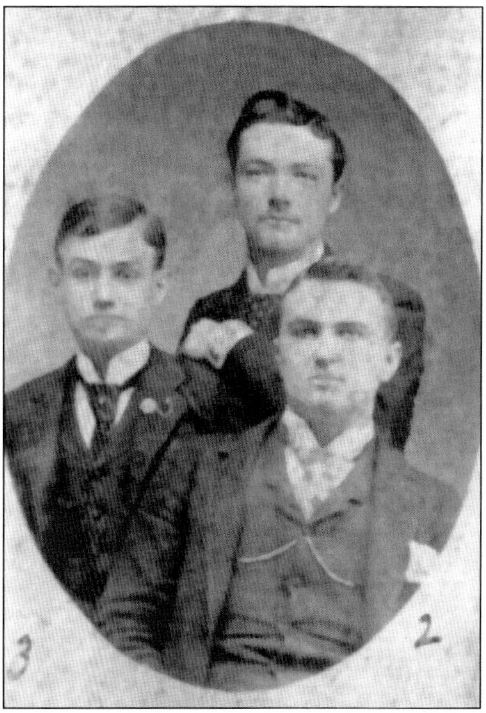

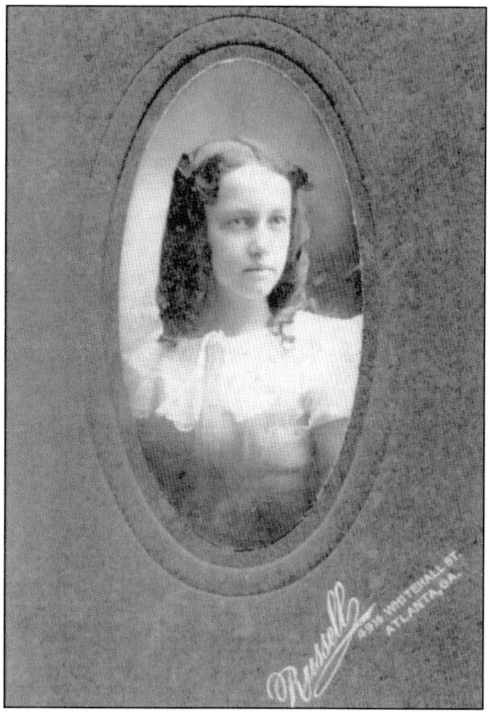

Left: Shown in this 1889 picture are, from left to right, T.W. Clanton, W.W. Pilcher, and M.L. Candler, a distinguished trio of young men. (Courtesy of G.L. Polatty.)
Right: Lucile Hatcher was photographed in 1900 by the studio listed at the bottom of this image. (Courtesy of G.L. Polatty.)

Shown here is Edna Ruth Paschal. Note the beautiful style of her dress. (Courtesy of Edna Ruth Paschal.)

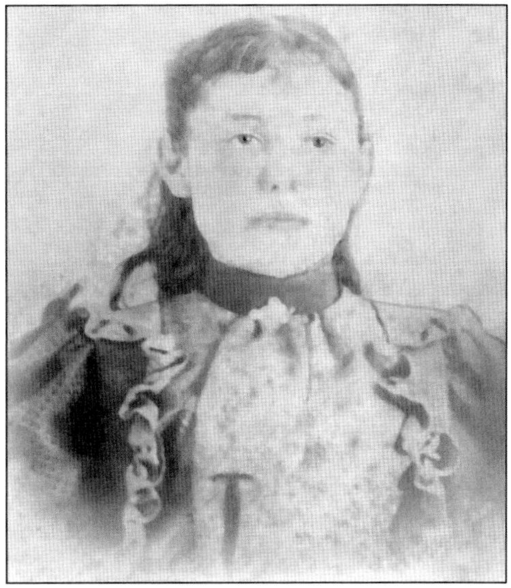

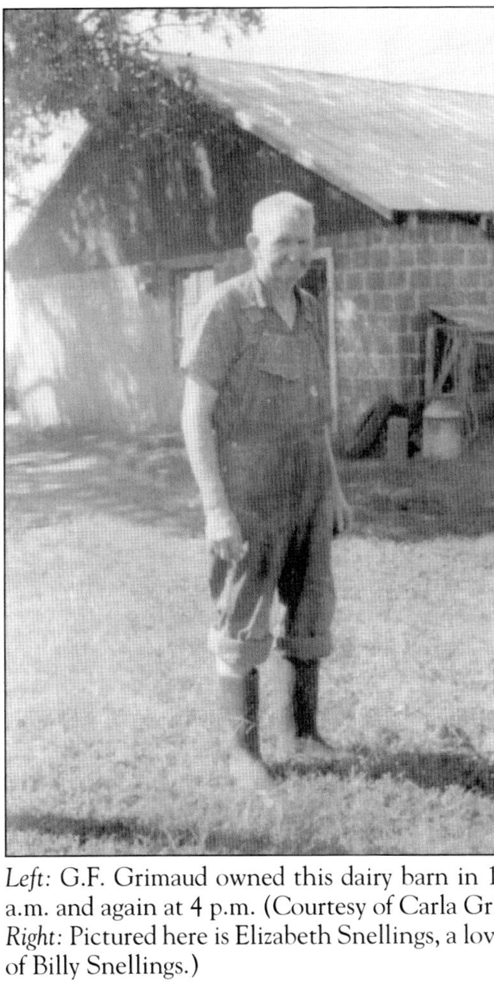

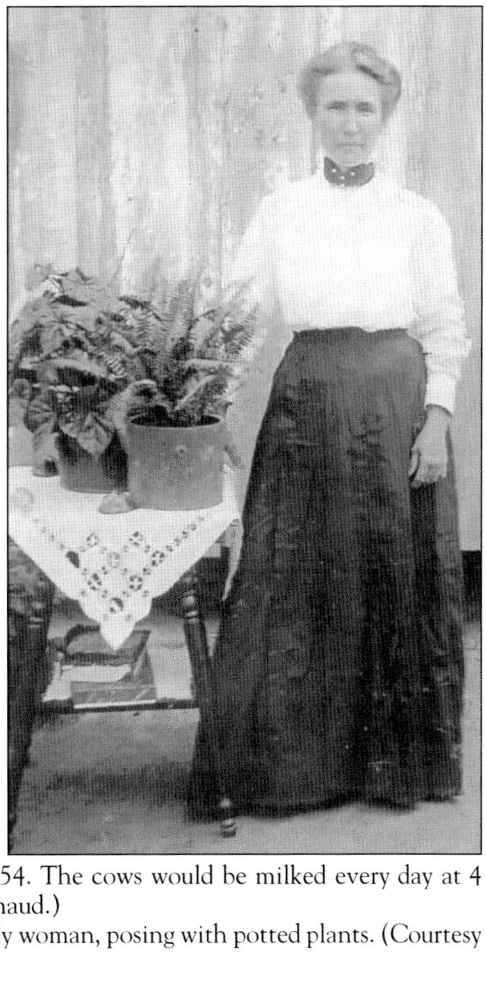

Left: G.F. Grimaud owned this dairy barn in 1954. The cows would be milked every day at 4 a.m. and again at 4 p.m. (Courtesy of Carla Grimaud.)
Right: Pictured here is Elizabeth Snellings, a lovely woman, posing with potted plants. (Courtesy of Billy Snellings.)

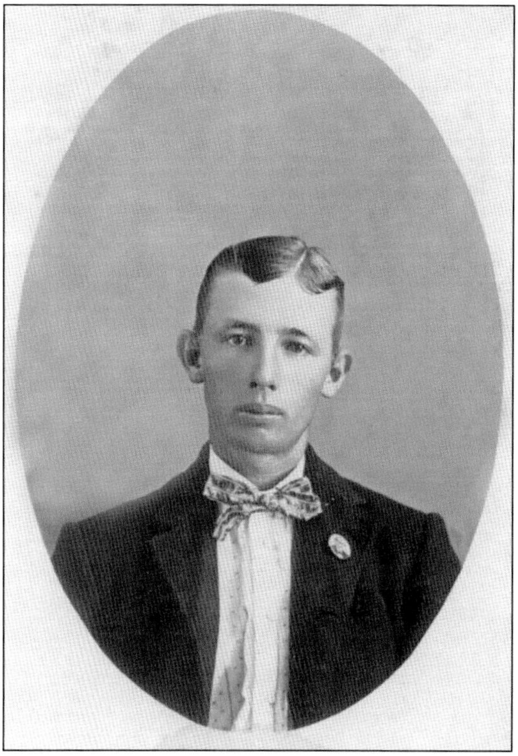

Benjamin Franklin Snellings, an earnest young man with plans for the future, had this smart photograph taken, c. 1890. (Courtesy of Billy Snellings.)

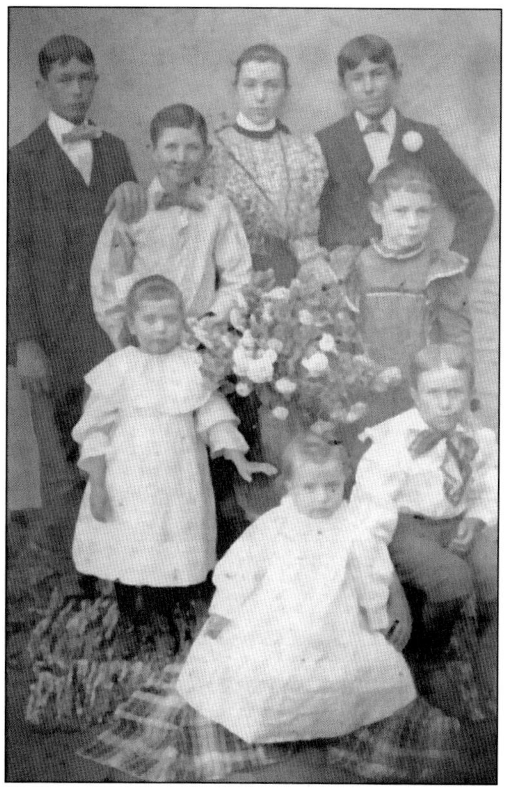

This family photograph of the Marshall children shows, in no particular order, Jody Howard Marshall, James Bailey Marshall, Carl Bonner Marshall, Lloyd Richard Marshall, Cora May Marshall, Willie Earl Marshall, Amie Echols Marshall, and Jabus Oliver Marshall, c. 1920. Note the family's studio pose and the beautiful flower arrangement. (Courtesy of Edna Ruth Marshall Paschal.)

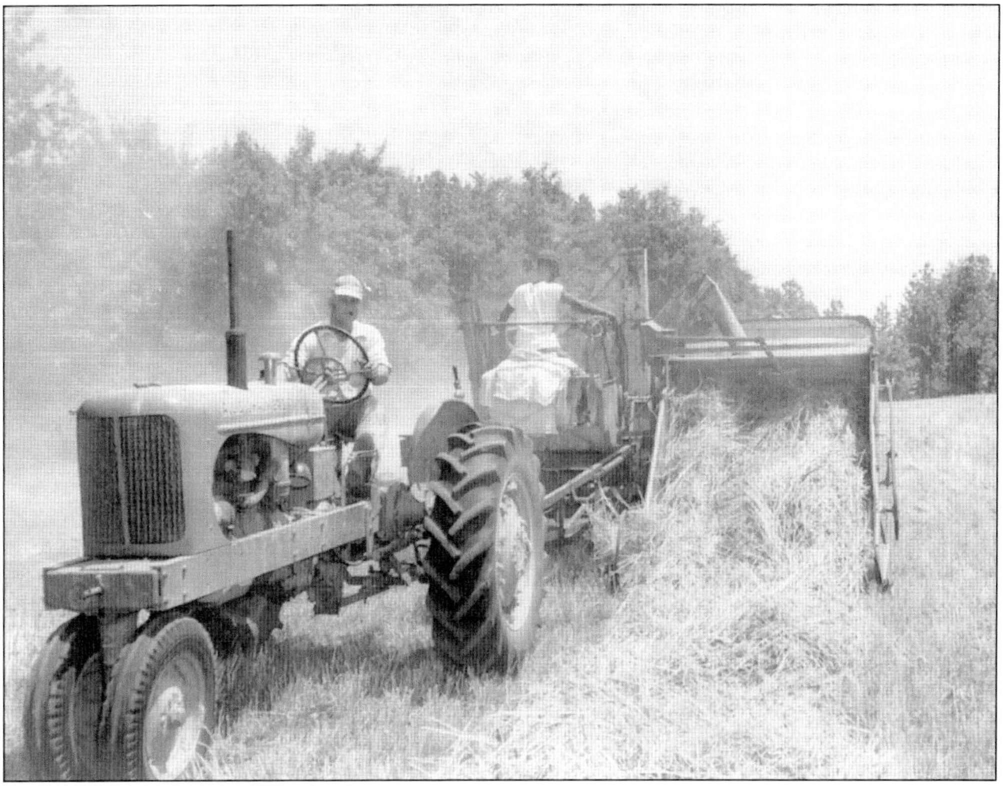

On the present site of the government complex in Evans, Georgia, is J.H. Marshall Jr. on his tractor, c. 1950. Notice the combine behind the tractor and the youth sitting on it and watching for problems. (Courtesy of Dan Marshall.)

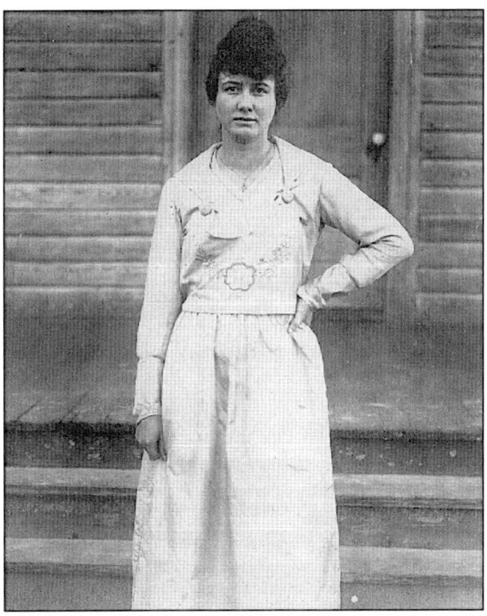

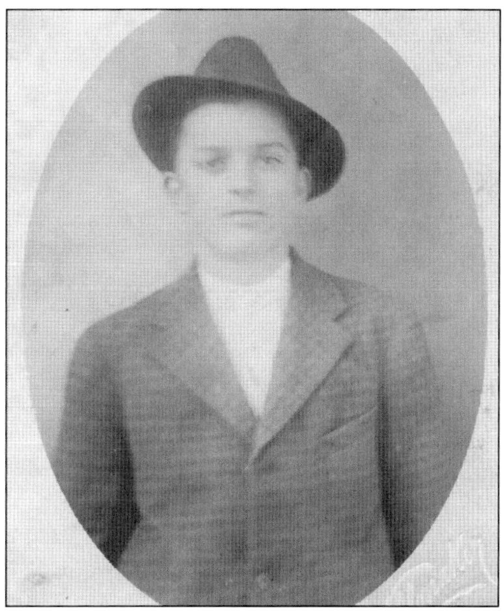

The bride-to-be of Dudley C. Young (at right) was Miss Laurie Palmer, shown here (at left) in 1918. (Courtesy of Carla Grimaud.)

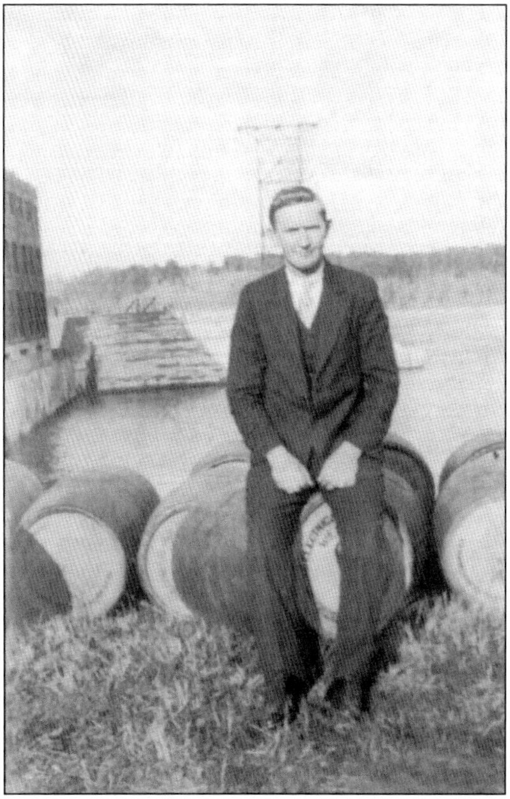

G.F. Gramaud Sr. poses at the Augusta Canal lock and dam in 1929. The lock and dam on the Savannah River supplied water for the Augusta Canal, on which crops and cargo were carried by boats to Augusta. Courtesy of Carla Grimaud.)

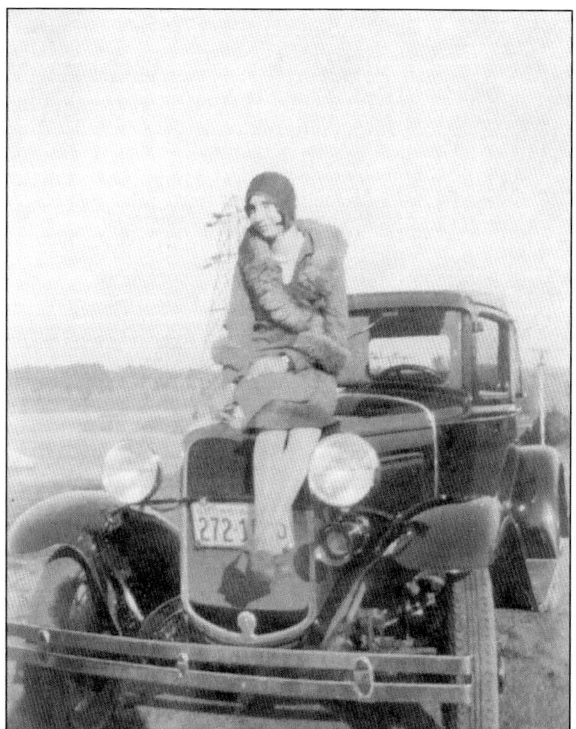

Fannie Wortham Grimaud, seated on a vintage automobile, is pictured at the Augusta Canal lock and dam. (Courtesy of Carla Grimaud.)

Shown in the rural natural beauty of Columbia County is the subject of this photograph, Reese Marshall, in 1914. This part of the county is still largely undeveloped. (Courtesy of Dan Marshall.)

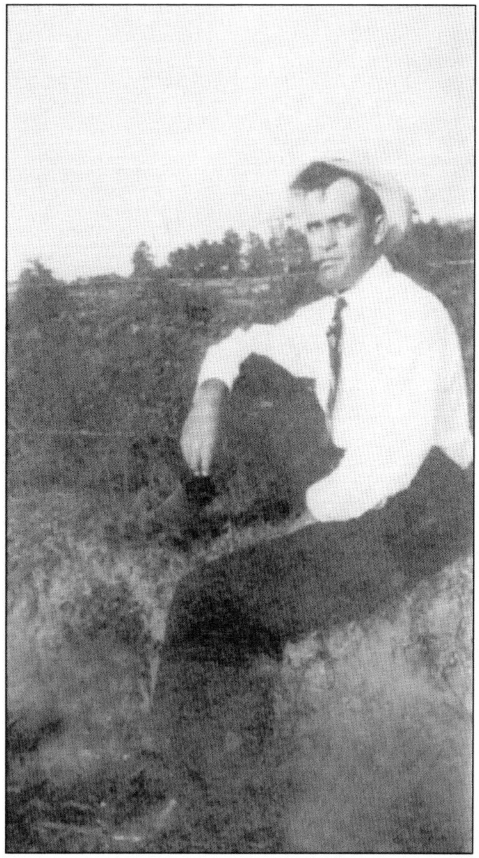

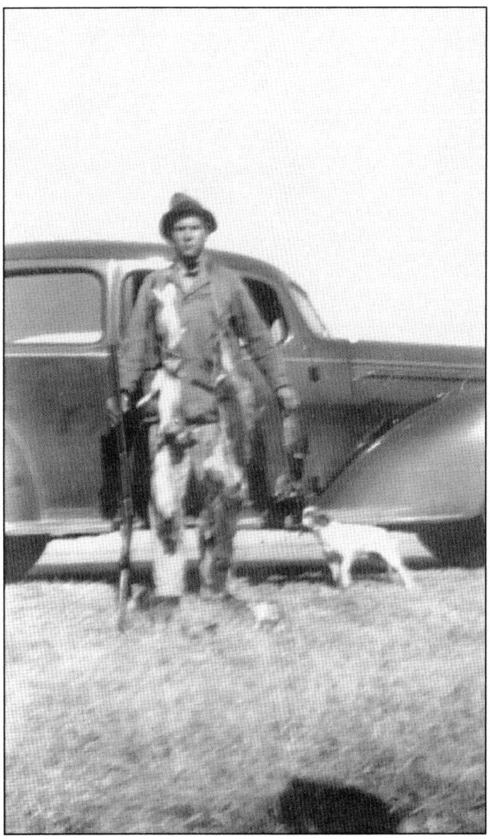

This is an unknown hunter in Columbia County. Bringing home meat from the fields and woods was not just a sport in those days. Note the hunting dogs and rabbits. (Courtesy of Dan Marshall.)

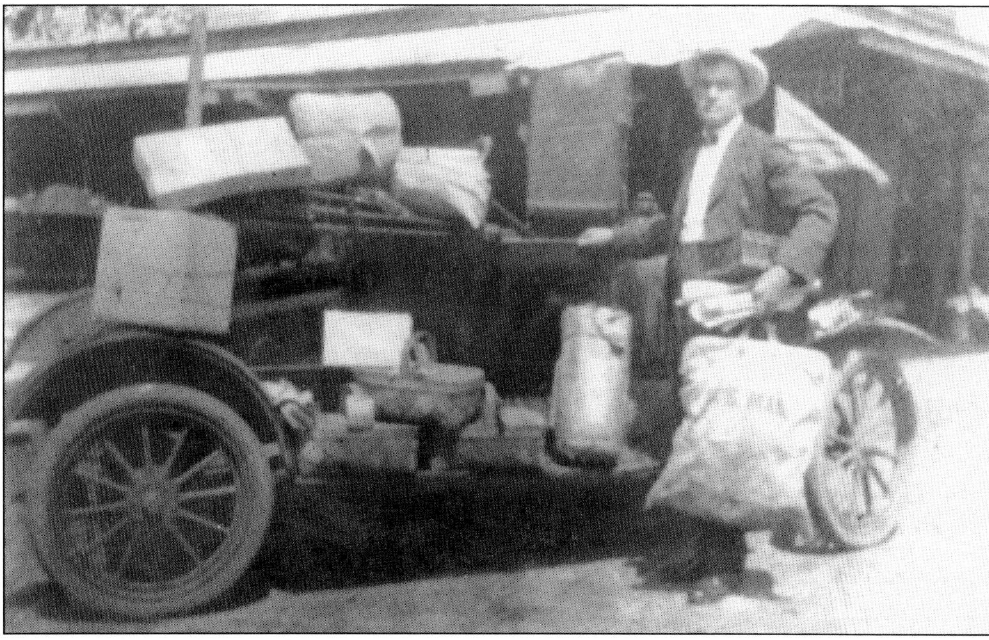

Reese Marshall and his mail car are pictured in this *c.* 1939 photograph. The "mail rider" in his Model T Ford not only brought the mail, but carried "notions" from the store to farm ladies and vegetables, eggs, and other products back to the store for bartering. (Courtesy of Dan Marshall.)

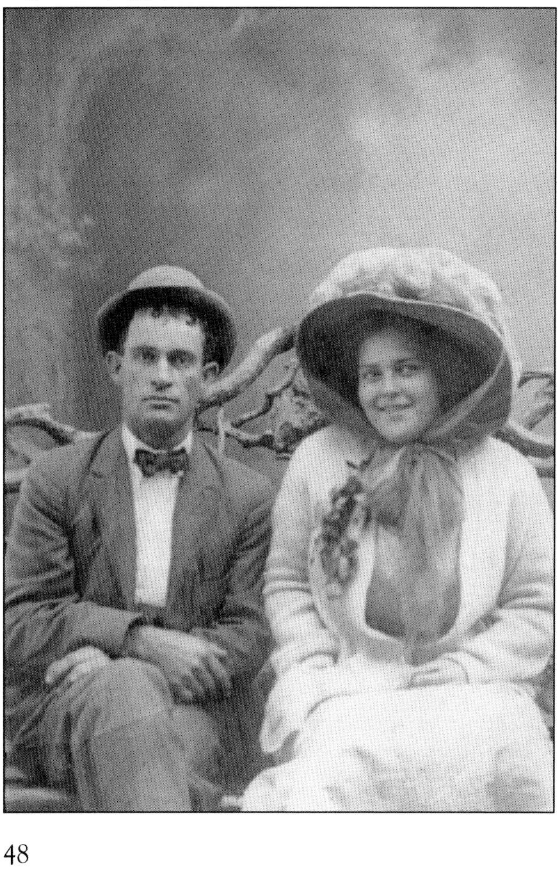

This is an unknown couple, *c.* 1900, in another studio shot. All "done up," these two may be newlyweds. (Courtesy of Dan Marshall.)

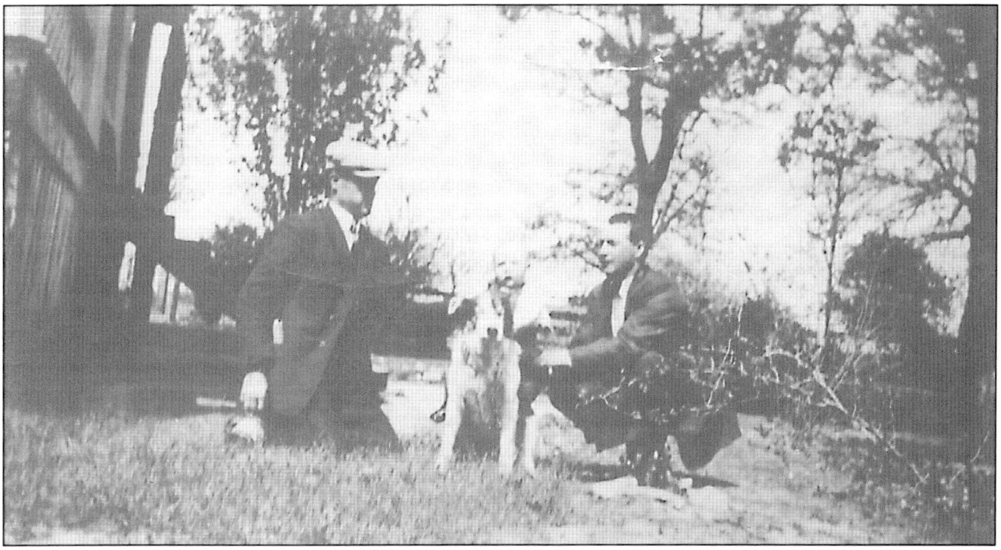

Here are Reese Marshall and J.H. Marshall Sr., with J.H. Marshall Jr. (seated on the dog) in front of the family home in Appling, 1914. (Courtesy of Dan Marshall.)

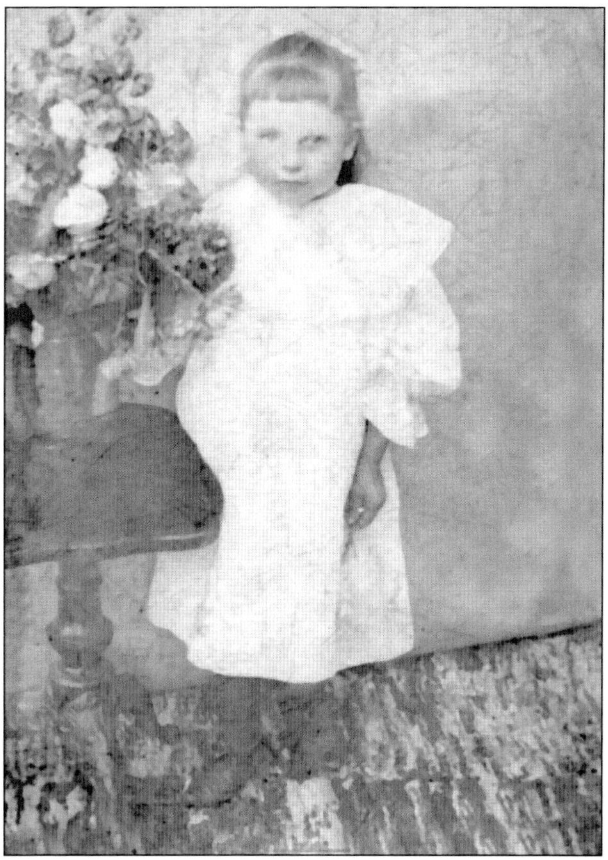

This 1890 photograph shows an unidentified four- or five-year-old girl. This lovely little lady is posed neat and trim. (Courtesy of Edna Ruth Paschal.)

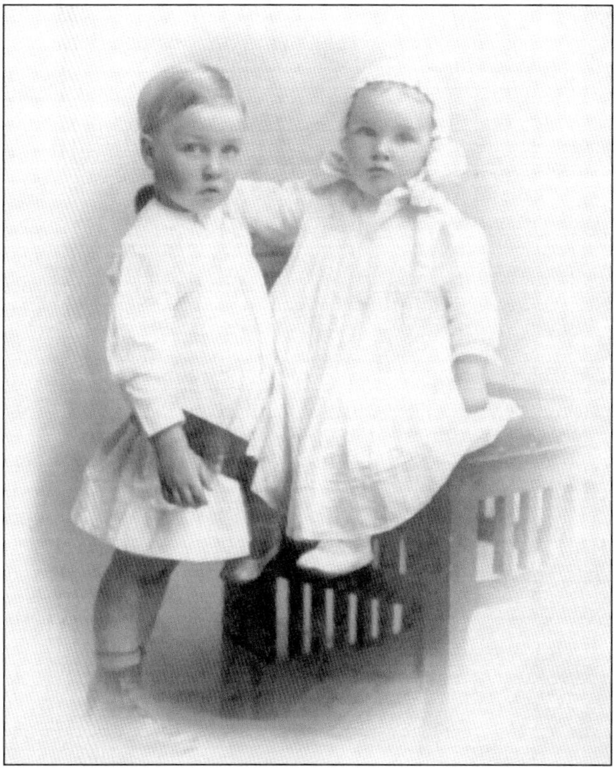

J.H. Marshall Jr. and his sister Ila Mae (Mrs. Nelson Cash) are seen here in this 1916 studio photograph. Even little boys wore dresses back then! (Courtesy of Dan Marshall.)

This family cemetery is located near Phinizy, Georgia in Old Brownsborough, one of the earliest communities in Columbia County. (Courtesy of Lallie Dozier Benkoski.)

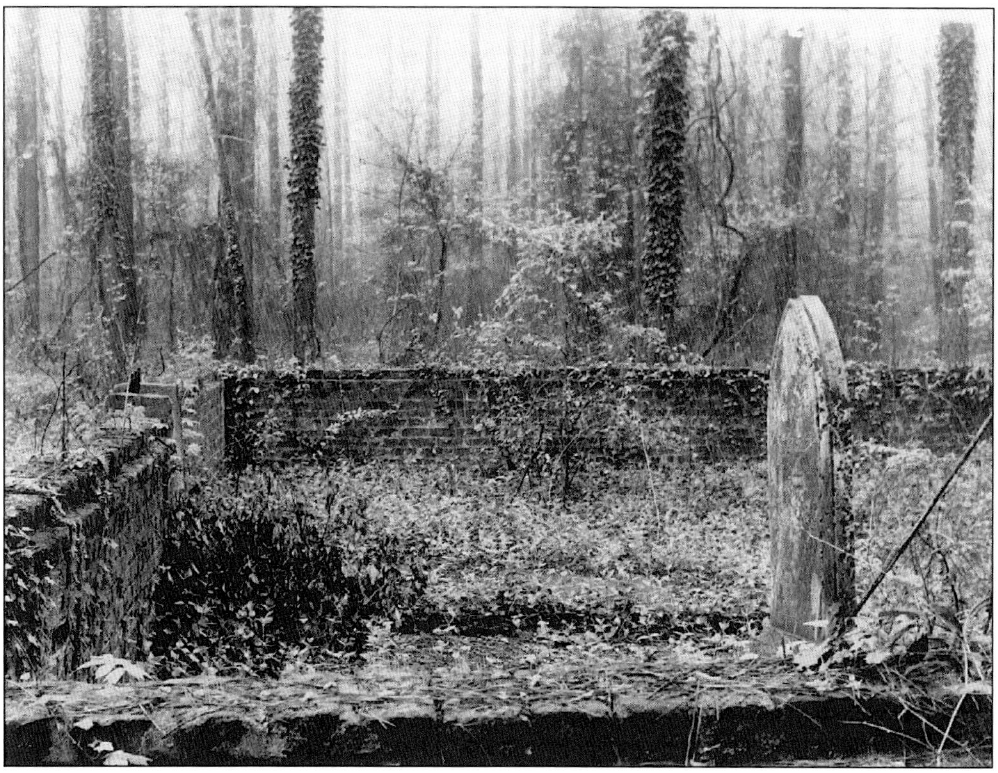

Andrew and Arthur Grimaud are in the foreground of this 1944 image with the farm on the old Callaway Plantation behind them. The little pooch is unidentified. (Courtesy of Carla Grimaud.)

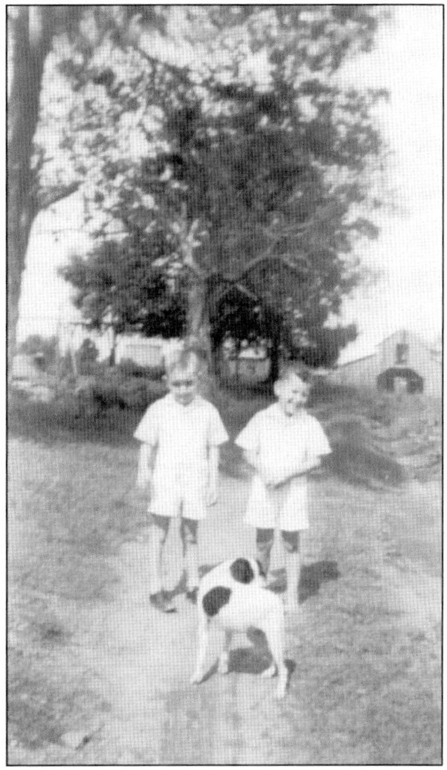

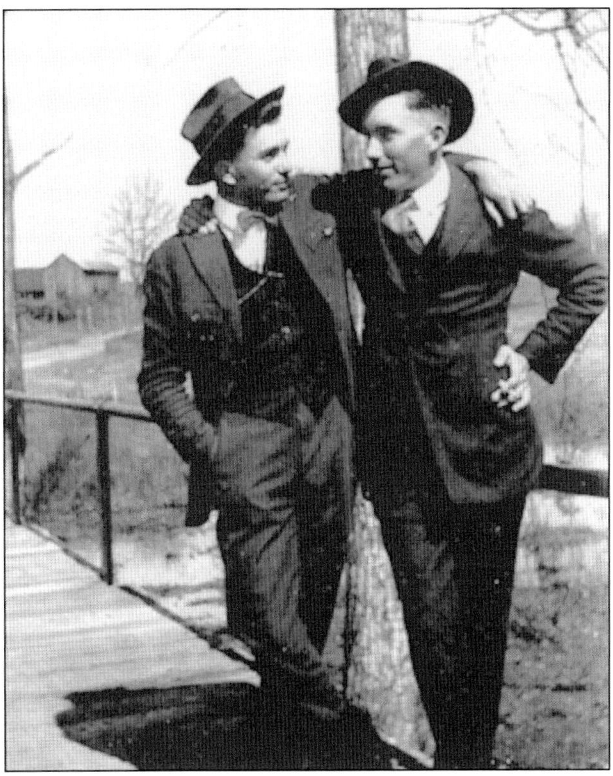

Seen here is the wooden bridge (now concrete) over Kiokee Creek in Appling, Georgia, c. 1940. The two pals posing for the camera are Gus Crawford and Ollie Marshall. (Courtesy of Lallie Dozier Benkoski.)

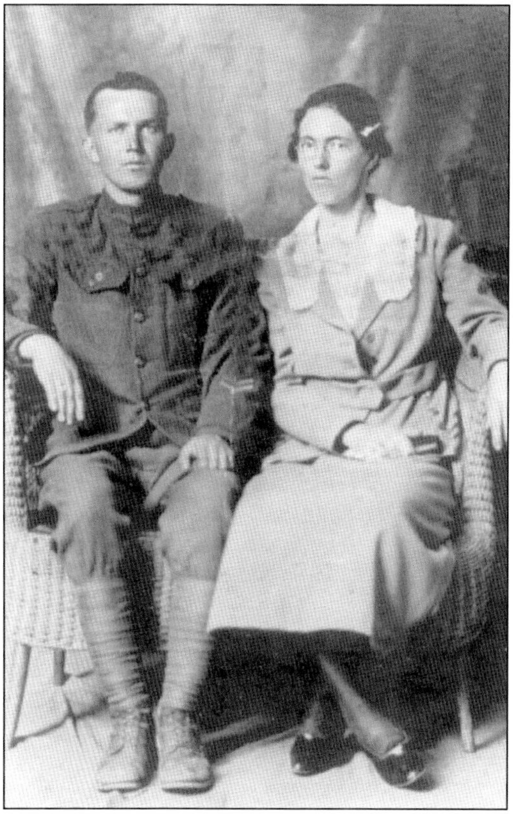

Shown are John Atkins, who served in the Army during World War I, and Margaret Bartles Atkins in 1917. (Courtesy of Jean Blackard.)

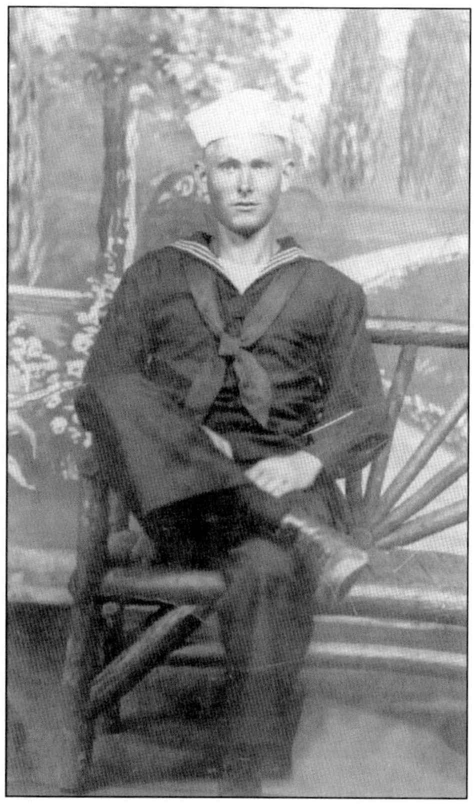

Tom Lewis Bartles was in the U.S. Navy in 1918. The studio backdrop of a forest scene does not quite match the Bartles's sailor uniform. (Courtesy of Jean Blackard.)

Two

HOMES

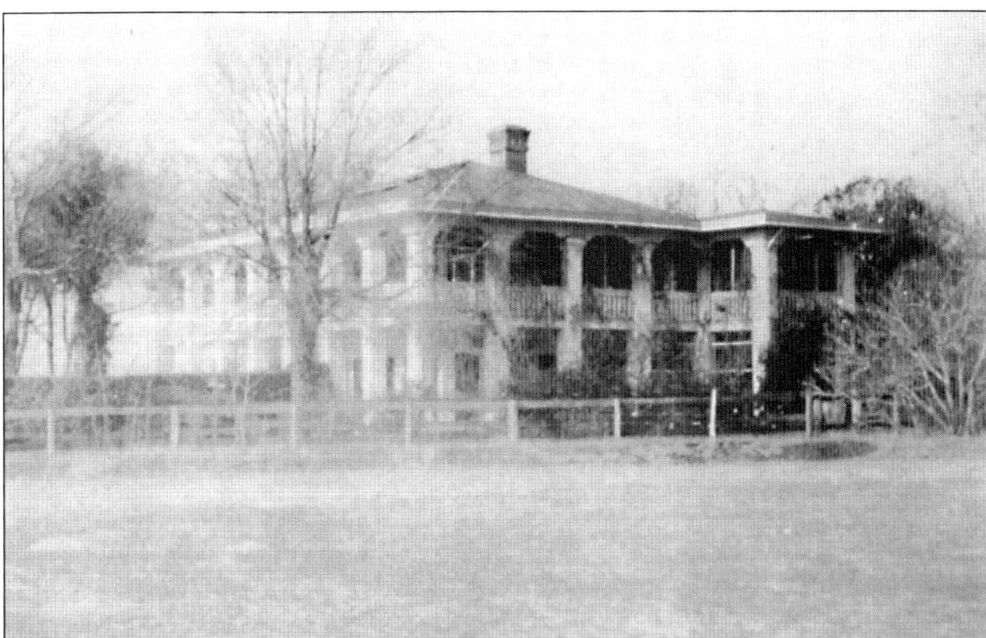

The photographer who took this c. 1900 photograph of the J.L. Dodge House in Grovetown, Georgia, was standing in a sulky racing track adjacent to the house. (Courtesy of G.J. Smith.)

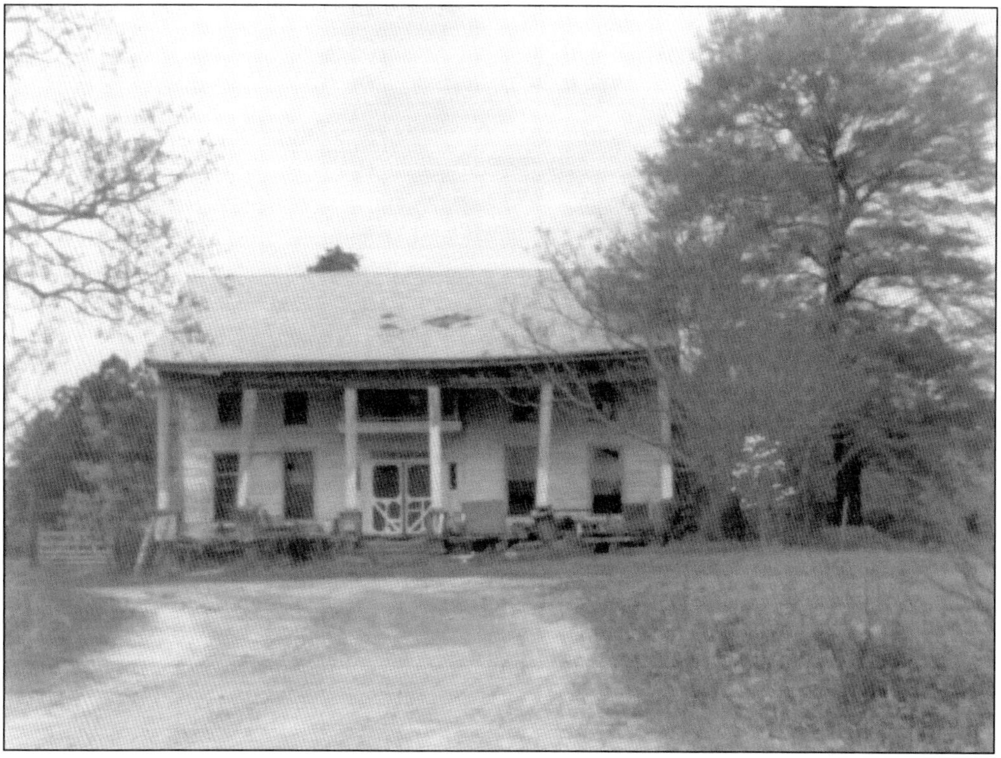

This is an unidentified 1839 plantation home. The photograph was taken *c.* 1940. (Courtesy of G.L. Polatty.)

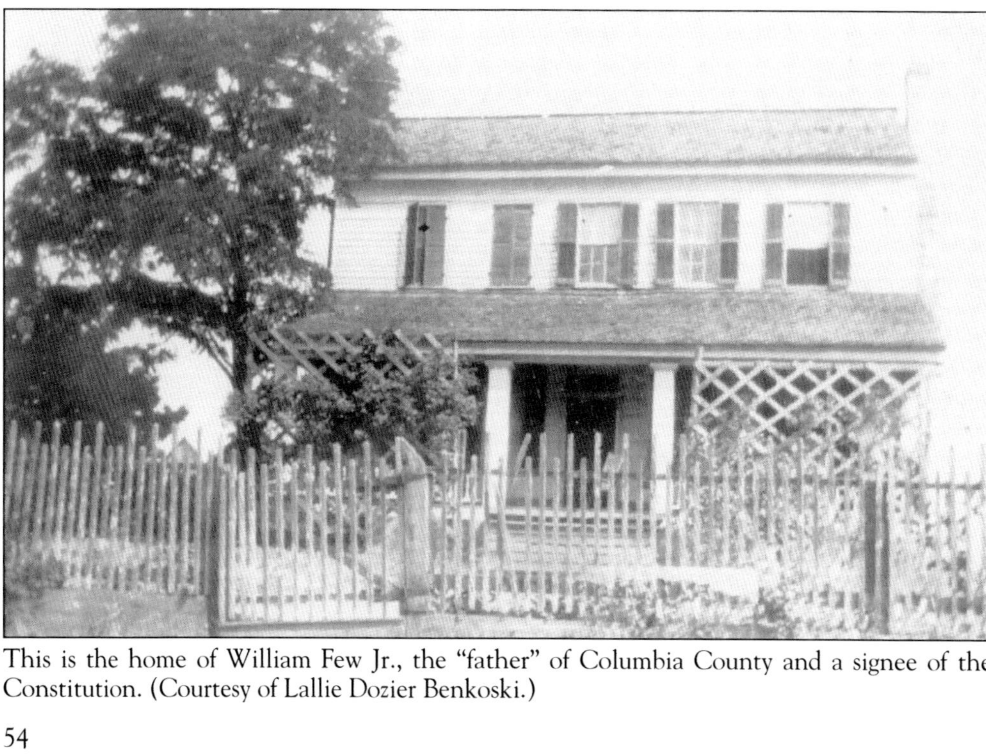

This is the home of William Few Jr., the "father" of Columbia County and a signee of the Constitution. (Courtesy of Lallie Dozier Benkoski.)

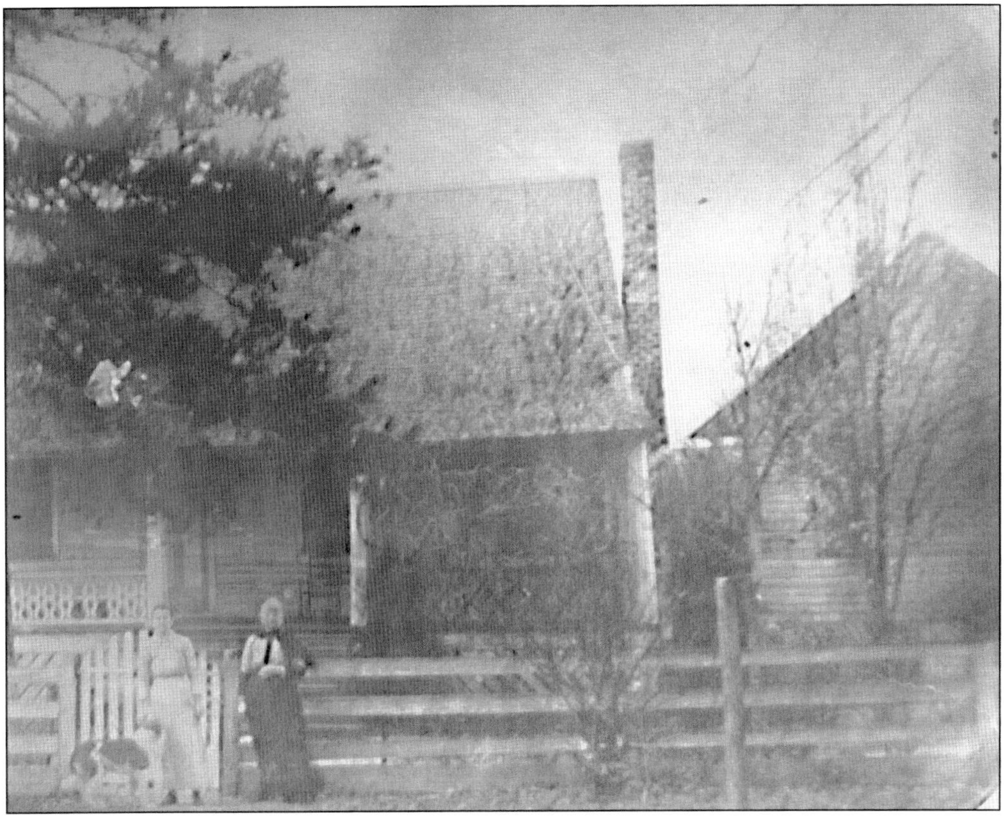

Here is the old Marshall homeplace in Appling, Georgia. (Courtesy of Dan Marshall.)

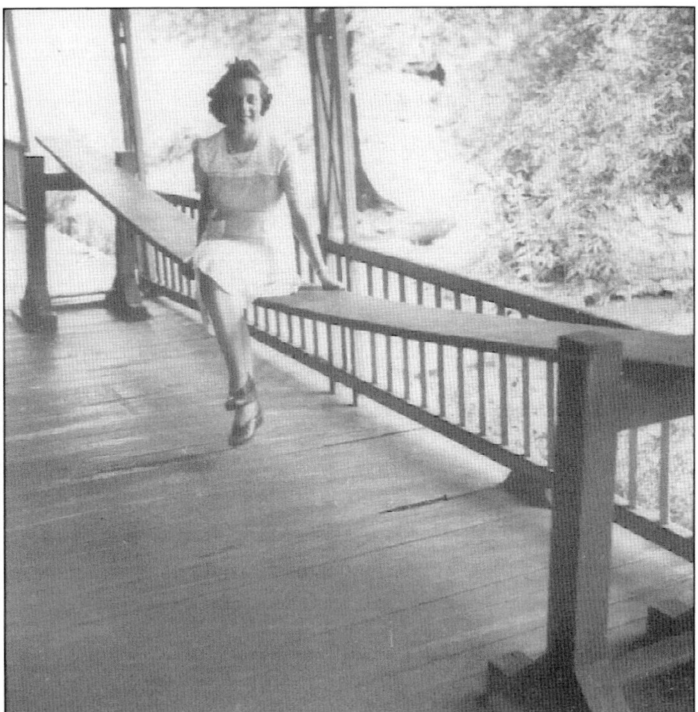

Elizabeth Benton Lamkin sits on a joggling board on the back porch of "The Oaks" plantation. (Courtesy of Elizabeth L. Johnson.)

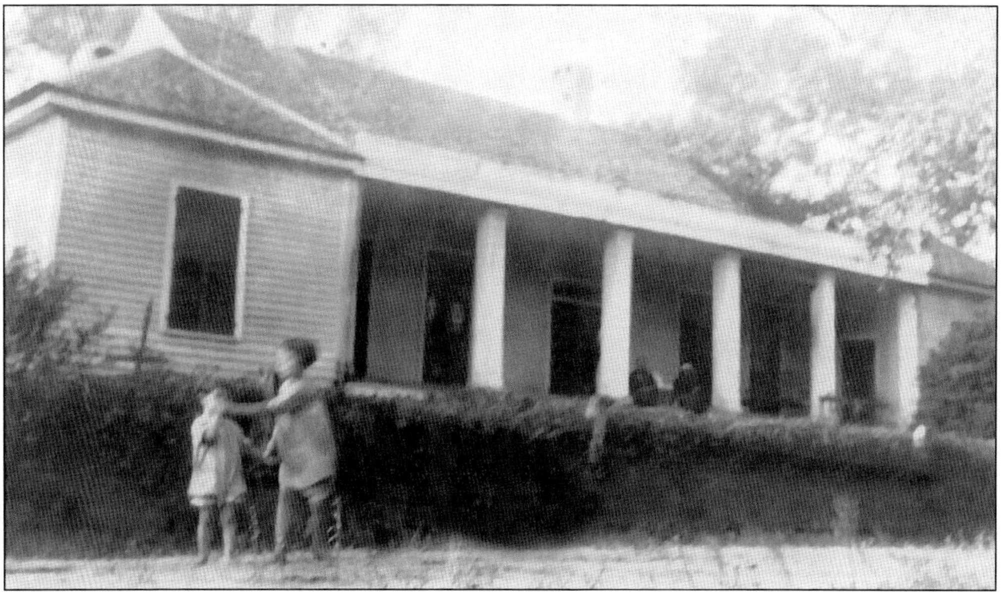

"The Oaks" plantation is home to Julian Barry Lamkin and Mary Talullah Benton Lamkin. The children playing in front are Walton Lamkin Jr. and Elizabeth Lamkin. (Courtesy of Elizabeth L. Johnson.)

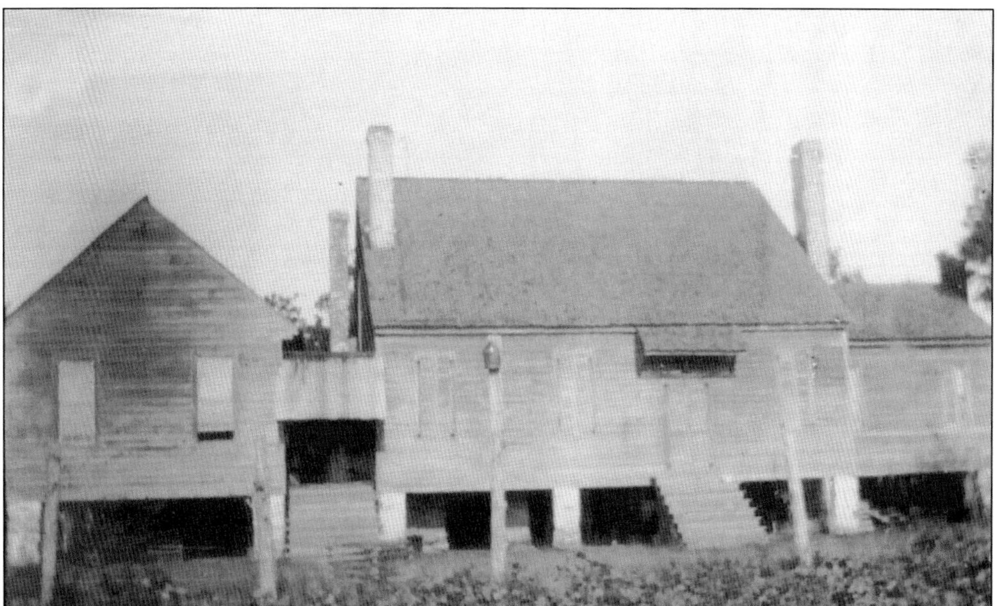

This is the rear view of the Marshall home in Appling, 1915. (Courtesy of Dan Marshall.)

This is the G.B. Pollard Sr. home in Appling, Georgia, *c.* 1940. It is now undergoing the process of restoration. The lady with the cat is schoolteacher Leone Pinson. (Courtesy of Lallie Dozier Benkoski.)

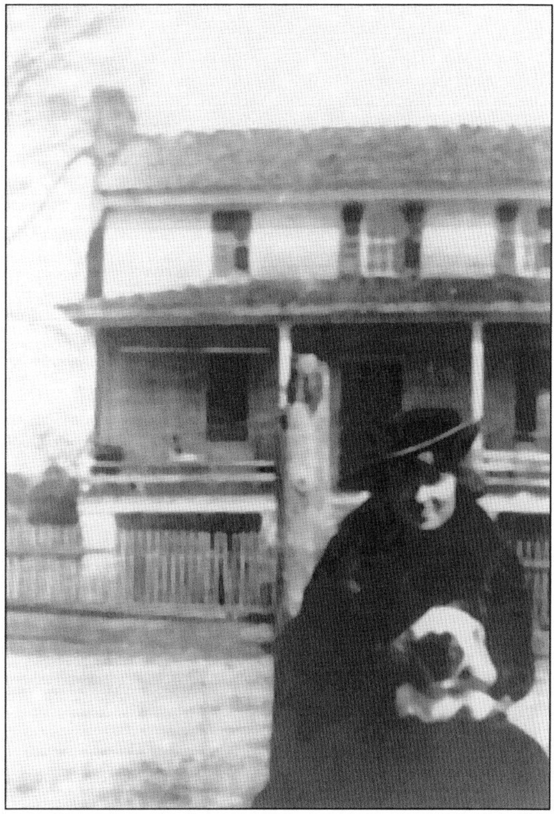

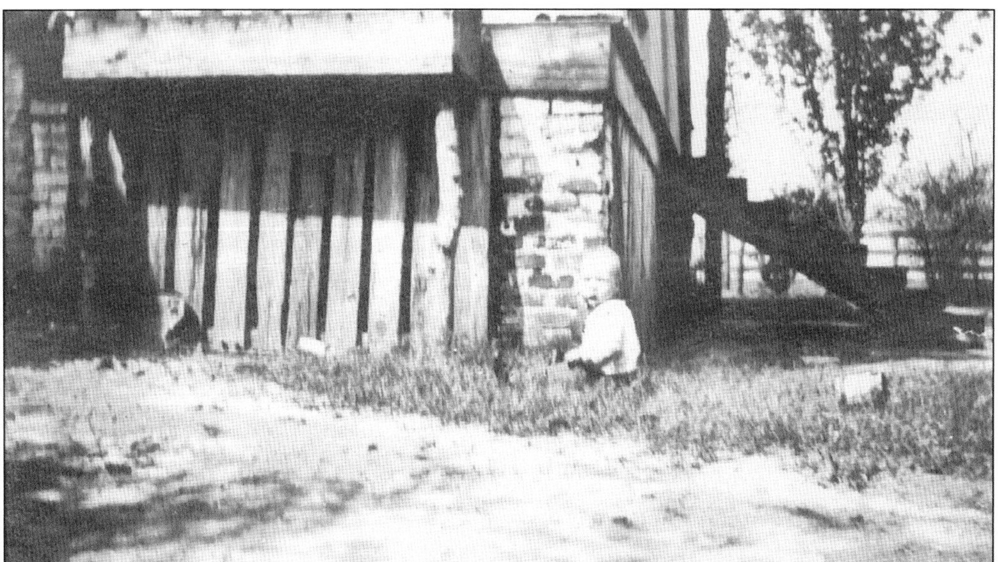

J.H. Marshall Jr. is pictured at Grandma's house in Appling, 1914. (Courtesy of Dan Marshall.)

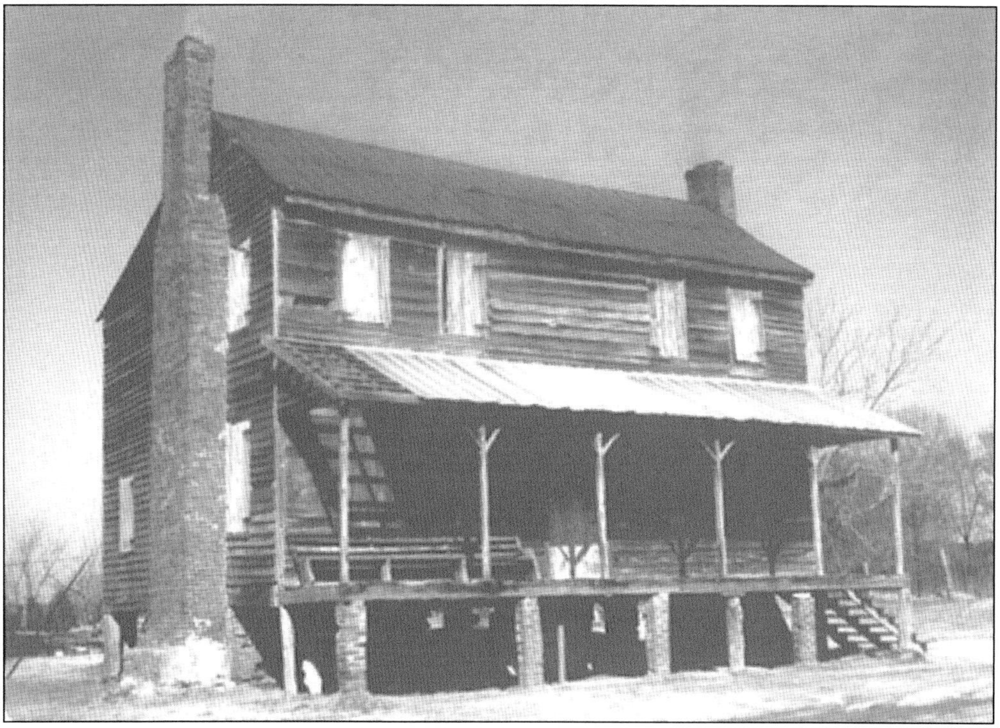

These photographs show two unidentified old houses in Winfield, *c.* 1930. The architectural style of the home above was very common at that time. The same can be said for the cottage-style of the home pictured below. (Both courtesy of Lallie Dozier Benkoski.)

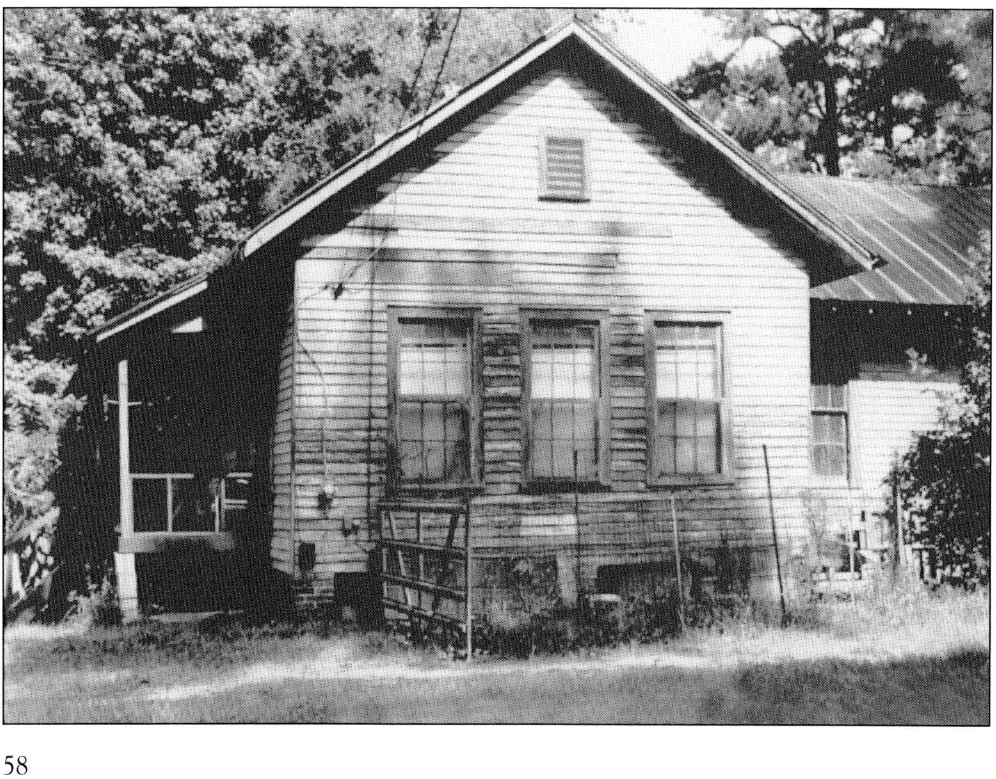

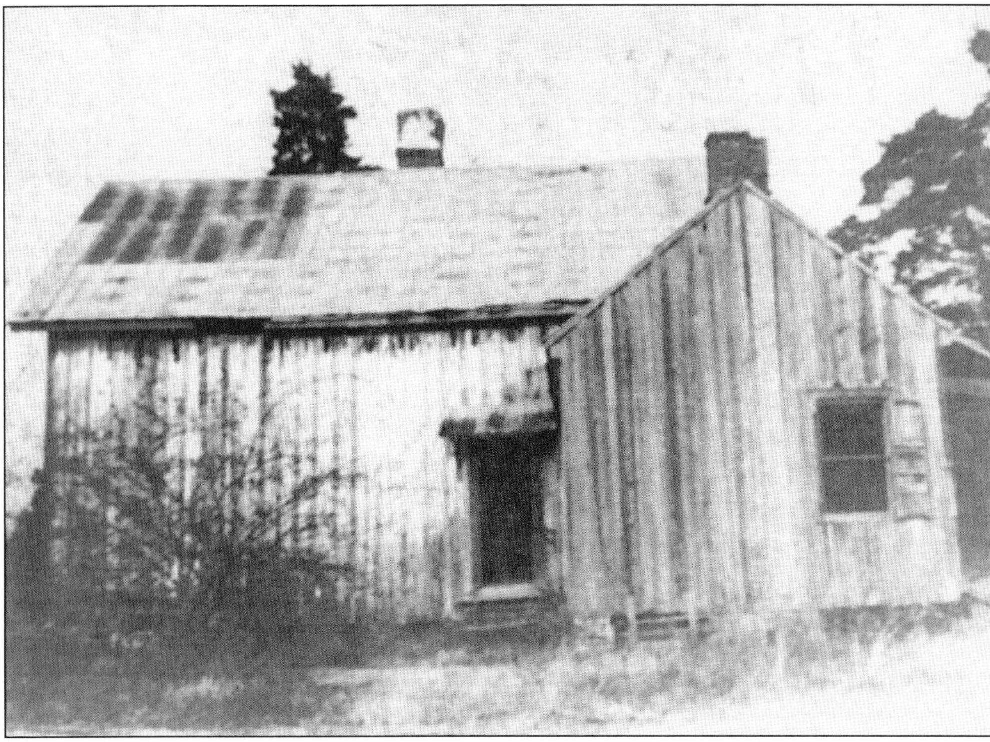

Copse Hill was the home of Paul Hamilton Hayne. This photograph was taken shortly before the structure was torn down in the 1960s. (Courtesy of Lallie Dozier Benkoski.)

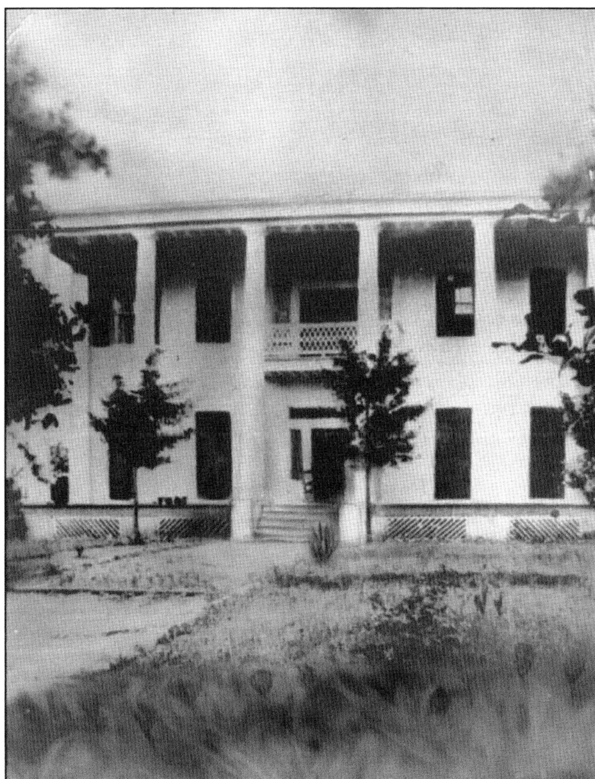

Waverly Hall is the home of Dr. H.R. Casey, an eminent doctor of medicine and a delegate to the Georgia Secession Convention. Dr. Casey was a leader in county politics before and after the Civil War and was a close friend of Alexander H. Stephens, the vice president of the Confederacy. (Courtesy of Lallie Dozier Benkoski.)

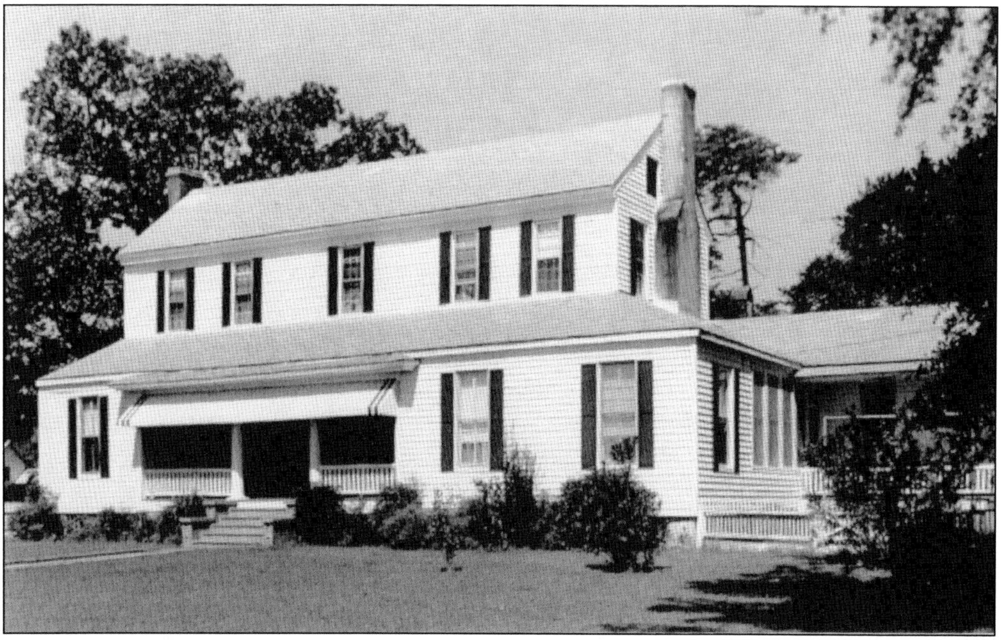

This photograph of the George McGruder home between Harlem and Highway 47 was taken in the 1950s. (Courtesy of Lallie Dozier Benkoski.)

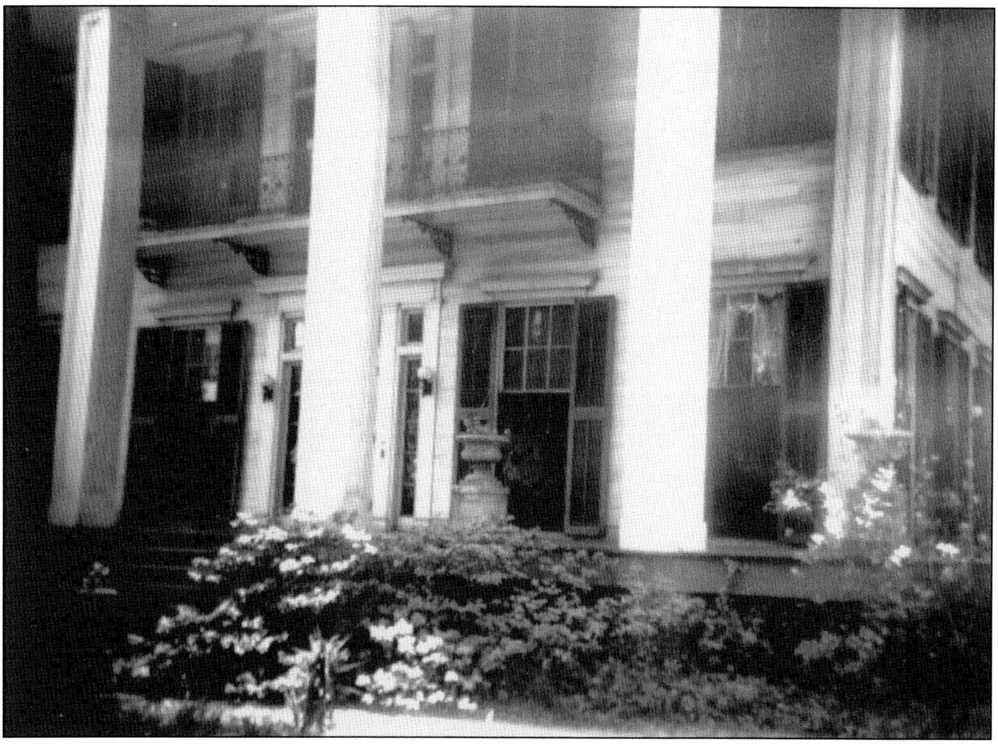

This is where William Harris Crawford lived as a youth in Phinizy, Georgia. The house burned in the first half of the 20th century. (Courtesy of Lallie Dozier Benkoski.)

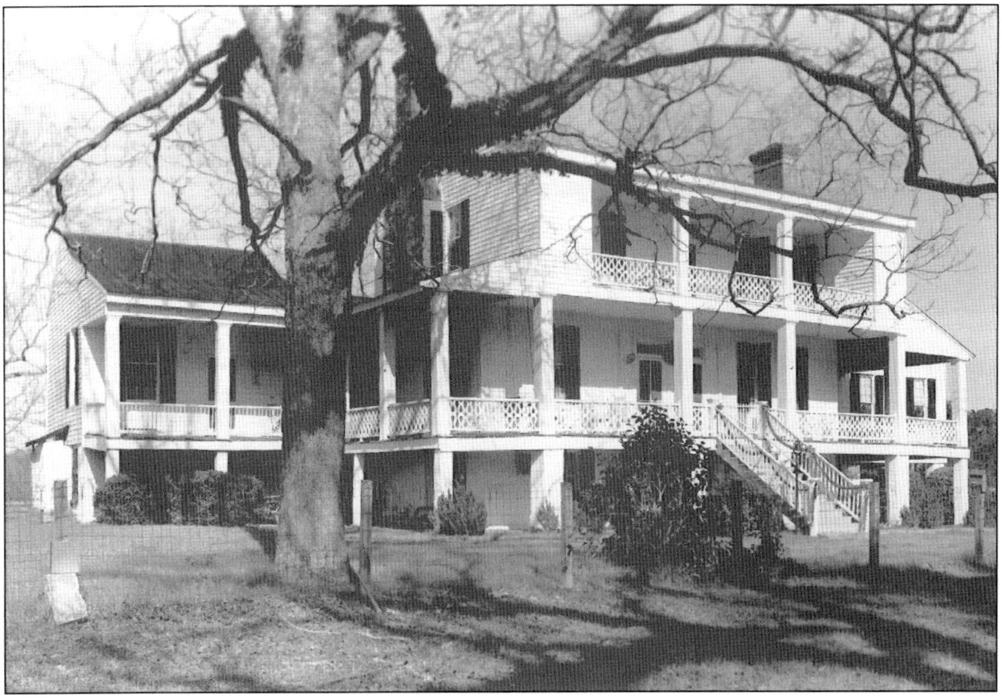

Woodville, the home of Dr. James Hamilton, is located near Phinizy on Dozier Road. (Courtesy of W.C. Blackard.)

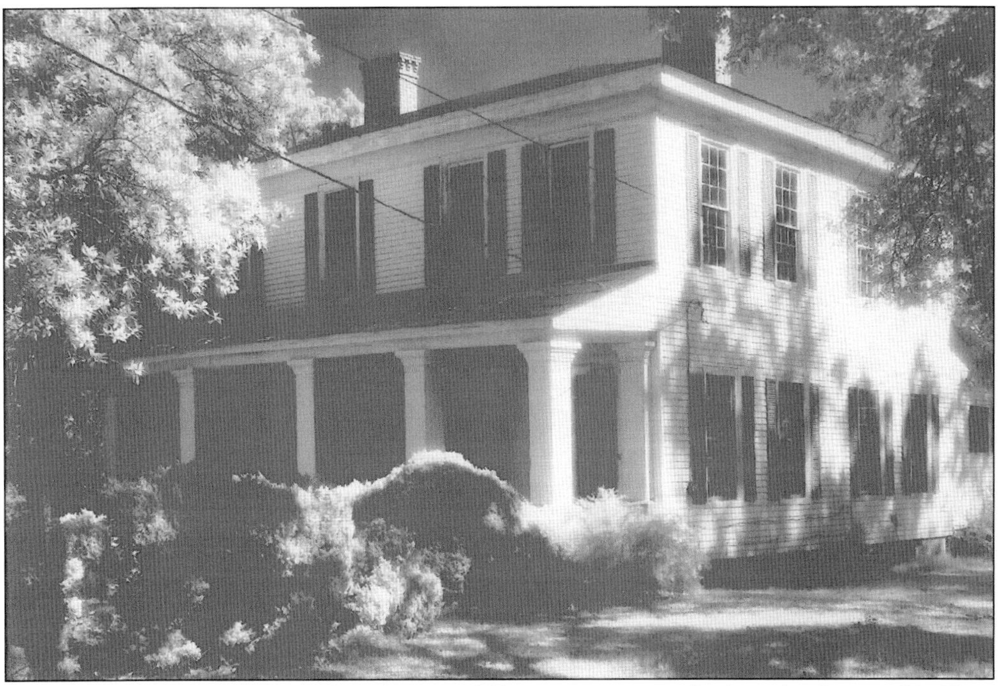

The home of Robert Lane, "Cedarvale" in Cobbham, Georgia was built on land granted by King George III. (Courtesy of Lallie Dozier Benkoski.)

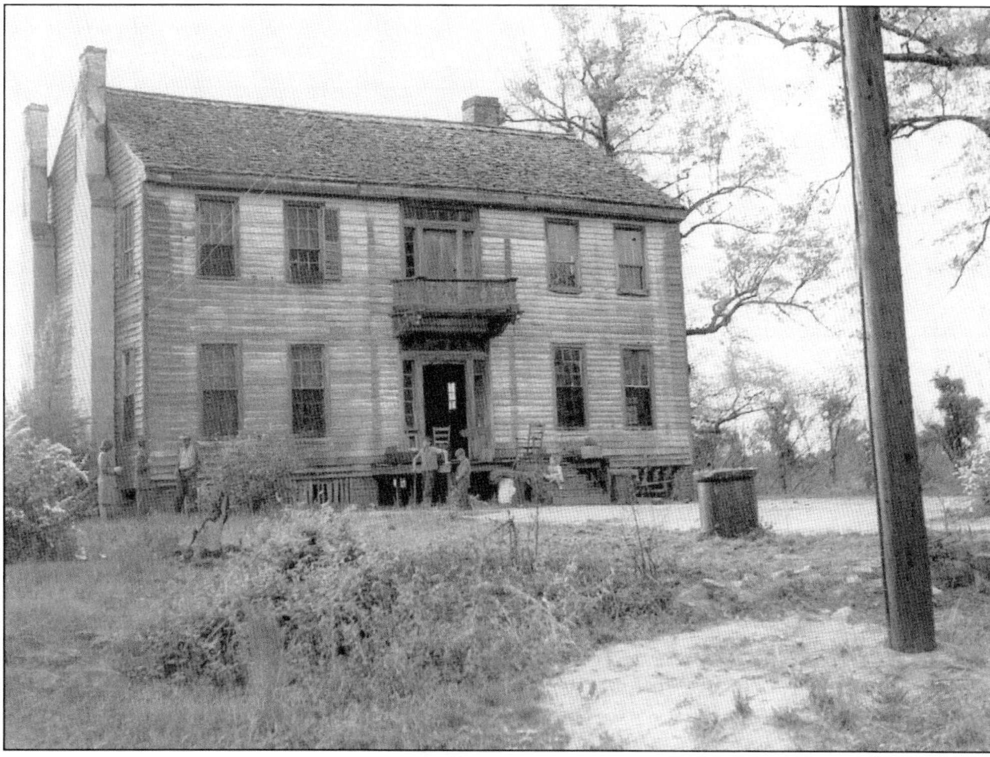

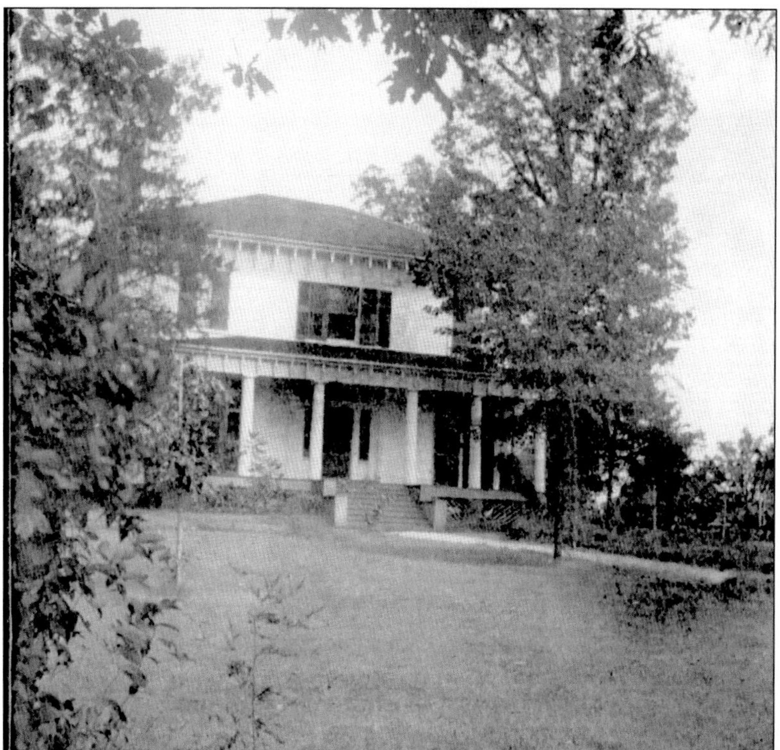

This is a picture of Liberty Point, the Walton estate, which was built *c.* 1835. (Courtesy of G.L. Polatty.)

This is a picture of the Lamkin home, *c.* 1940. Columbia County had many large plantations in the 1800s. Several, like this home, are still standing. (Courtesy of G.L. Polatty.)

Three

Towns and other Places

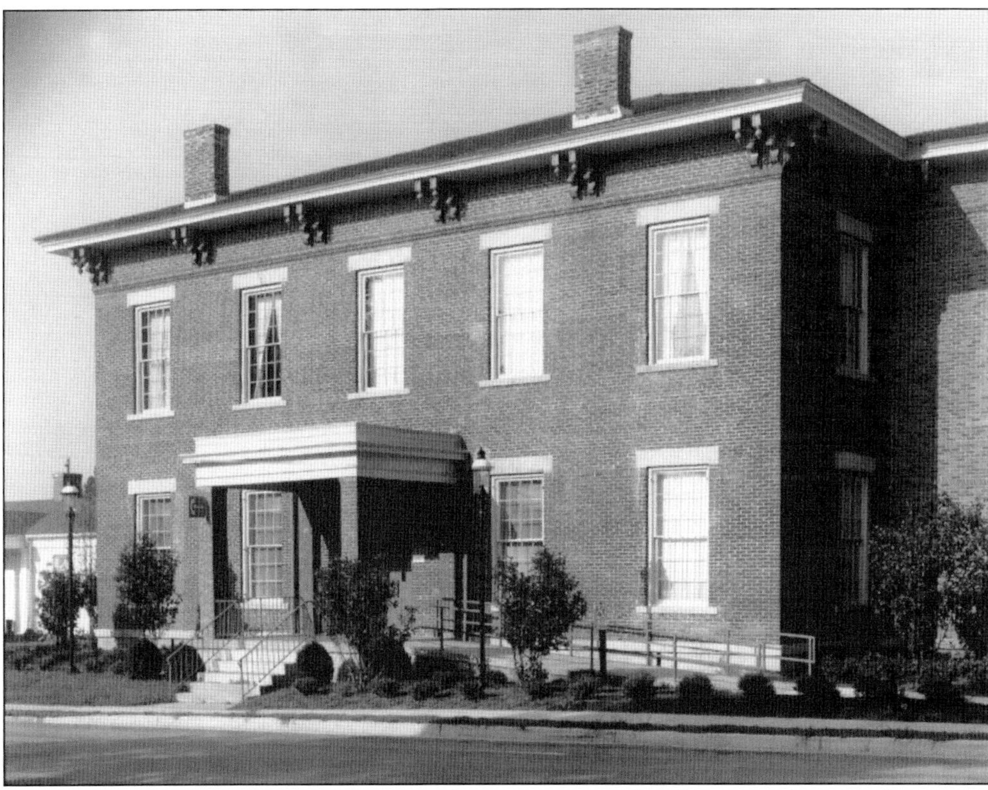

The Columbia County Courthouse in Appling, Georgia, is the oldest courthouse still in use in the state. It was built in 1854. (Courtesy of W.C. Blackard.)

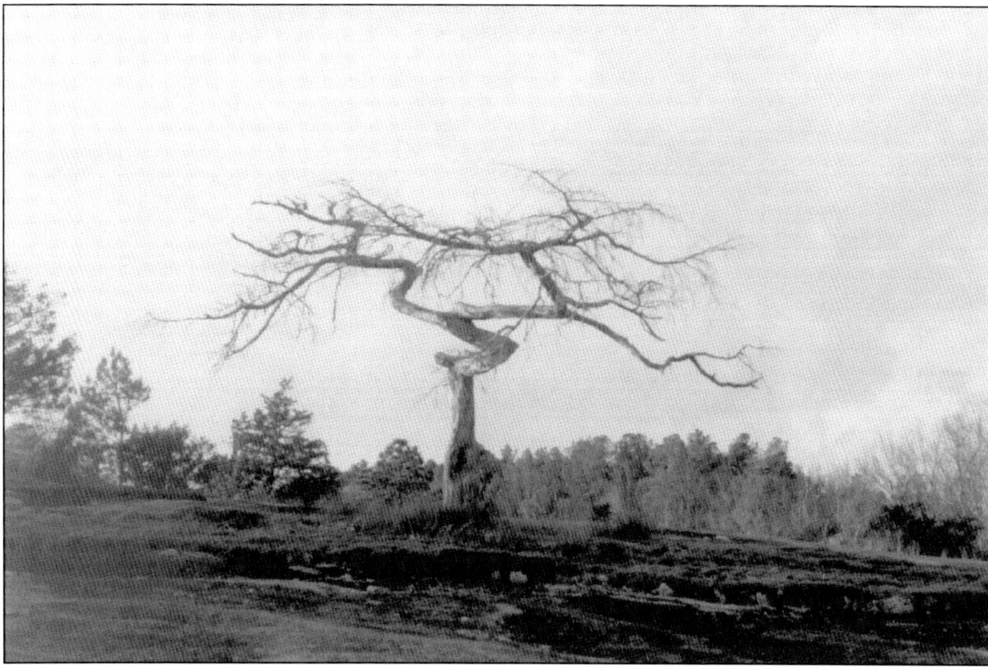

An autumn scene was photographed at Heggie Rock near Appling, c. 1985. (Courtesy of Pat Blanchard.)

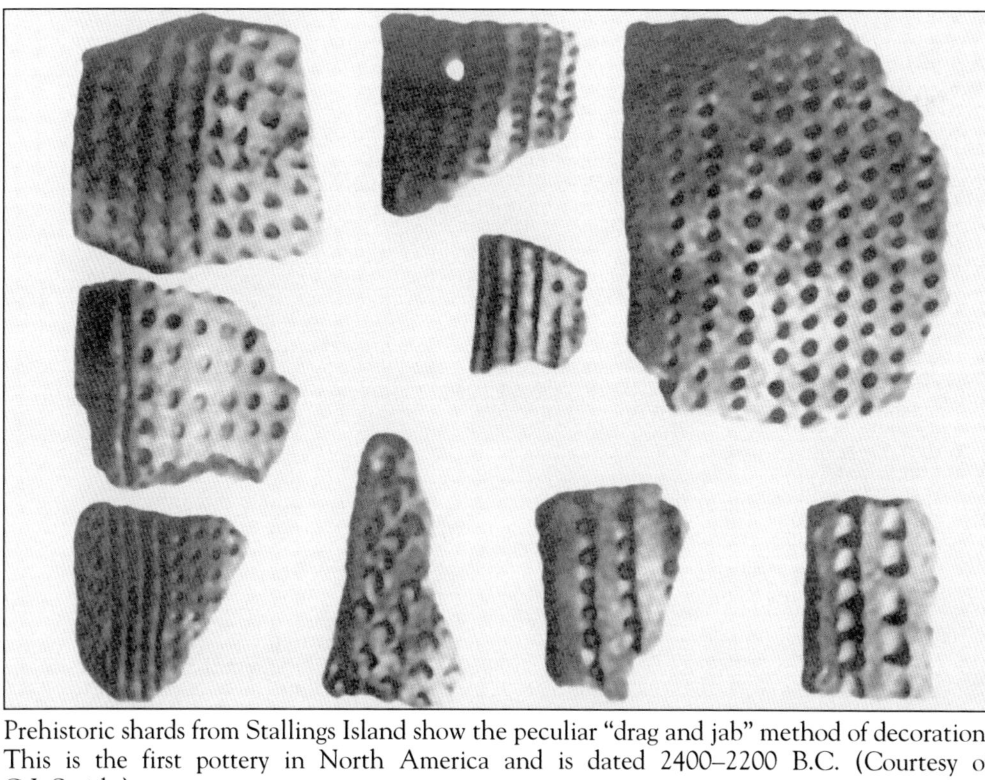

Prehistoric shards from Stallings Island show the peculiar "drag and jab" method of decoration. This is the first pottery in North America and is dated 2400–2200 B.C. (Courtesy of G.J. Smith.)

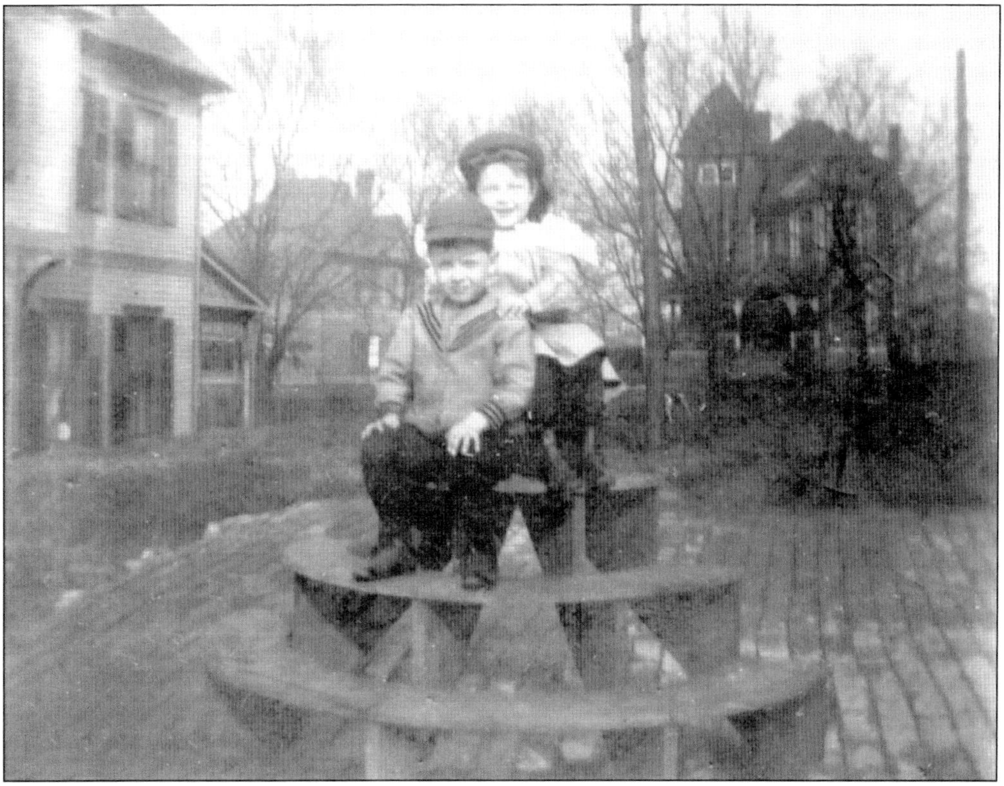

These are unidentified children, in Harlem, Georgia, *c.* 1940. (Courtesy of G.L. Polatty.)

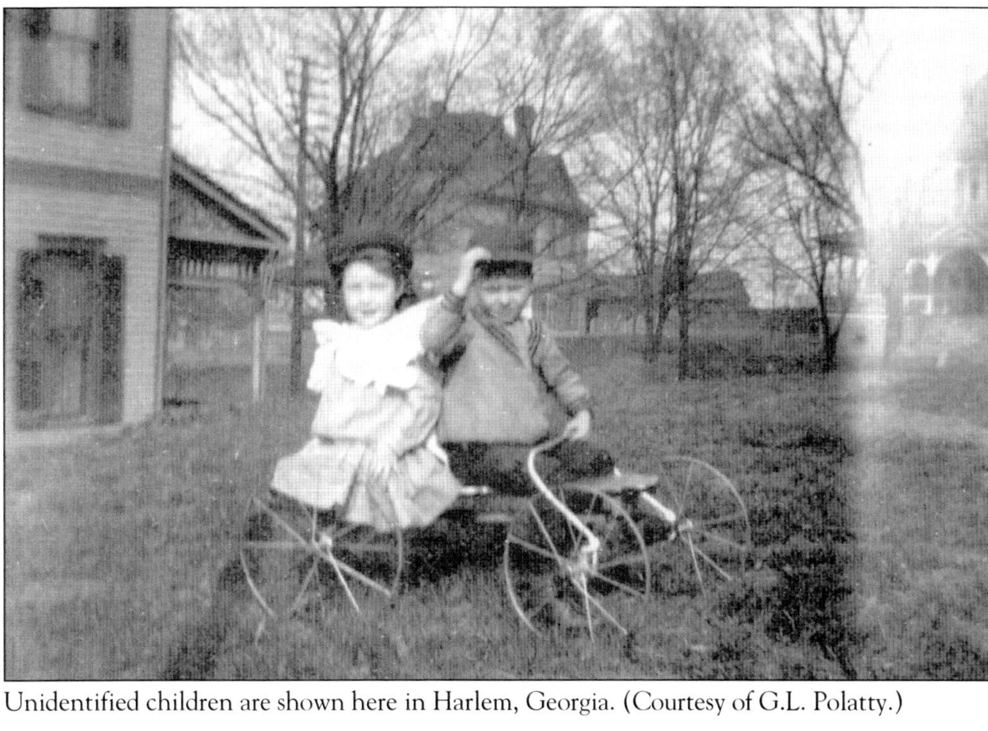

Unidentified children are shown here in Harlem, Georgia. (Courtesy of G.L. Polatty.)

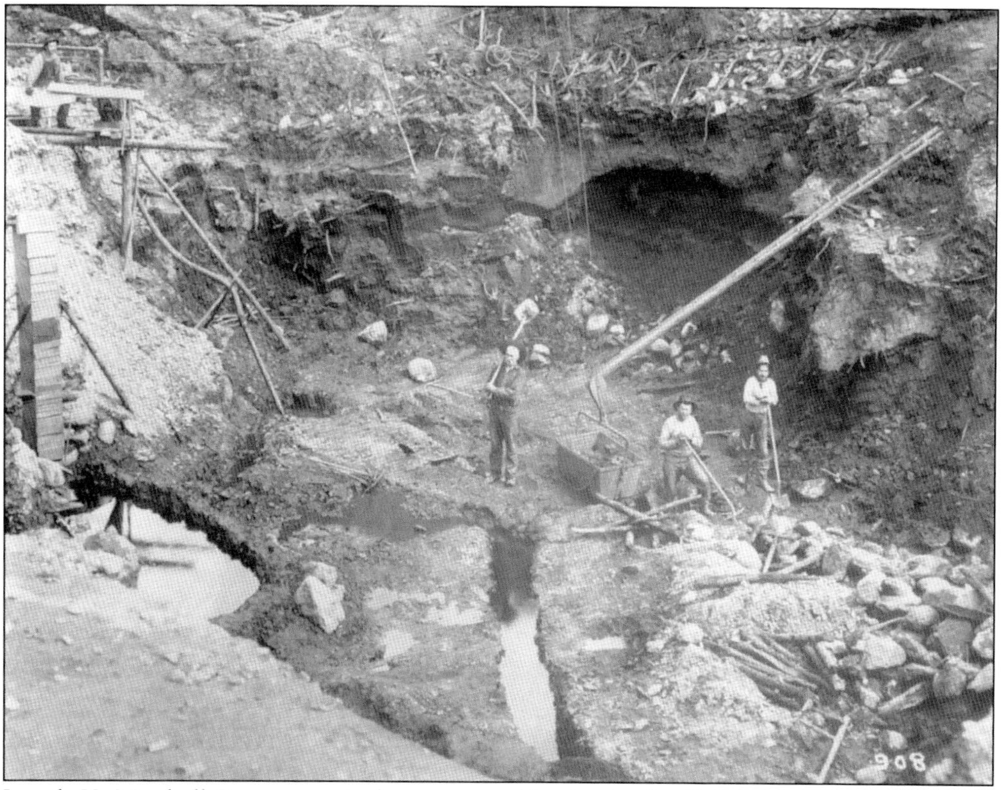

Joseph H. Marshall Sr., center, is shown at a gold mine in the Yukon Territory in the early 1900s. (Courtesy Dan Marshall.)

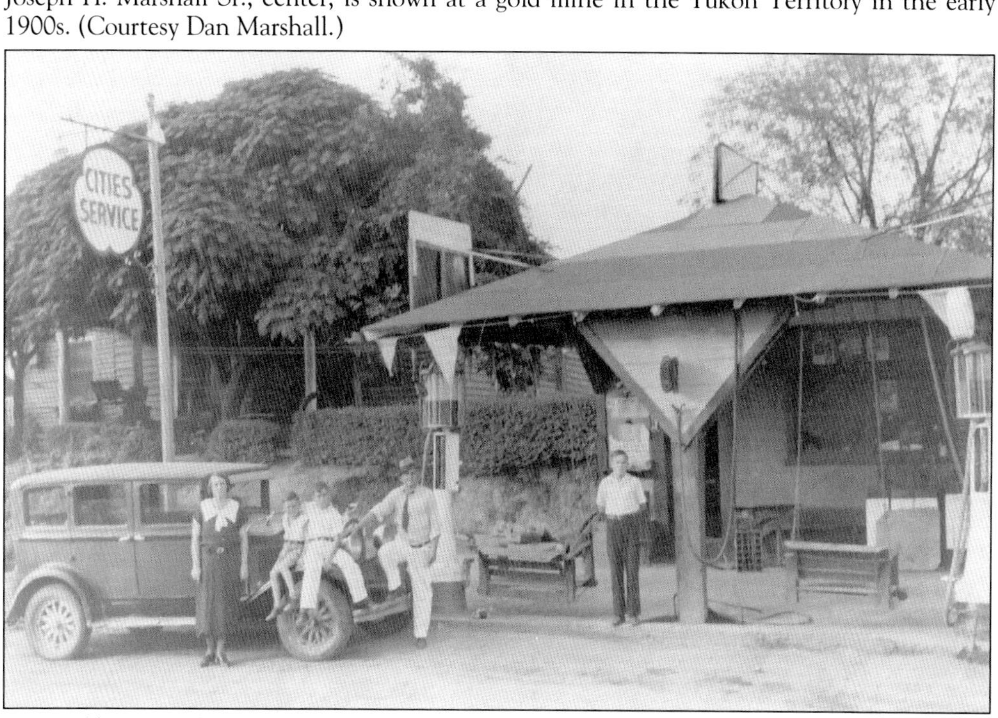

Pictured here is Polatty's Cities Service Gas Station in Evans, Georgia, c. 1940.

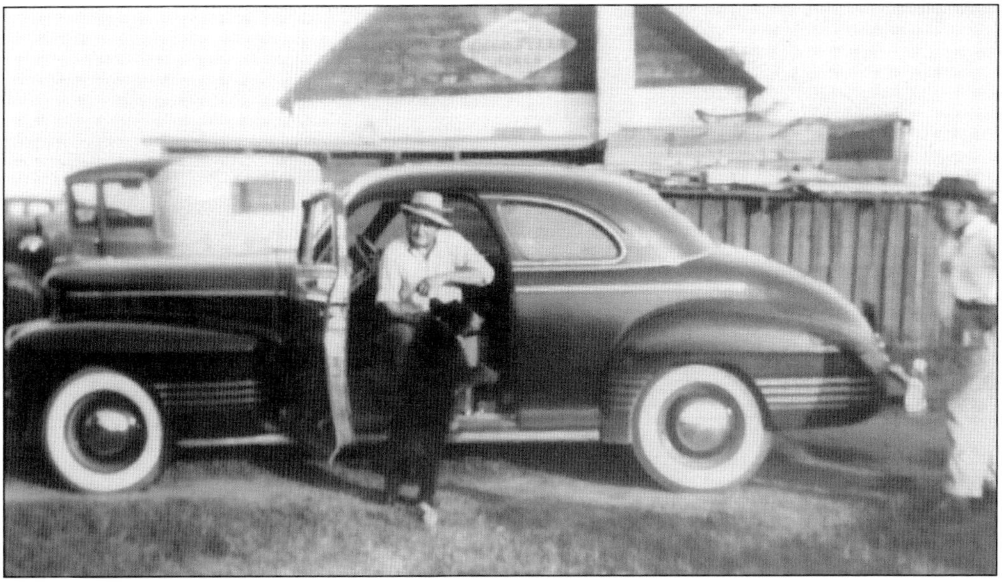

Ernest Polatty, Calvin Polatty, and a bear are pictured in Evans, Georgia, *c.* 1940. Mr. Polatty kept animals at his service or "filling station" for his customers to admire. (Courtesy of G.L. Polatty.)

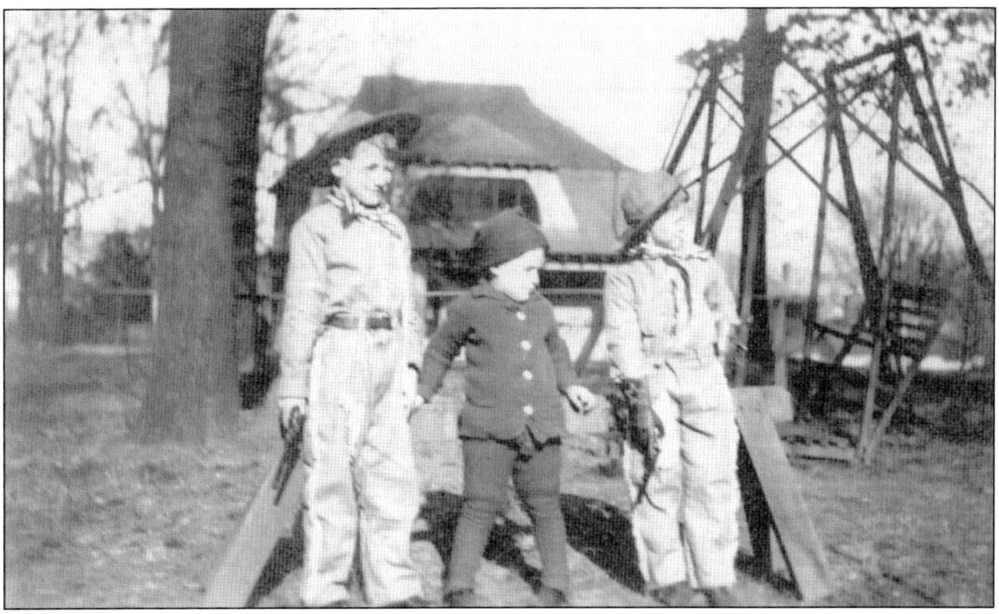

These unidentified children dressed in cowboy attire and carrying "cap" pistols are shown in a *c.* 1940 image from Harlem, Georgia. (Courtesy of G.L. Polatty.)

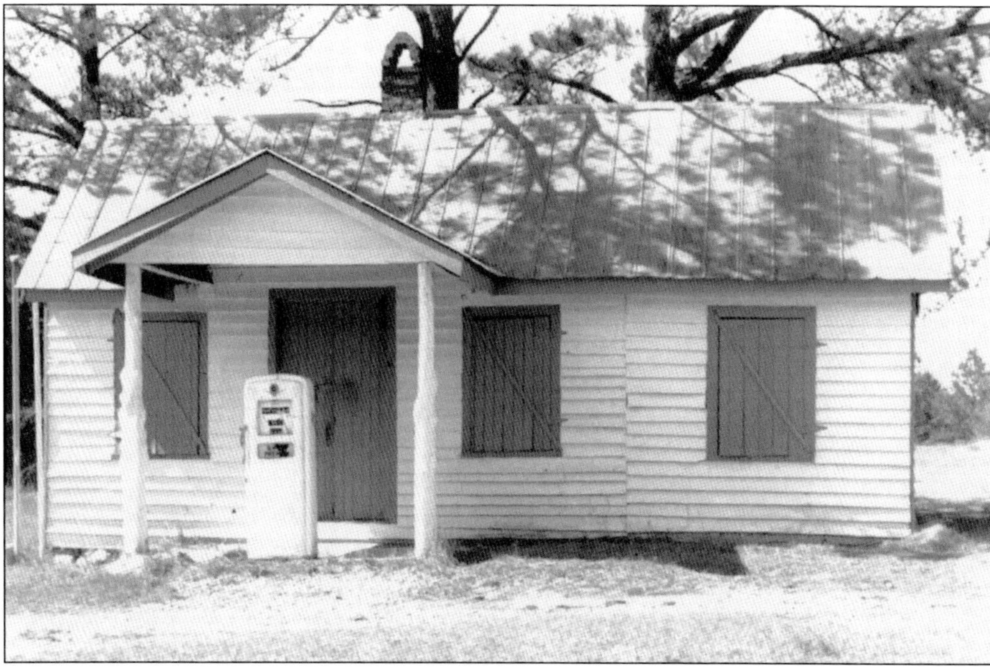

This country store, c. 1950, was owned by Marvin Neal in Winfield, Georgia. (Courtesy of Lallie Dozier Benkoski.)

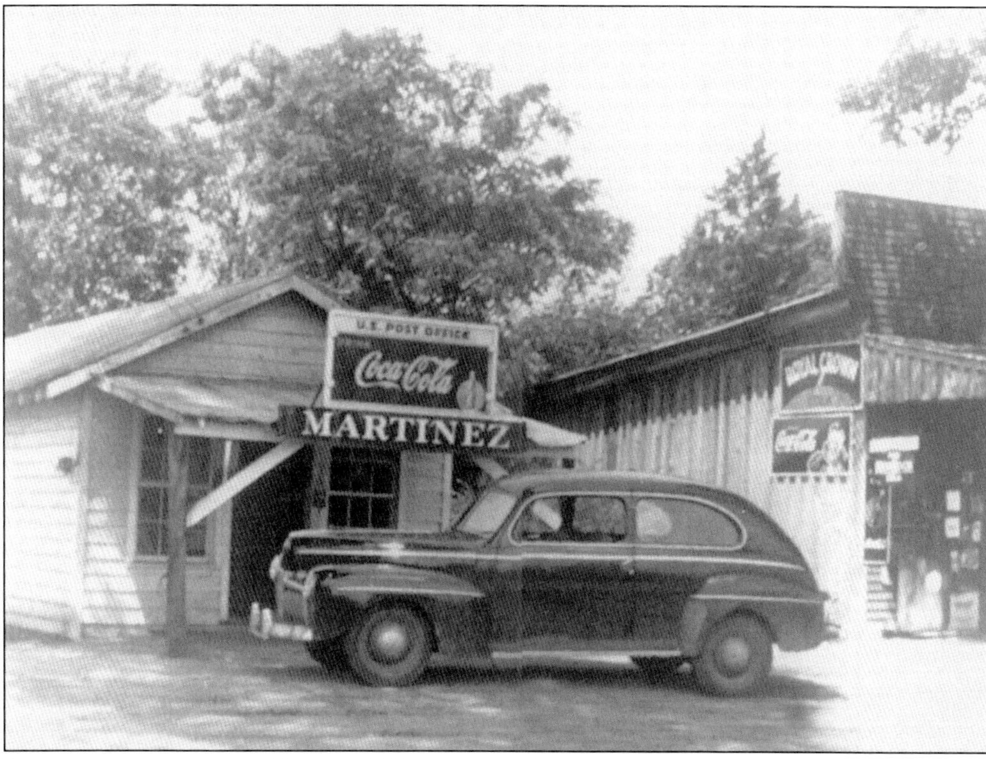

This picture shows the U.S. Post Office and neighboring store in Martinez, Georgia, in the 1930s. (Courtesy of Carole Davis.)

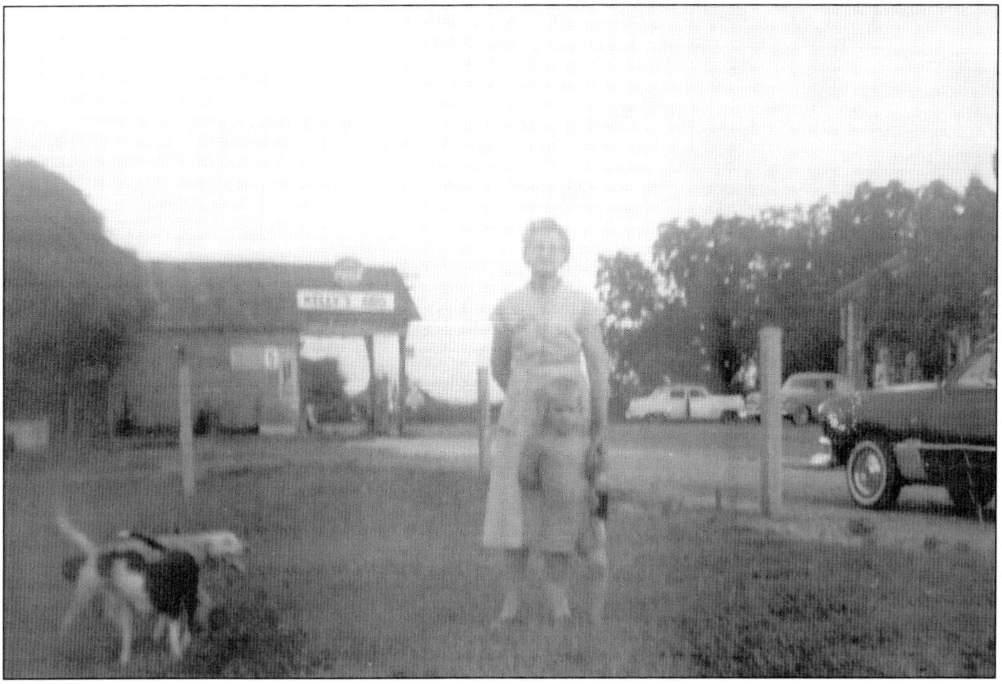

Pictured are Mrs. A.C. Wallace and her grandson at Wallace's Store in Phinizy in the 1950s. (Courtesy of Jimmy Wallace.)

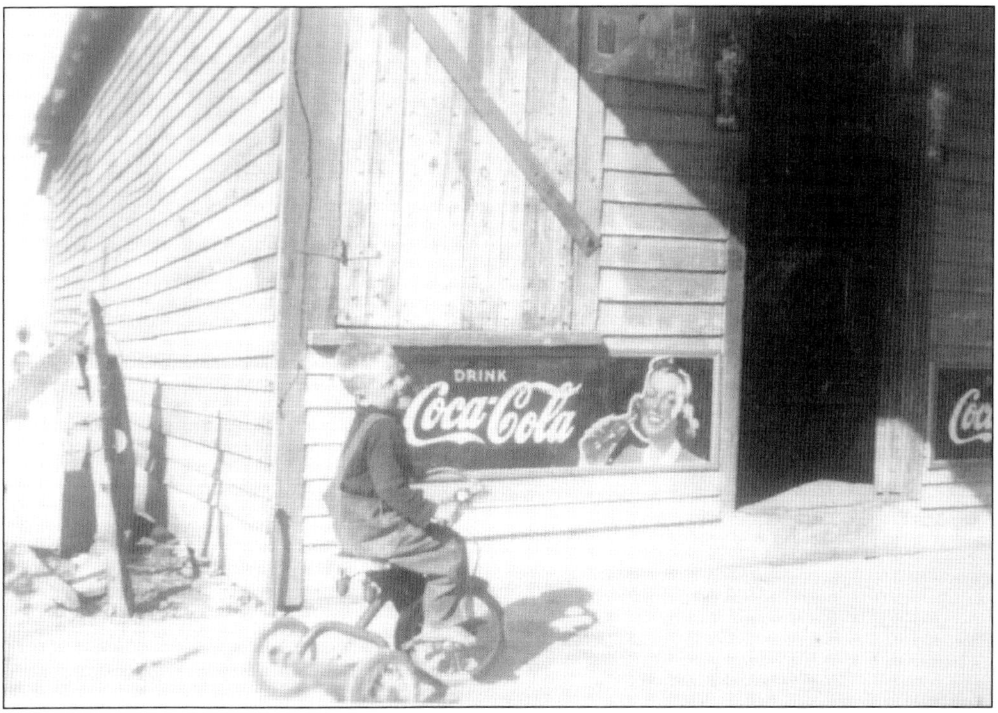

Young Jimmy Wallace rides a tricycle to Wallace's Store in the 1950s. Maybe he'll buy a soda pop, a moon pie, or a jawbreaker. (Courtesy of Jimmy Wallace.)

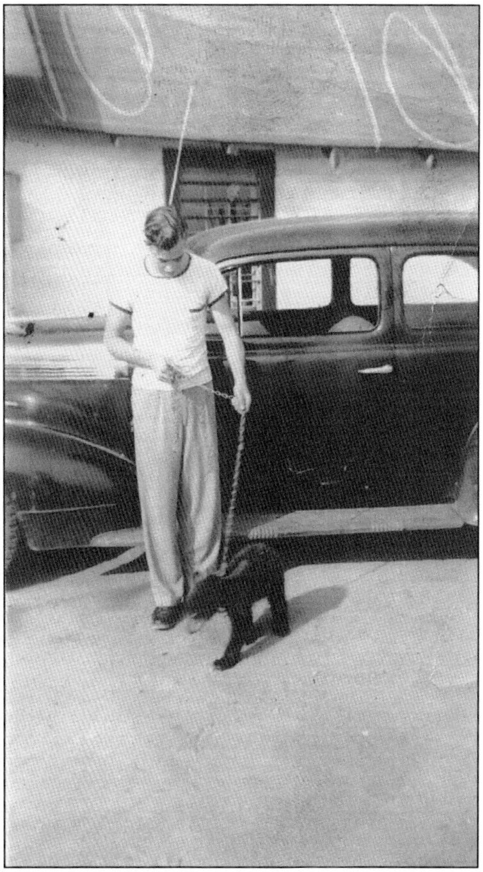

Russell Hensley and a bear cub are pictured here c. 1940. A tourist and customer attraction for several years, the little cub is the same animal that appears on page 67. (Courtesy of G.L. Polatty.)

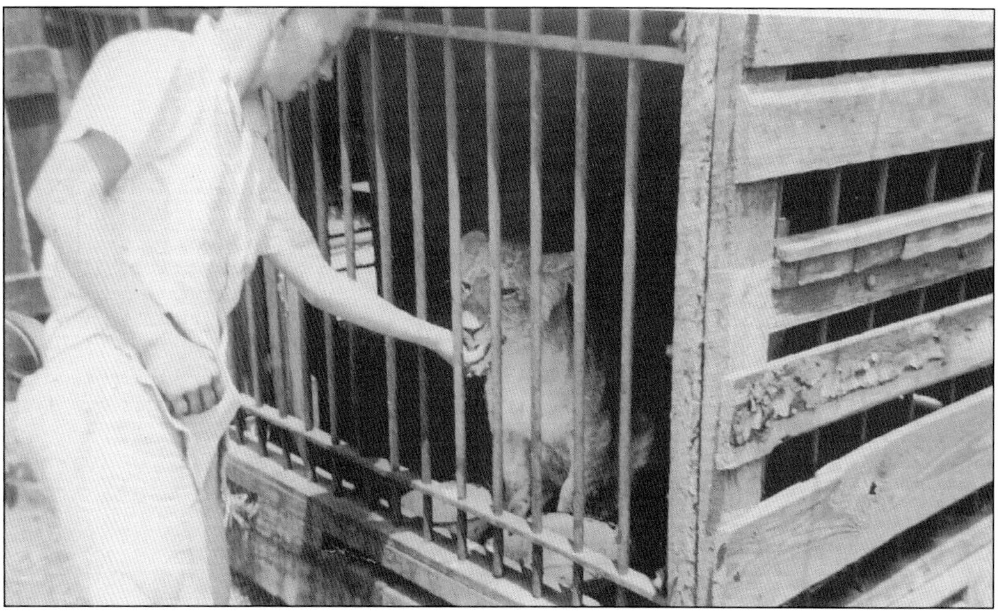

Howard Hensley must be on intimate terms with this lion cub, c. 1940. (Courtesy of G.L. Polatty.)

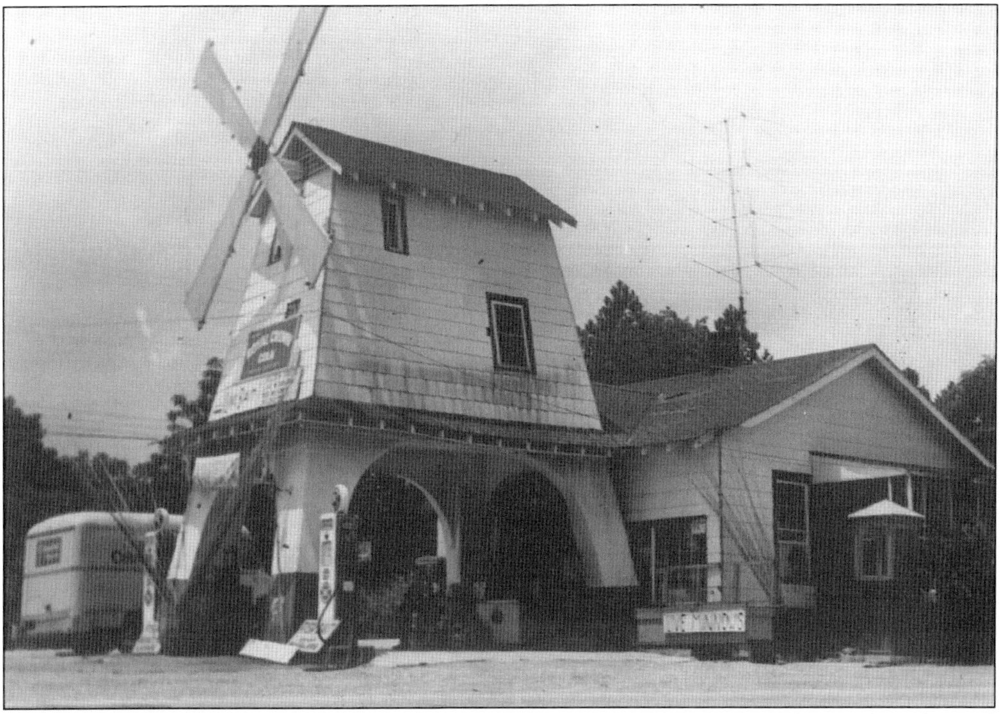

In this 1950s view, the old general store in Martinez, Georgia is seen with a Colonial Bread truck on the side and a huge windmill in front. (Courtesy of Bill Jackson.)

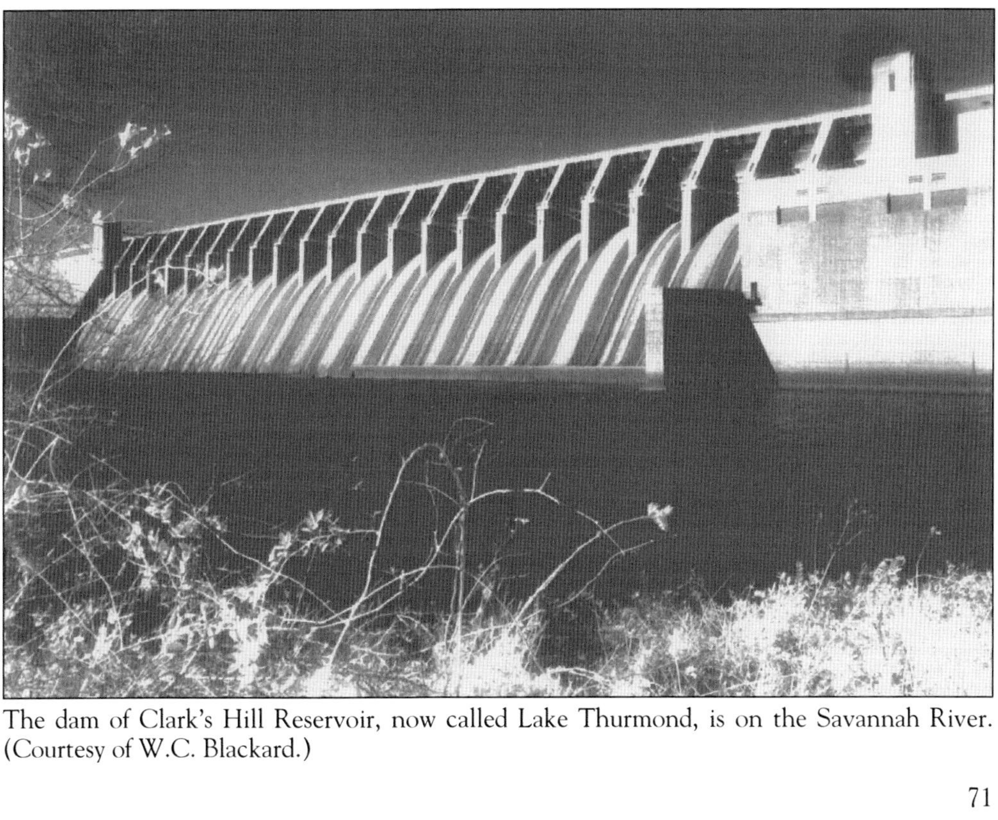

The dam of Clark's Hill Reservoir, now called Lake Thurmond, is on the Savannah River. (Courtesy of W.C. Blackard.)

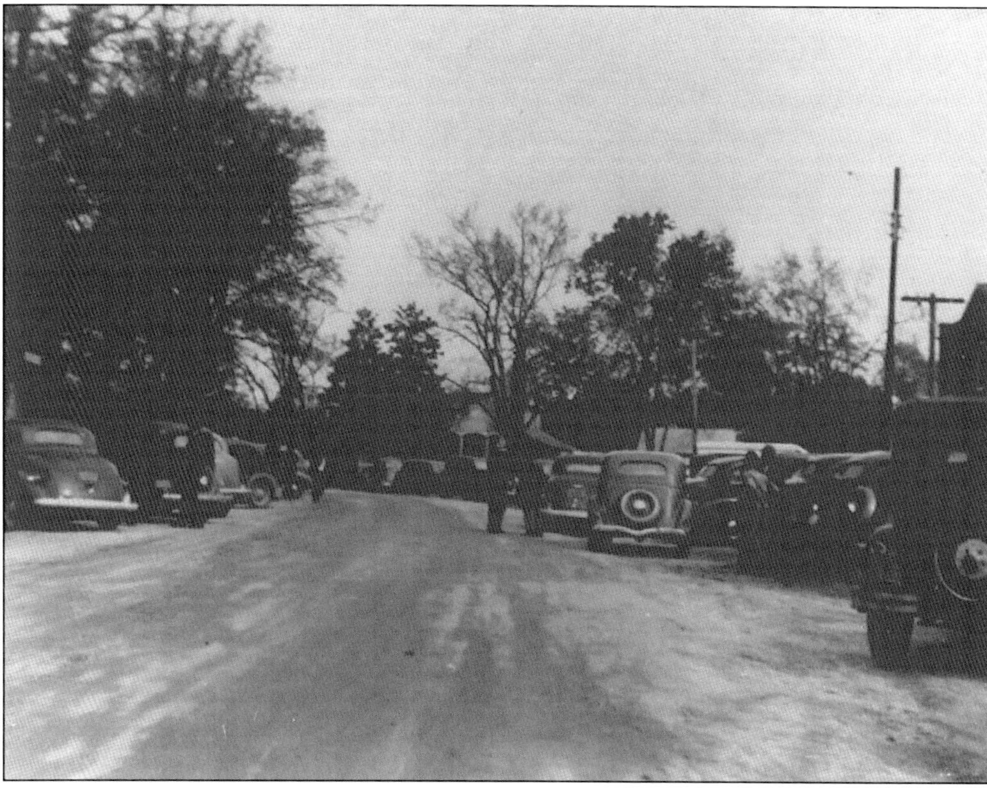

Pictured here is "court day" in Appling, Georgia, c. 1930. Court day, which could last a week or more every month, was the time in which all the legal business of a community, from grand juries to criminal trials to hangings, would be held. This would draw many people from miles away to town. (Courtesy of Jake Pollard.)

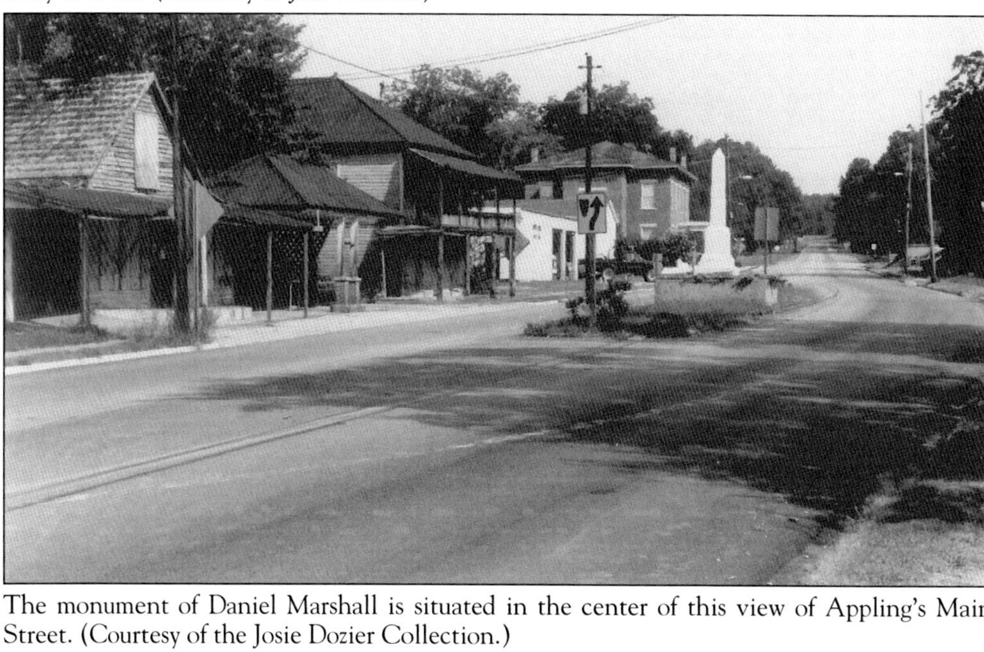

The monument of Daniel Marshall is situated in the center of this view of Appling's Main Street. (Courtesy of the Josie Dozier Collection.)

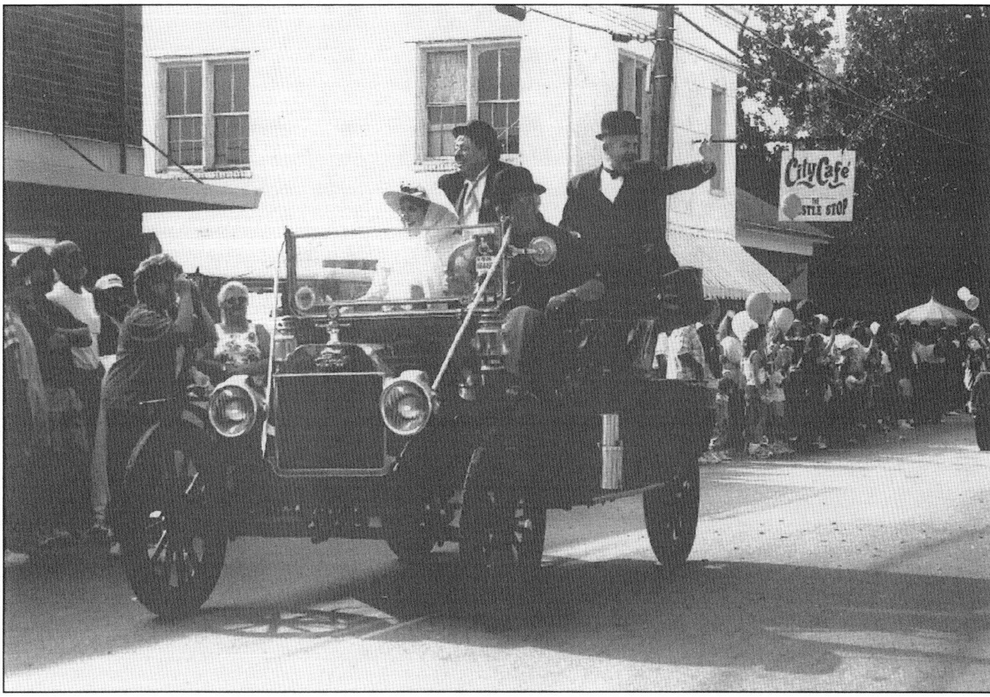

Laurel and Hardy impersonators ride in a Model T Ford in the Oliver Hardy Festival in Harlem, Georgia. (Courtesy of the City of Harlem.)

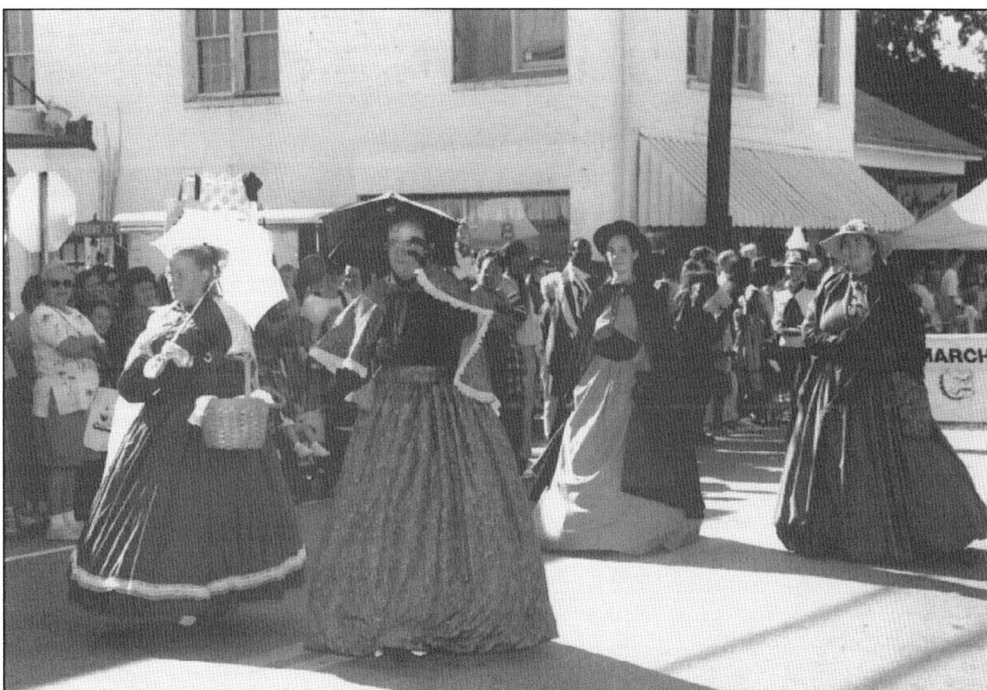

Unidentified women in period dress participate in the Hardy Festival parade. (Courtesy of the City of Harlem.)

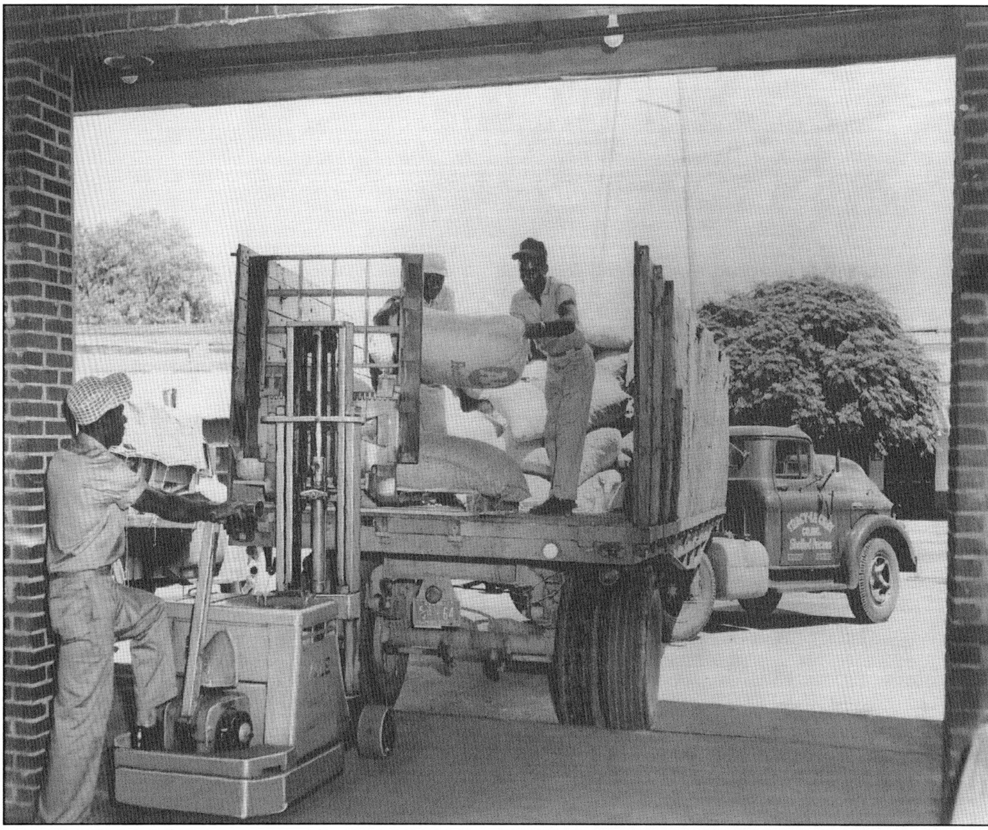

Men load a truck at Tracy-Lucky Pecan Company in Harlem, Georgia, in the 1970s. (Courtesy of Francis Tracy.)

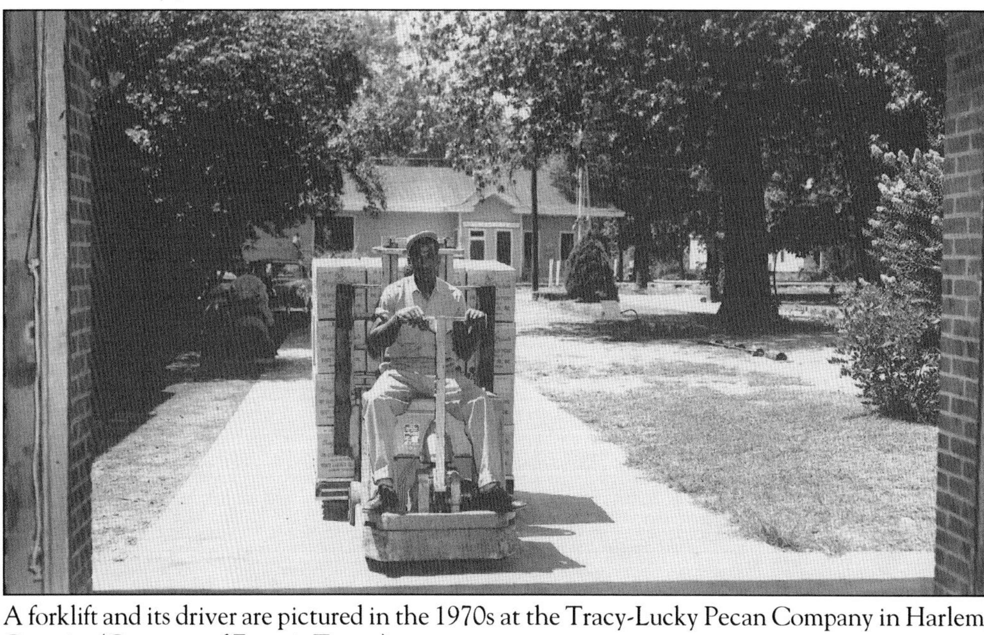

A forklift and its driver are pictured in the 1970s at the Tracy-Lucky Pecan Company in Harlem, Georgia. (Courtesy of Francis Tracy.)

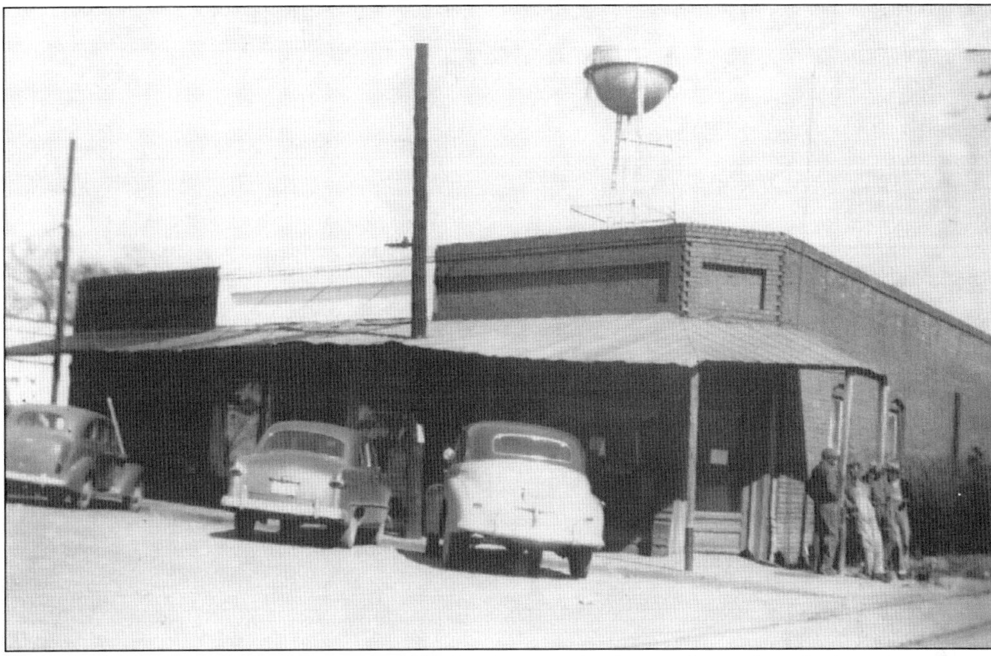

Here is a corner store in Harlem, c. 1950. Such stores had everything for sale from hairpins to plows and also served as gathering places for townsfolk to pass the time and visit with friends and neighbors. (Courtesy of Francis Tracy.)

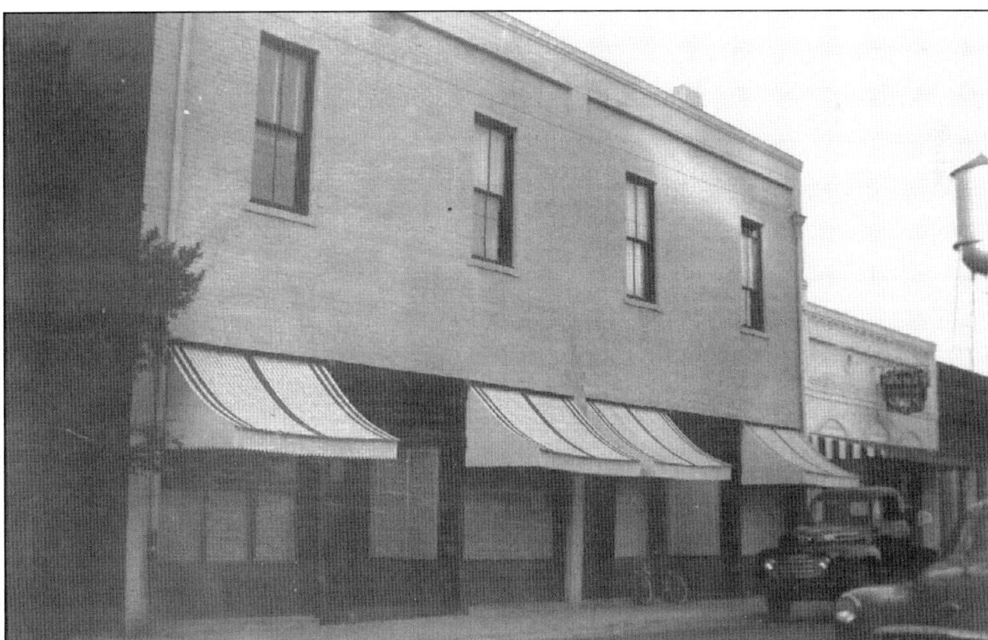

This c. 1950 photograph shows the Tracy-Lucky Pecan Company in Harlem, Georgia. (Courtesy of Francis Tracy.)

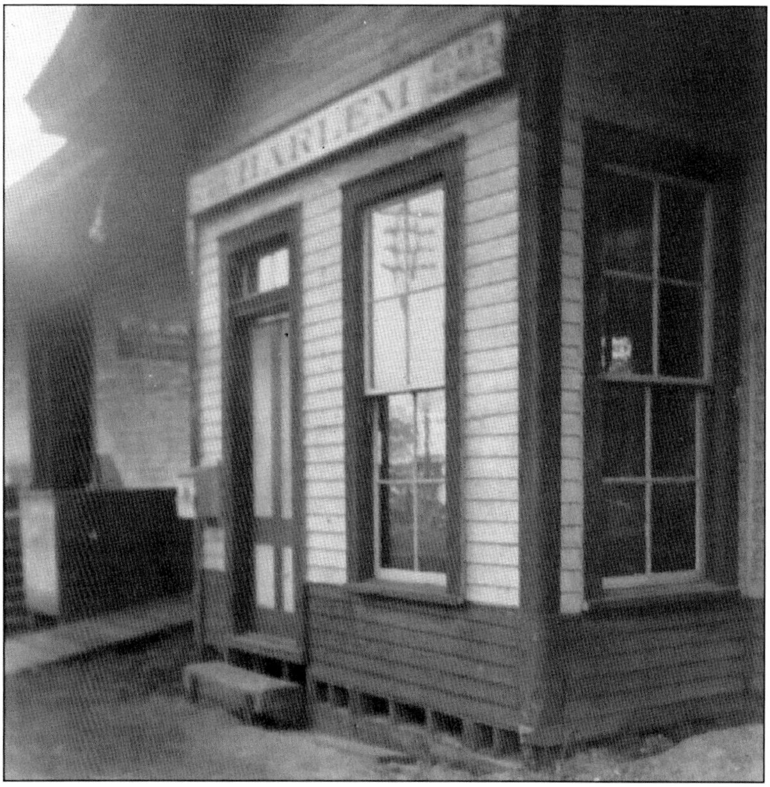

The depot at Harlem, Georgia had this little room that jutted out from the building so that the telegrapher inside could see both ways as trains approached. This picture was taken in 1950. (Courtesy of Francis Tracy.)

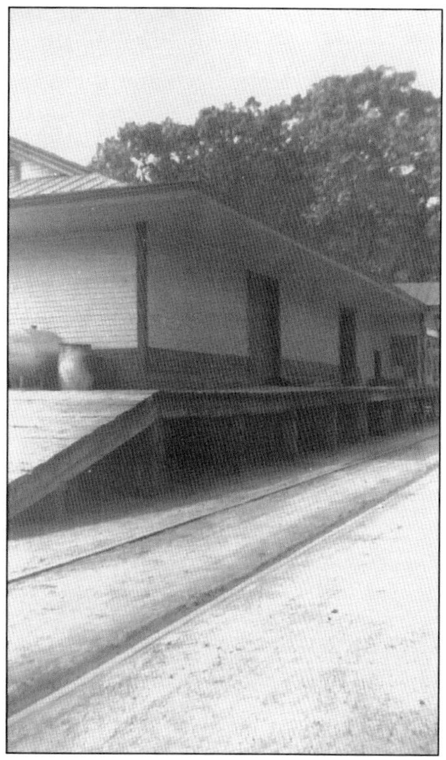

This 1958 view of the Harlem Depot shows the loading platform, a very busy place during cotton season. Mail freight was also loaded and unloaded here, and young boys used the site to play and watch for trains. (Courtesy of Francis Tracy.)

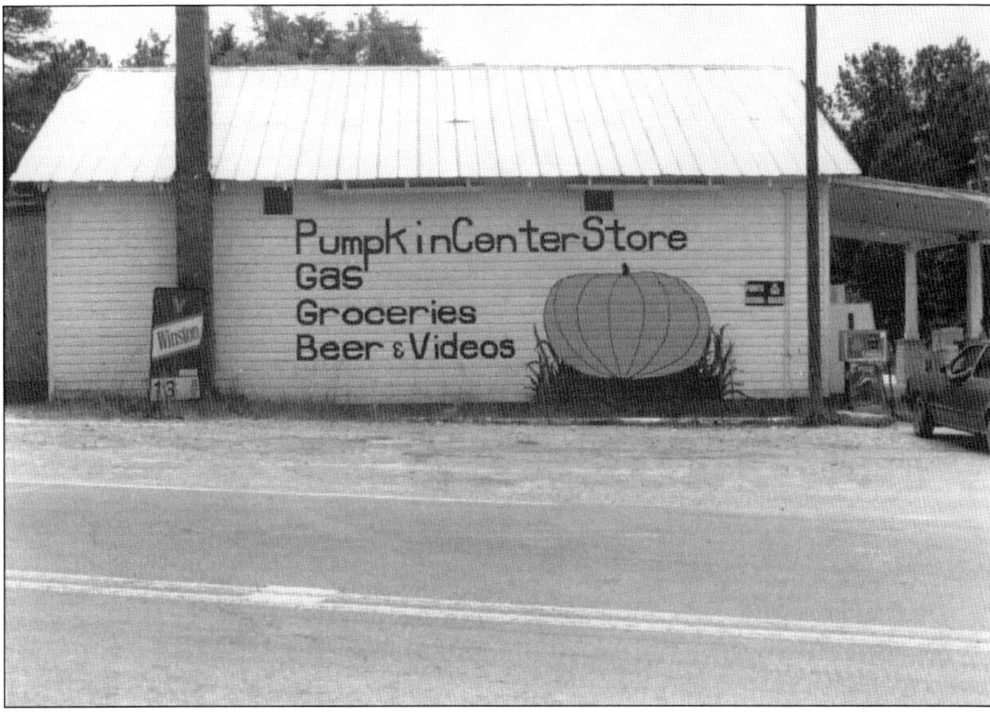

This 1960 photograph shows the store at the Pumpkin Center crossroads community between Appling and Harlem. (Courtesy of Lallie Dozier Benkoski.)

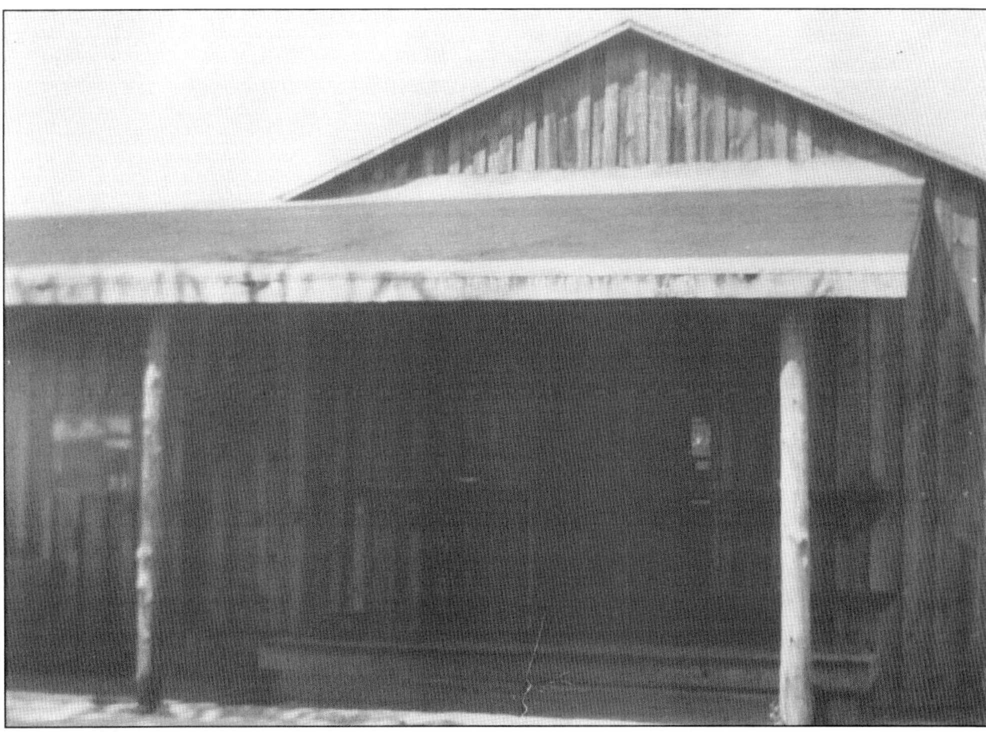

Here is a view of the post office in Appling, *c.* 1950. (Courtesy of Jake Pollard Jr.)

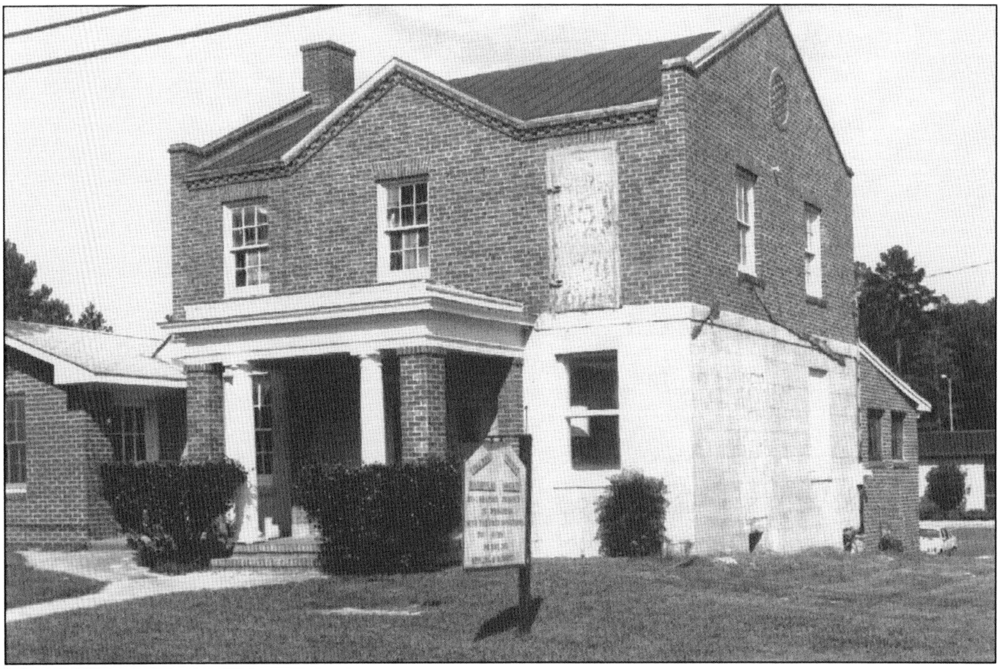

The old jail in Appling, Georgia is now the headquarters of the Columbia County Historical Society. (Courtesy of the Columbia County Historical Society.)

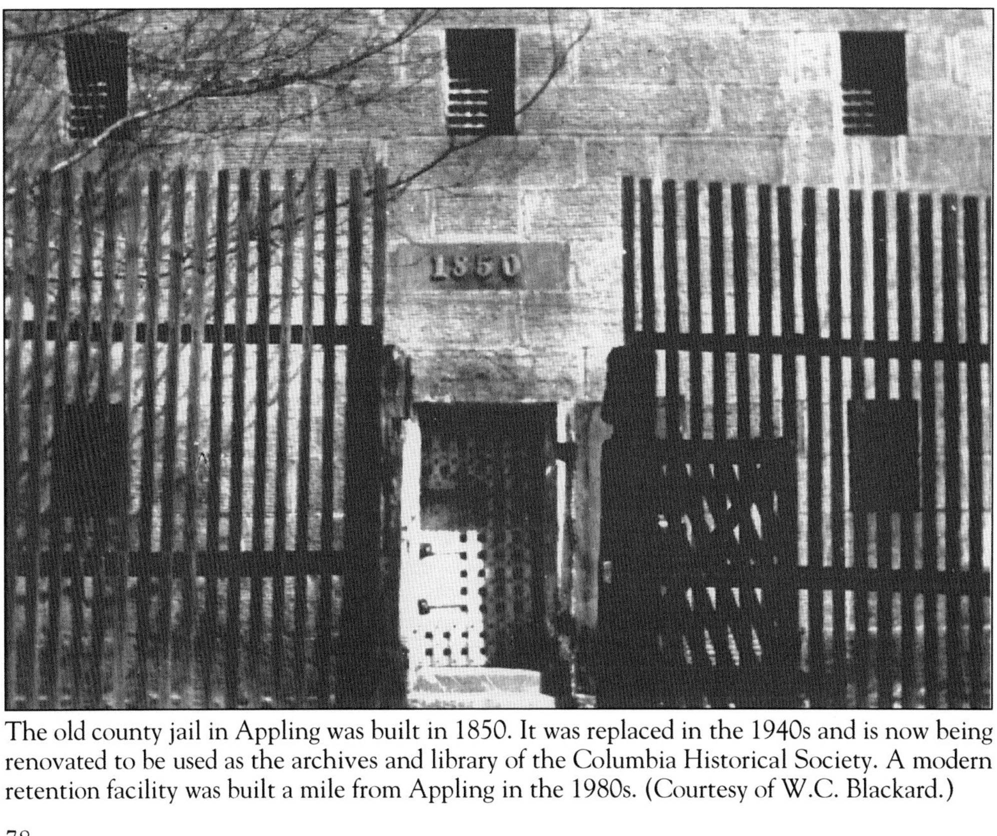

The old county jail in Appling was built in 1850. It was replaced in the 1940s and is now being renovated to be used as the archives and library of the Columbia Historical Society. A modern retention facility was built a mile from Appling in the 1980s. (Courtesy of W.C. Blackard.)

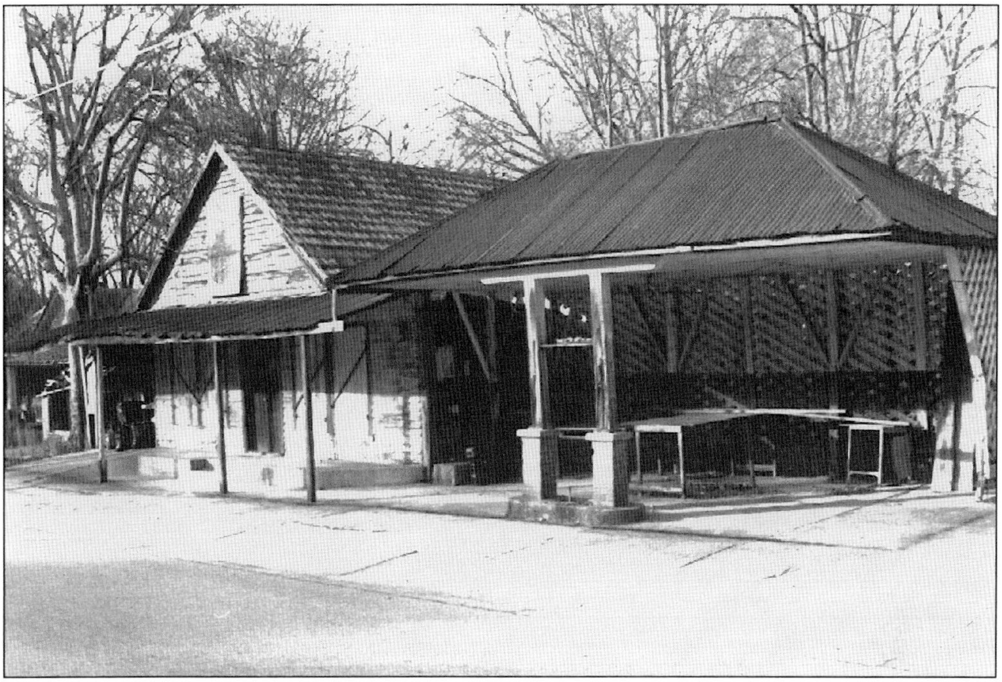

This 100-year-old store in Appling is now a flea market, but such stores were once critical in the local life of a town. It was there that residents could find and purchase the necessities of life. (Courtesy of W.C. Blackard.)

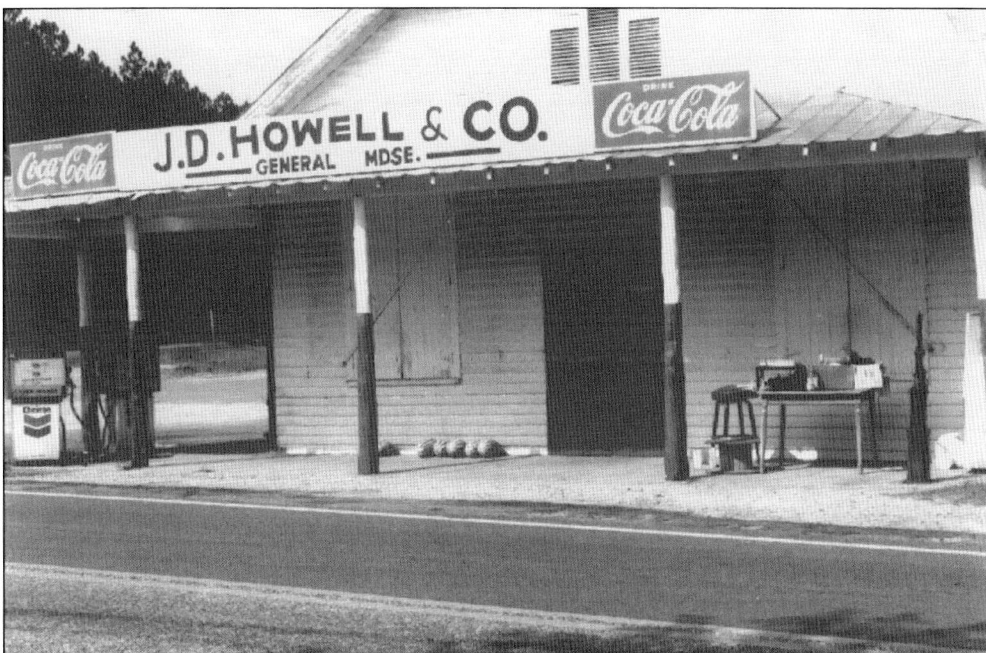

J.D. Howell's store in Appling, Georgia looked like this in the 1950s. The structure still stands, but it is unoccupied. (Courtesy of W.C. Blackard.)

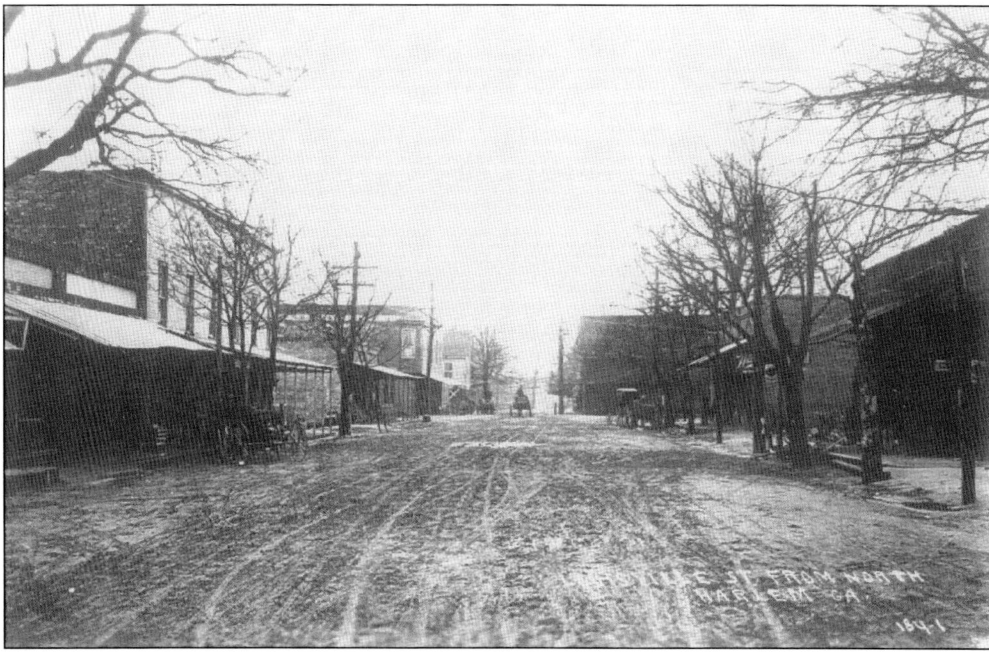

This is a remarkable *c.* 1900 postcard of the City of Harlem. Notice the wagon wheel ruts in the dirt road. (Courtesy of Darwin Morris.)

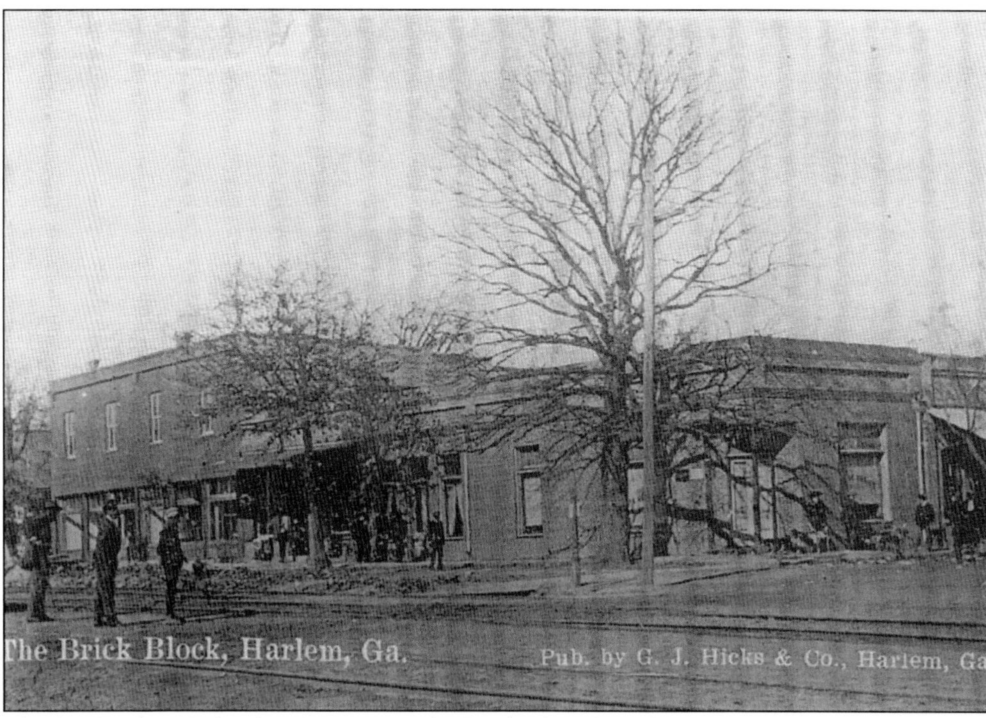

The first bank in Columbia County was the Bank of Harlem. (Courtesy of Darwin Morris.)

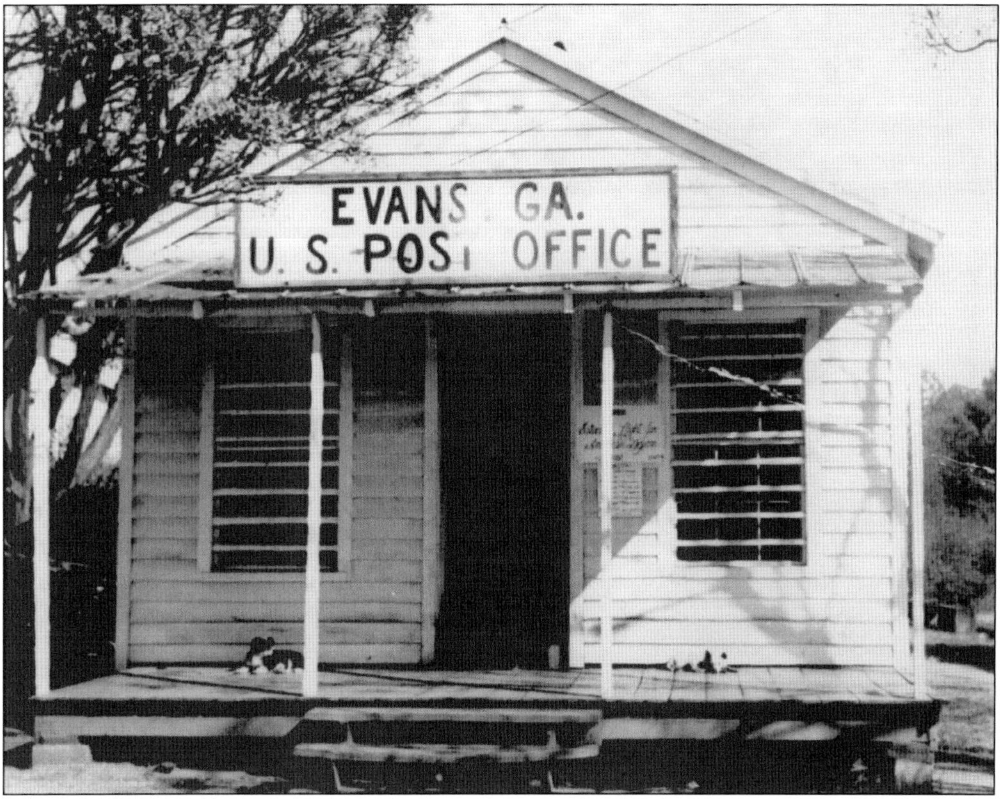

Here is the Evans Post Office, *c.* 1940. (Courtesy of W.C. Blackard.)

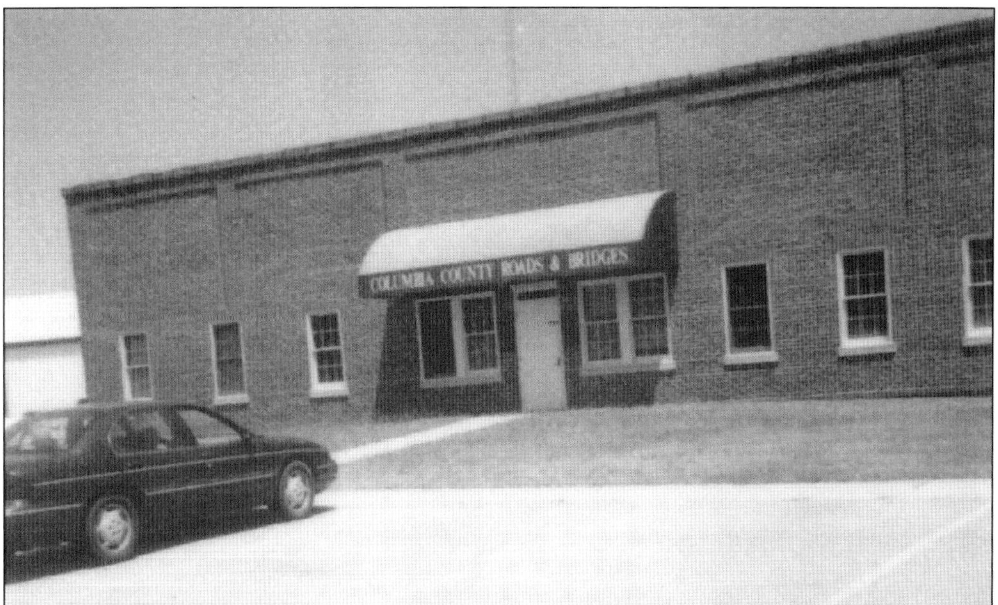

The old convict camp in Appling is now the Columbia County Roads and Bridges Office. (Courtesy of Lewis Bartles.)

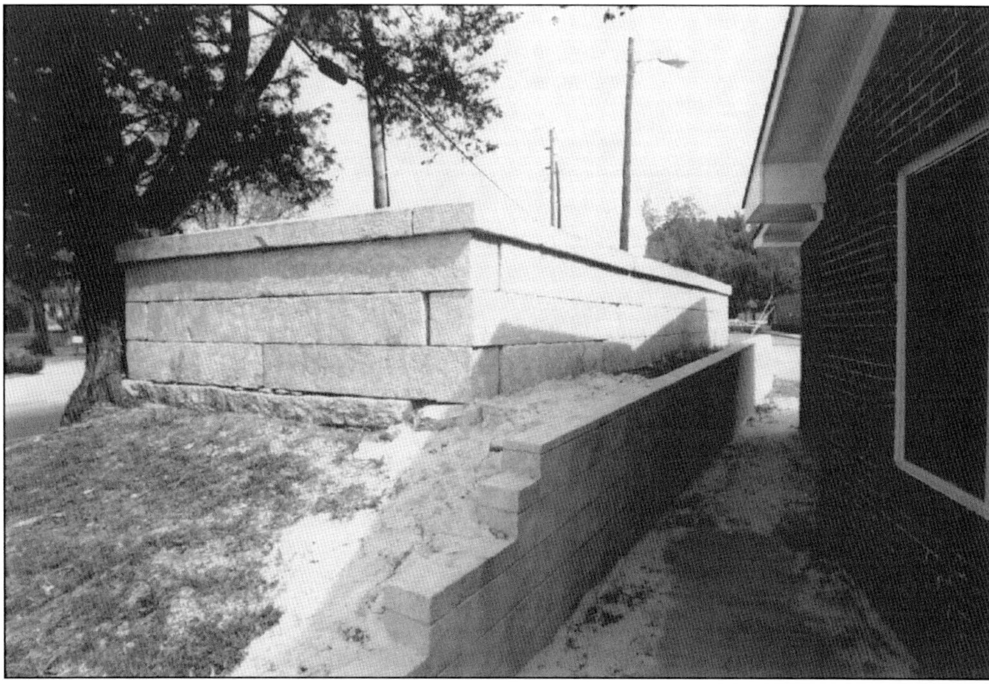

The oldest-known grave site in Columbia County is that of the Ray family. The two graves within this cement enclosure were there when the land for the courthouse was deeded in the 1790s. (Courtesy of W.C. Blackard.)

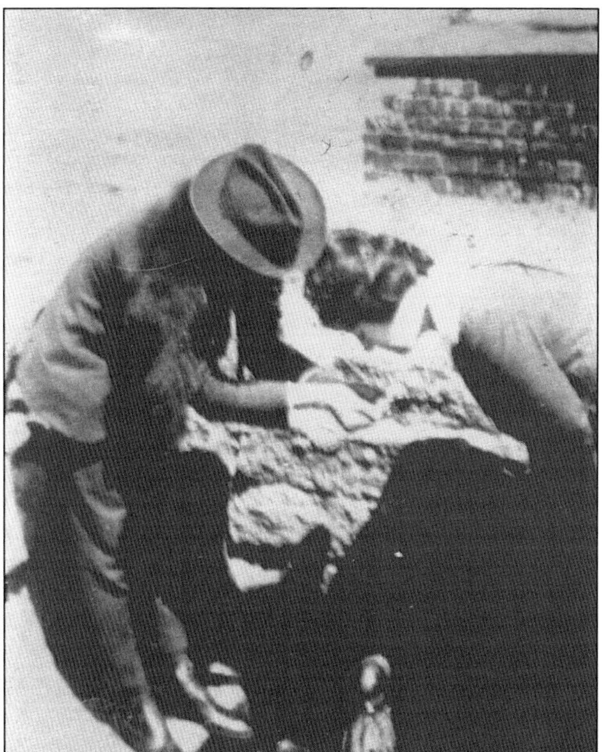

This public spring in Appling, Georgia was quite a welcome relief on hot, muggy days. Courtesy of Jake Pollard Jr.)

Four

Bicentennial Celebration

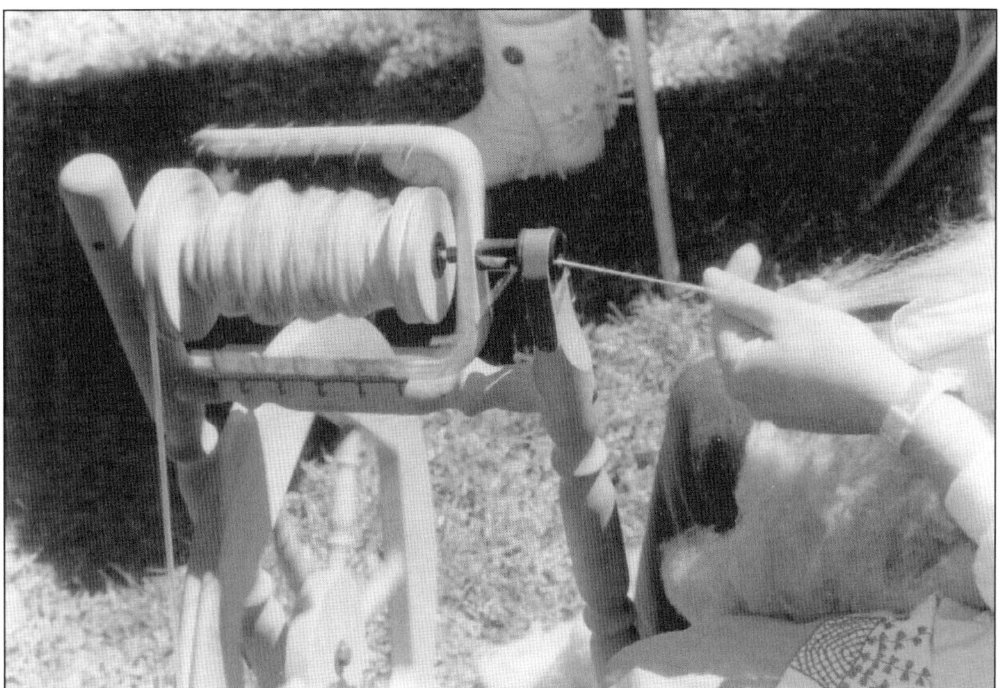

This is the close-up view of a bobbin and thread on the flax wheel, c. 1976. (Courtesy of the Josie Dozier Collection.)

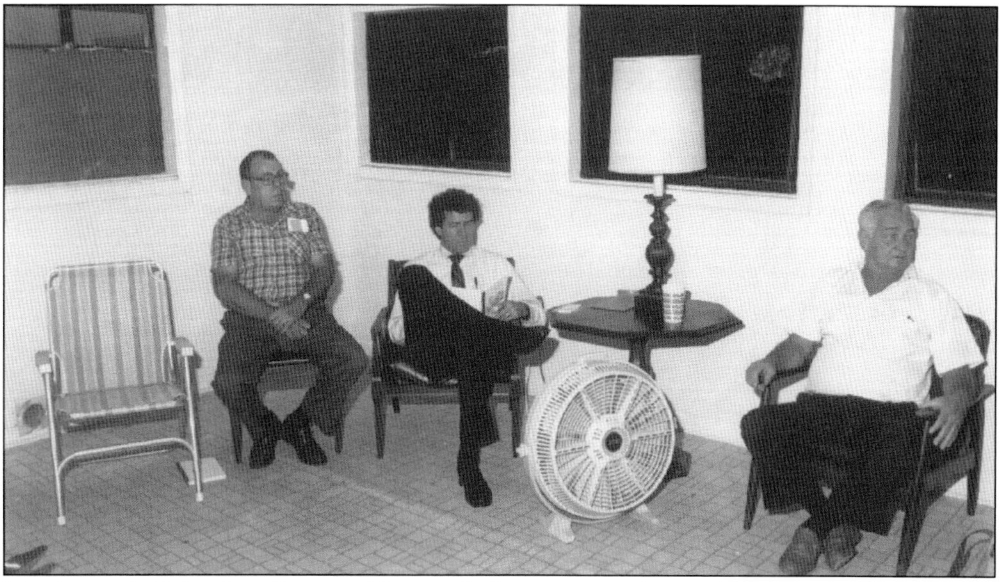

Members of Columbia County Historical Society are shown here in the 1970s. The man in the center is Phil Blanchard; the others are unidentified. (Courtesy of the Josie Dozier Collection.)

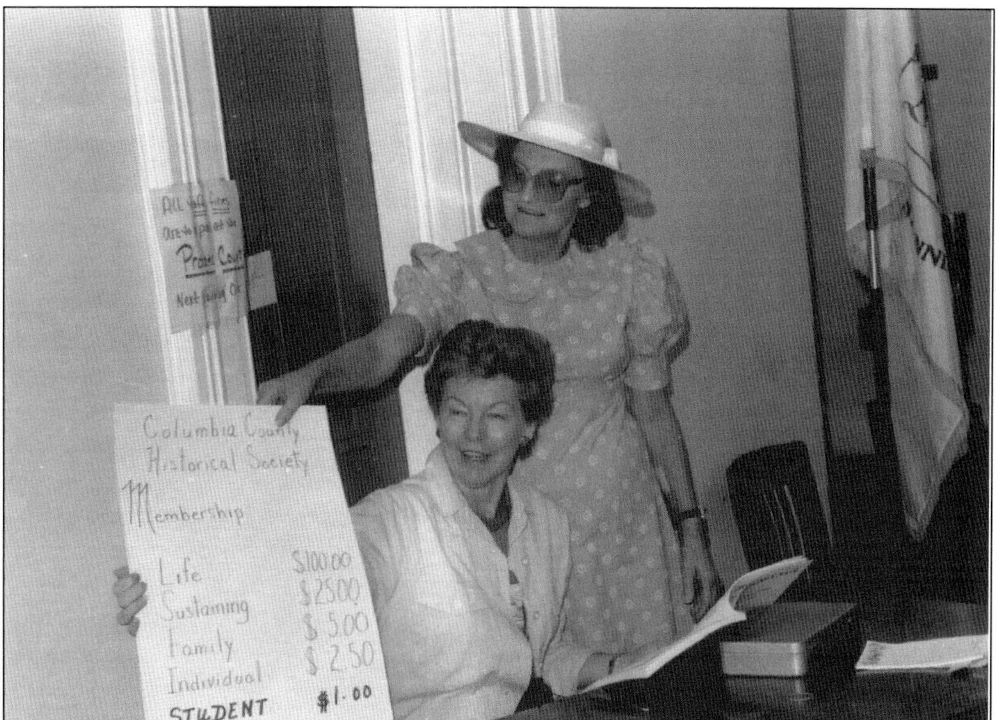

Pictured is a membership drive of the Columbia County Historical Society. (Courtesy of the Josie Dozier Collection.)

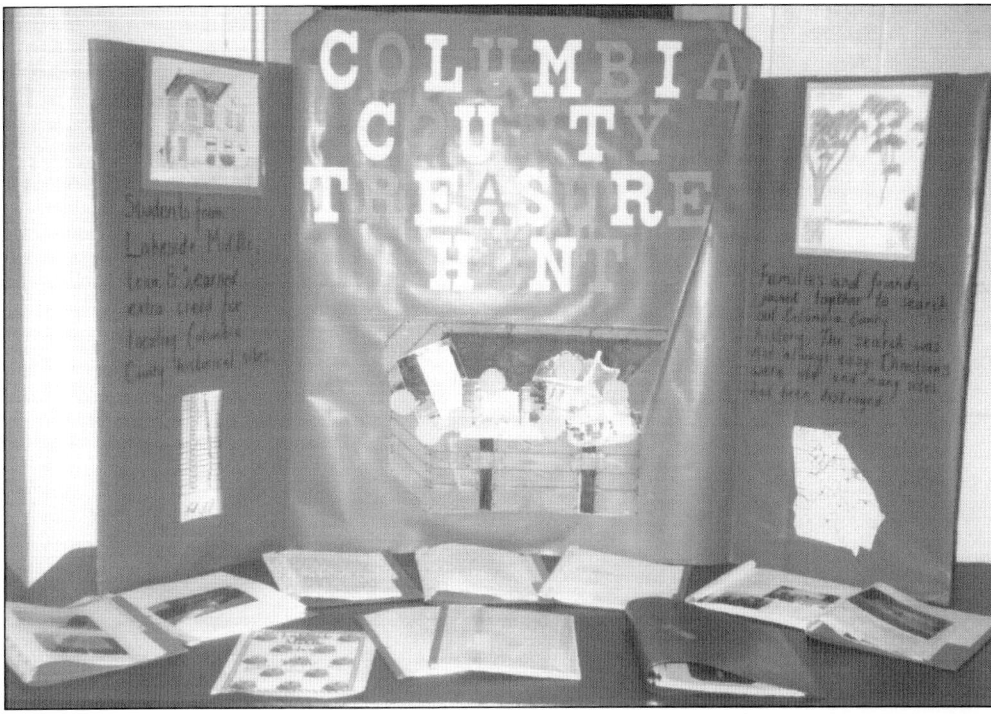

This is a bicentennial display. (Courtesy of the Josie Dozier Collection.)

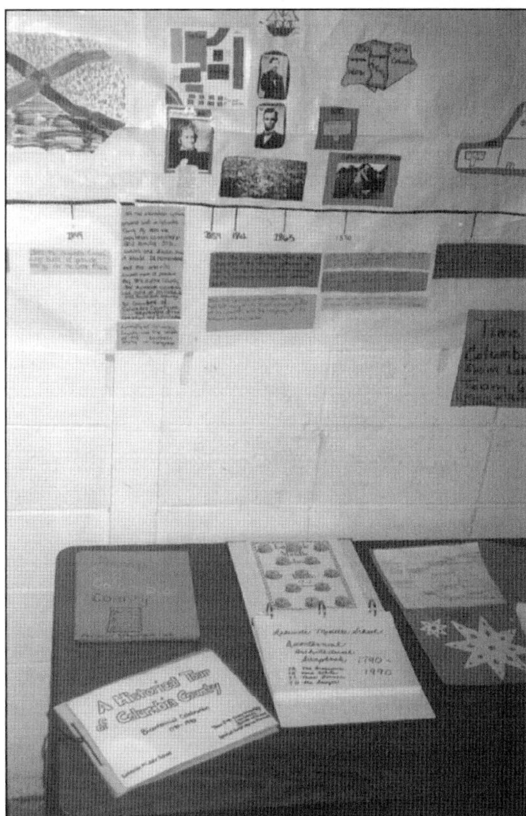

This 1976 school display was a Columbia County history project. Schoolchildren were eager and creative helpers in preparing for the bicentennial celebration. They made displays, dioramas, quilts, and histories. (Courtesy of the Josie Dozier Collection.)

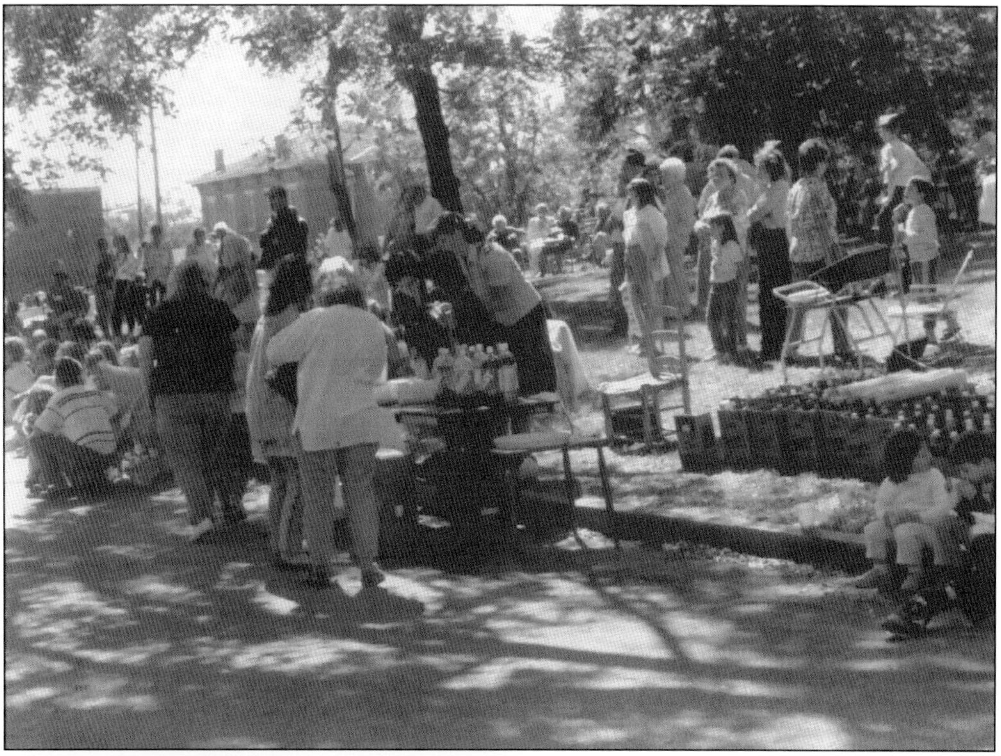

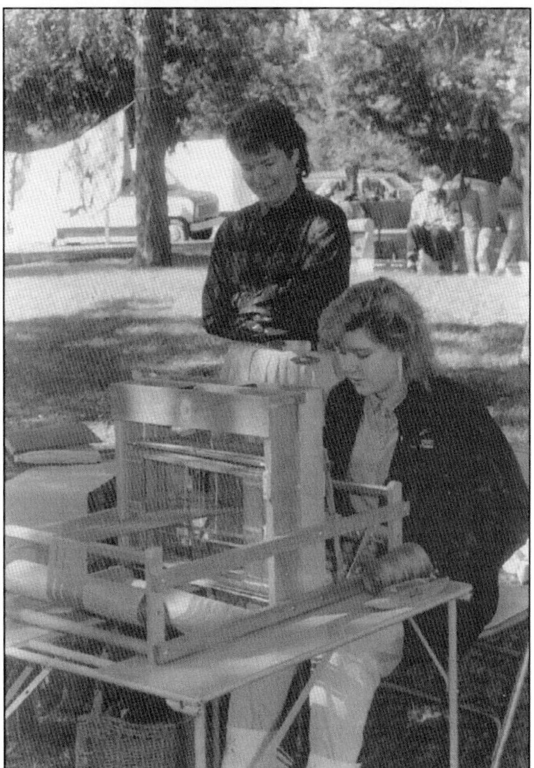

A bicentennial gathering took place at Old Kiokee Church in 1976. (Courtesy of the Josie Dozier Collection.)

Cloth is made here on an old loom. The spinning wheel and loom were indispensable items in colonial Columbia County. (Courtesy of the Josie Dozier Collection.)

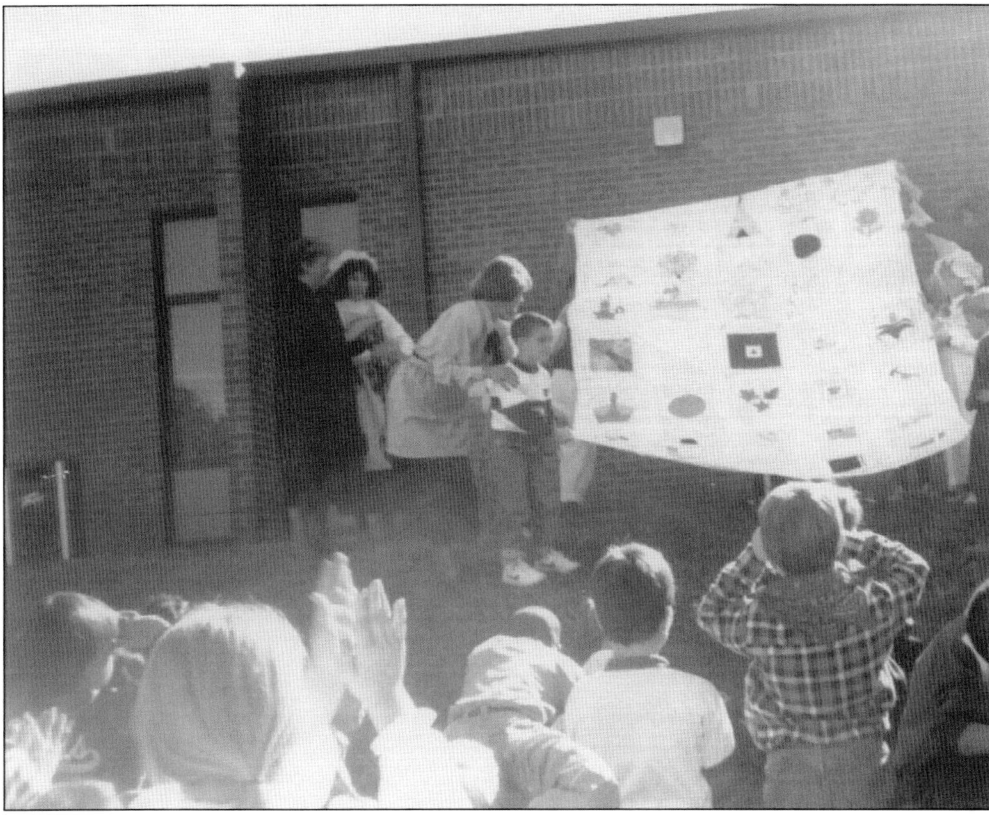

The Bicentennial Quilt is presented in 1976. (Courtesy of the Josie Dozier Collection.)

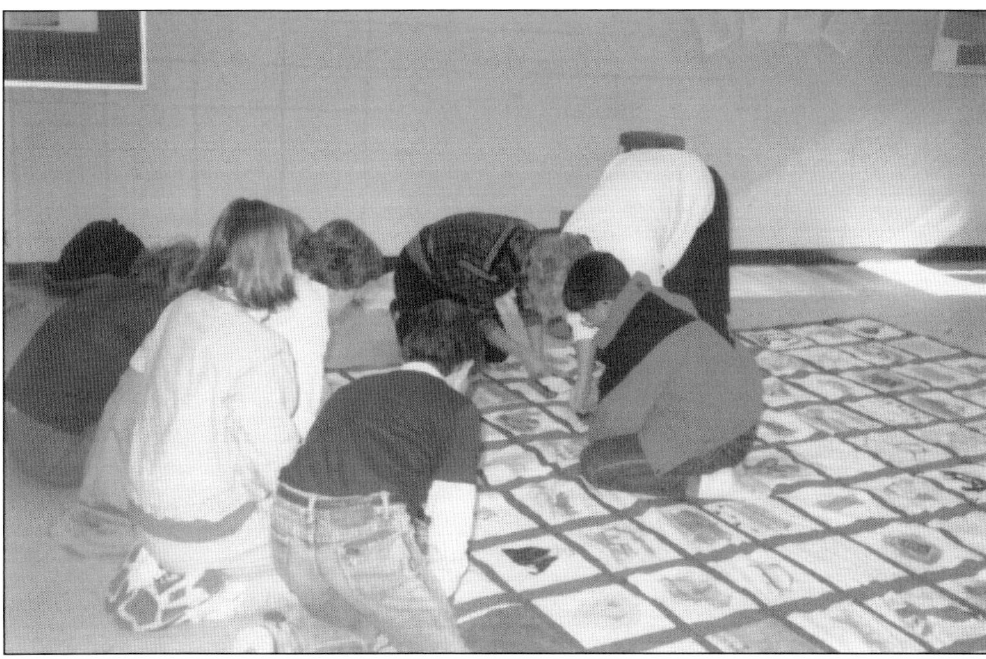

Youngsters work on making a quilt. (Courtesy of the Josie Dozier Collection.)

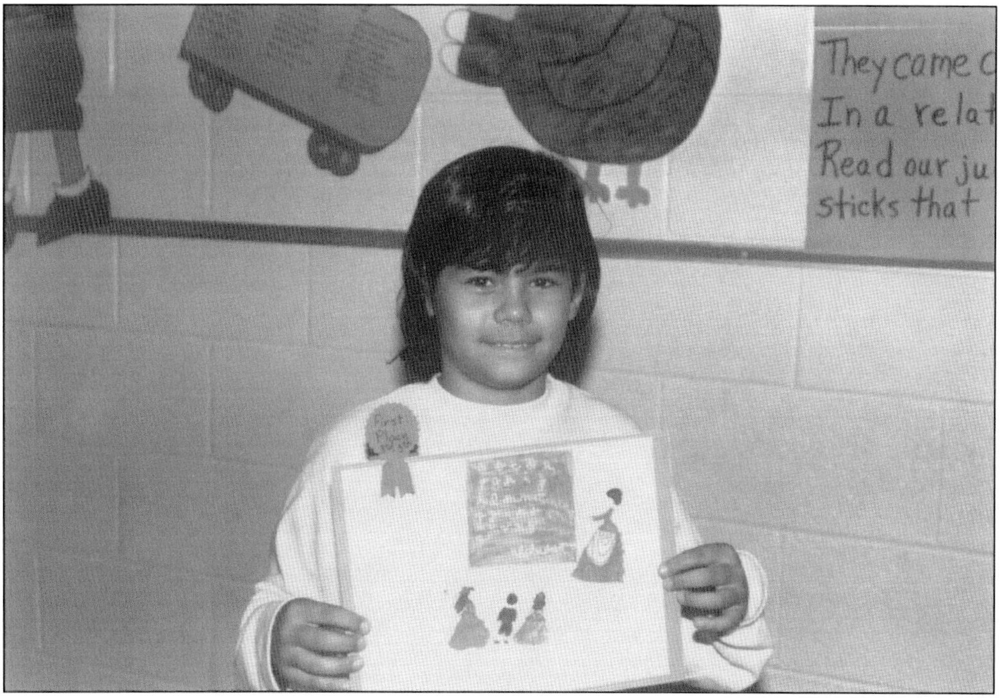

Children were rightfully proud of their artistic creations! (Courtesy of the Josie Dozier Collection.)

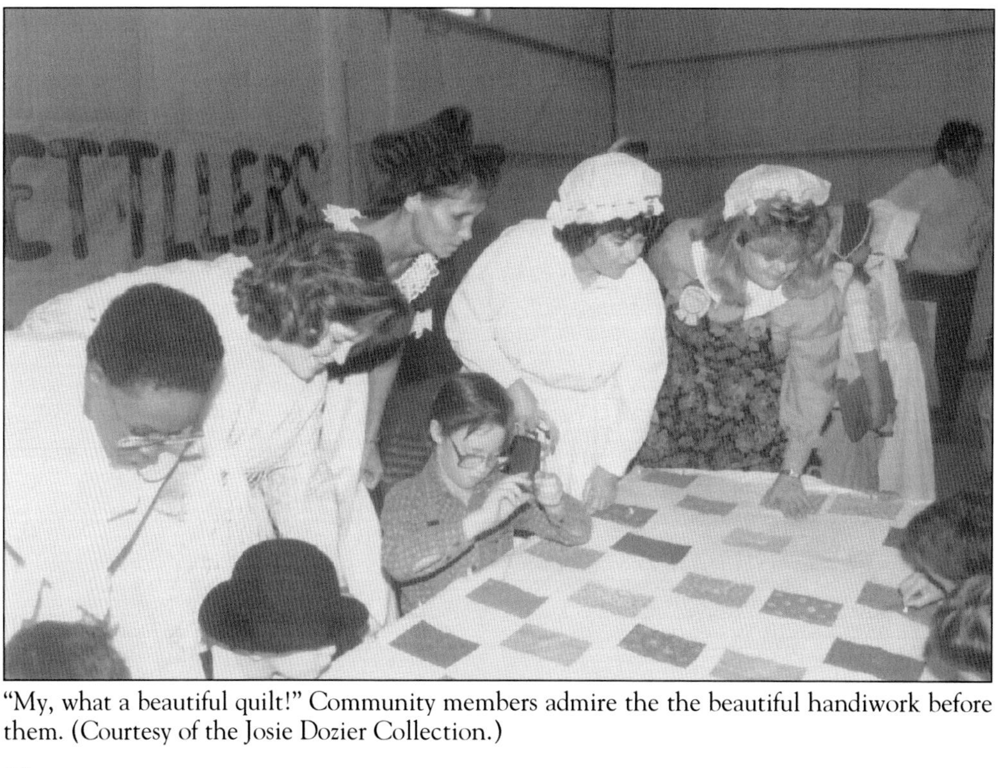

"My, what a beautiful quilt!" Community members admire the the beautiful handiwork before them. (Courtesy of the Josie Dozier Collection.)

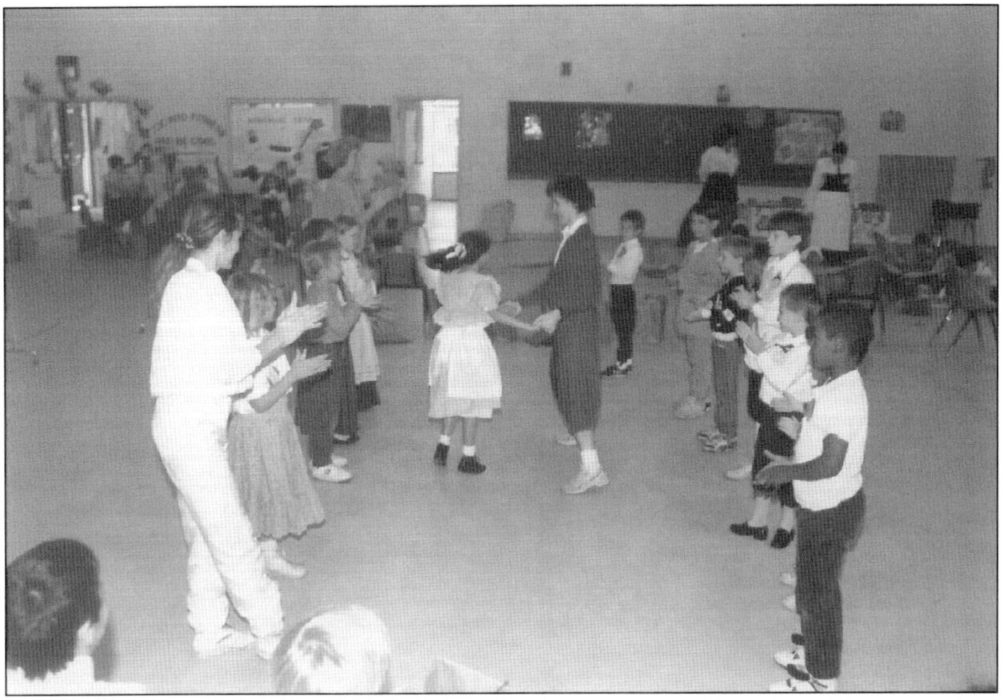

Students dance the Virginia Reel, a very popular dance in the "olden" days. (Courtesy of the Josie Dozier Collection.)

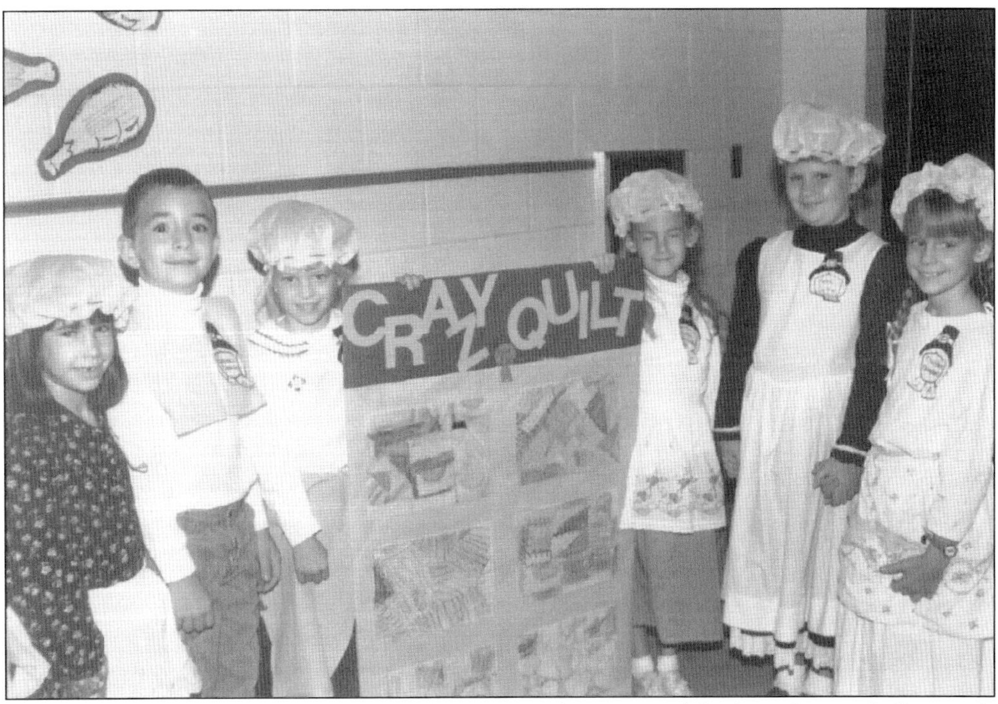

These children are seen with "Crazy Quilt" in 1976. (Courtesy of the Josie Dozier Collection.)

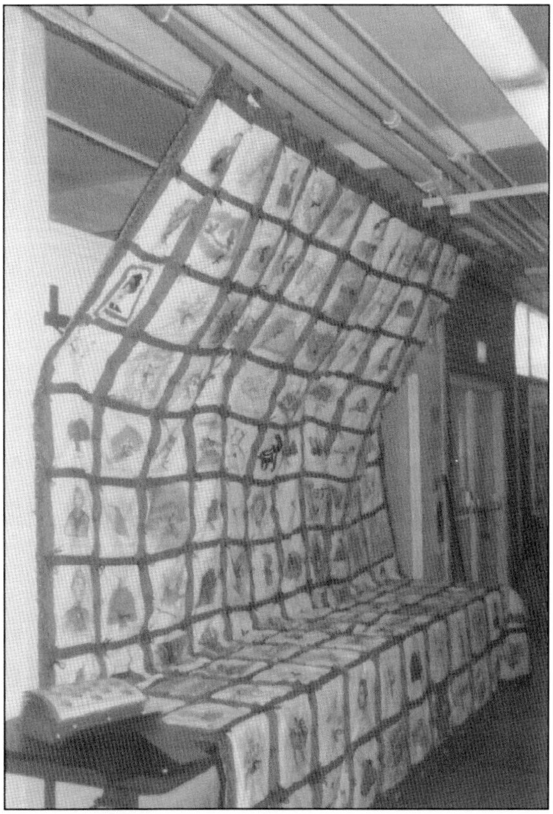

This is another photograph of the Bicentennial Quilt. Hanging from its frame, this quilt is a marvelous piece of work that involved many folks, young and old. Quilting is still a creative and fascinating hobby for many. (Courtesy of the Josie Dozier Collection.)

Here, people are hard at work making the Bicentennial Quilt. (Courtesy of the Josie Dozier Collection.)

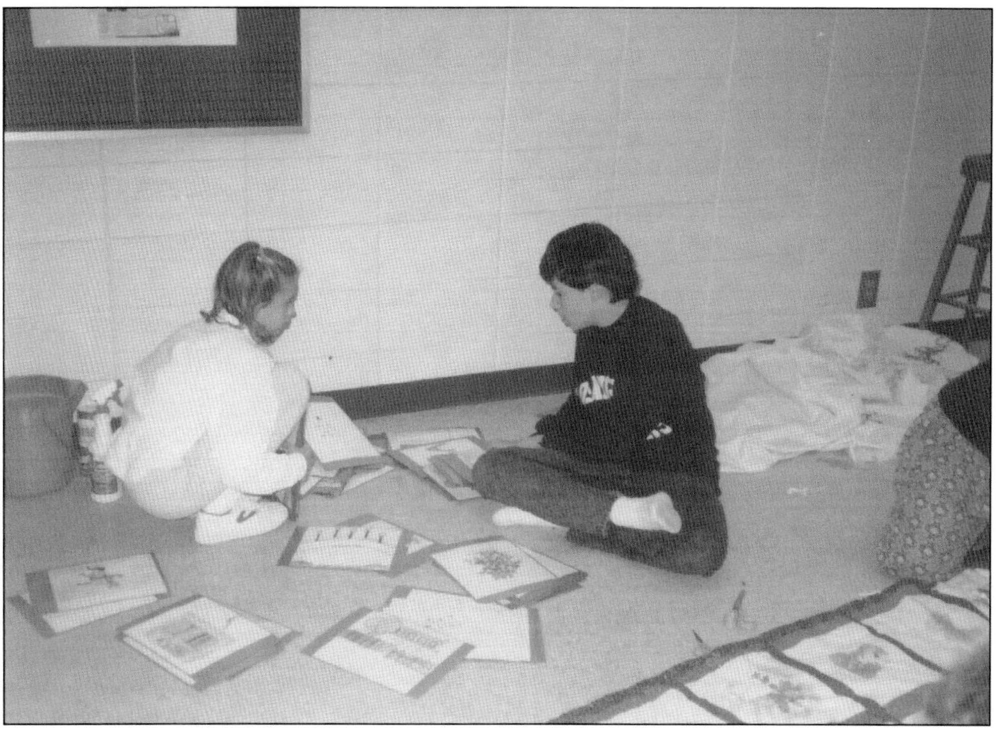

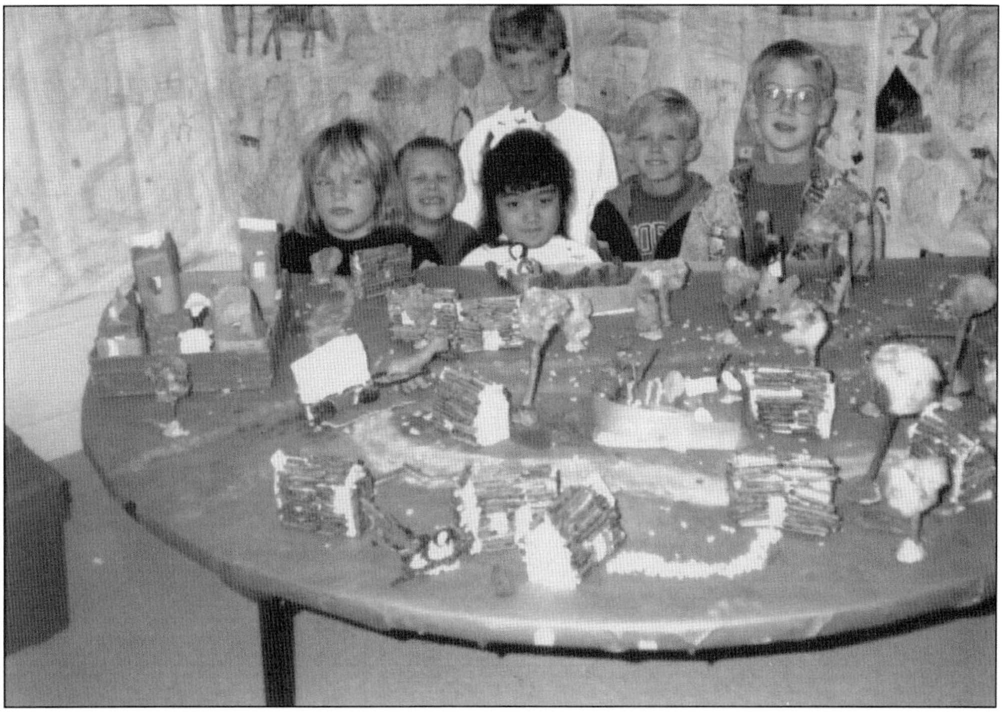

Children made this diorama of frontier Columbia County complete with a fort and log cabins. Good work, kids! (Courtesy of the Josie Dozier Collection.)

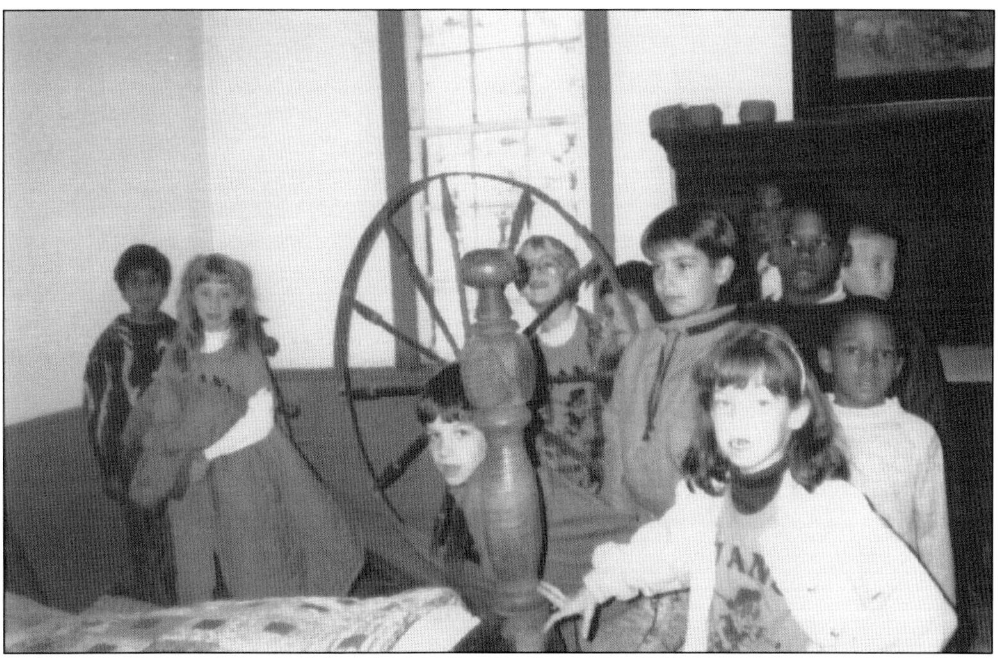

This photograph shows schoolchildren with a spinning wheel in 1976. (Courtesy of the Josie Dozier Collection.)

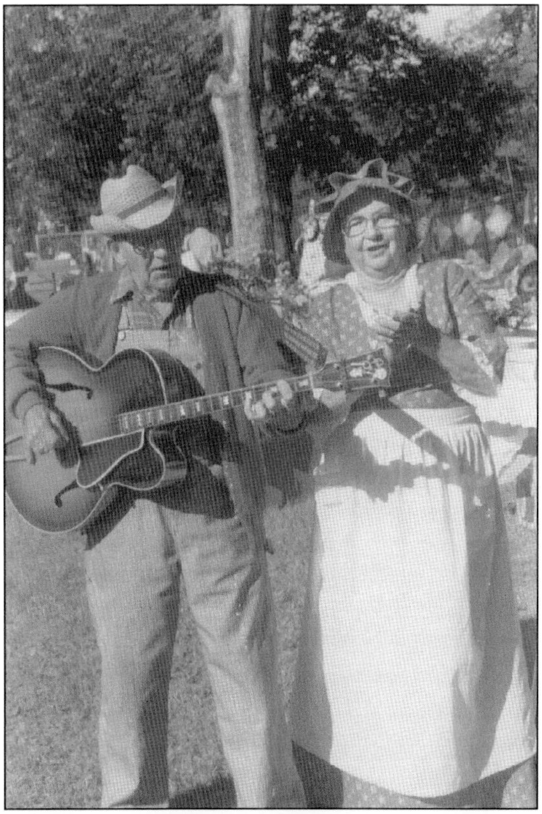

Participants in the bicentennial celebration say, "Let's have a hoe-down!" Guitars, banjos, and mandolins—all were sure to appear at informal gatherings. In the days before television and radio, this was recreation and entertainment, perhaps at its best! (Courtesy of the Josie Dozier Collection.)

Columbia County citizens are shown in this picture. (Courtesy of the Josie Dozier Collection.)

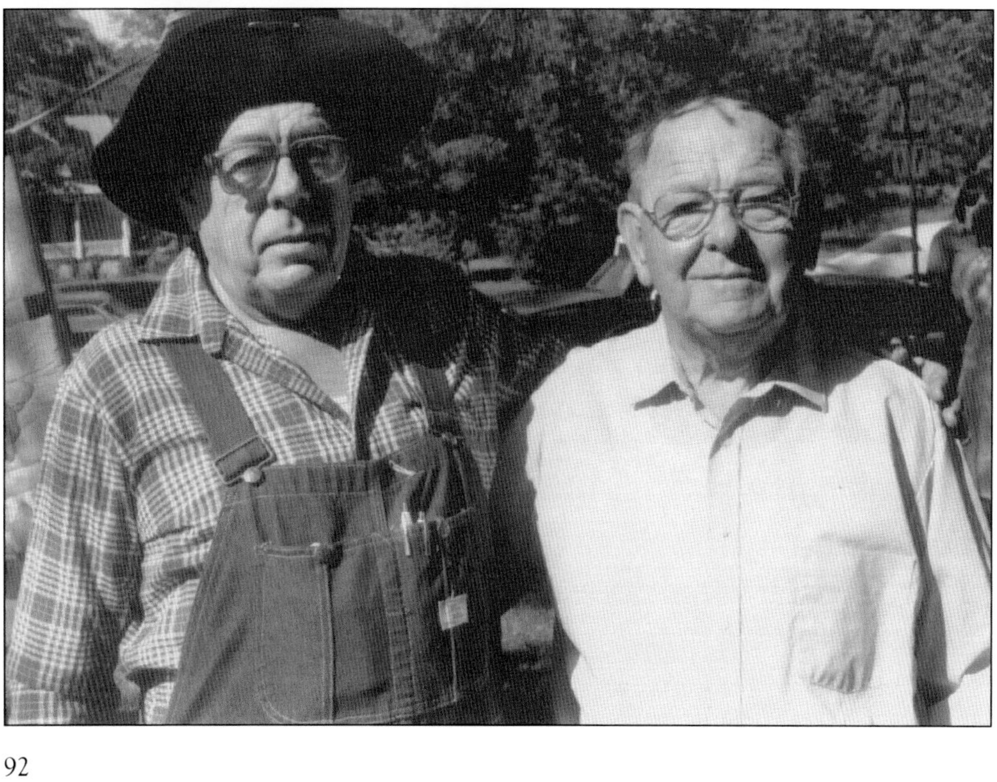

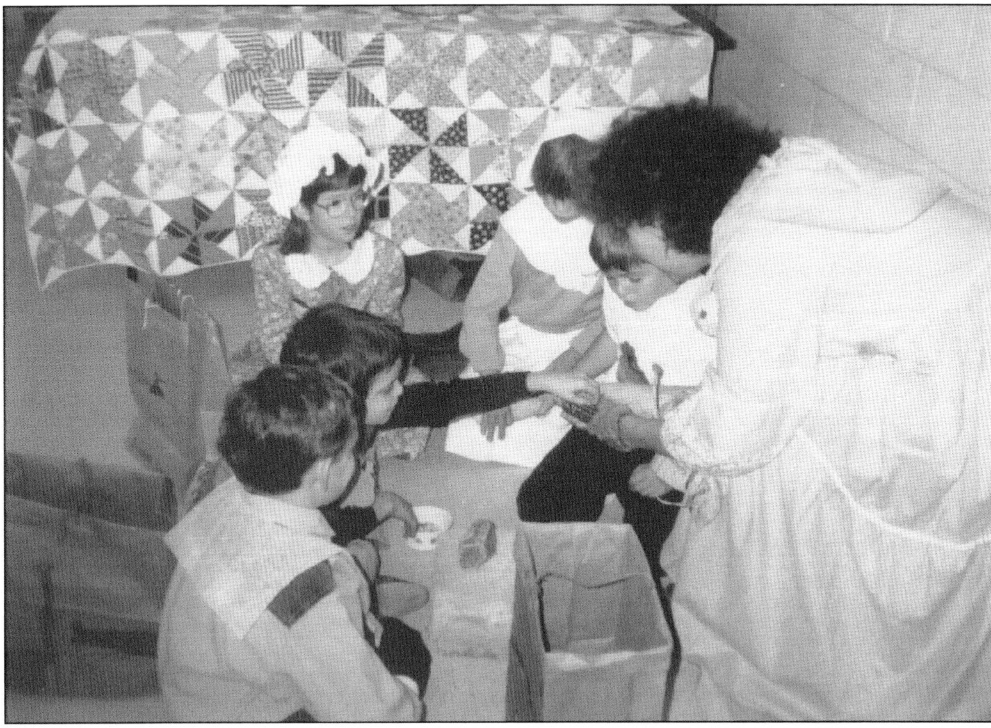

Children and adults dress in period costumes. (Courtesy of the Josie Dozier Collection.)

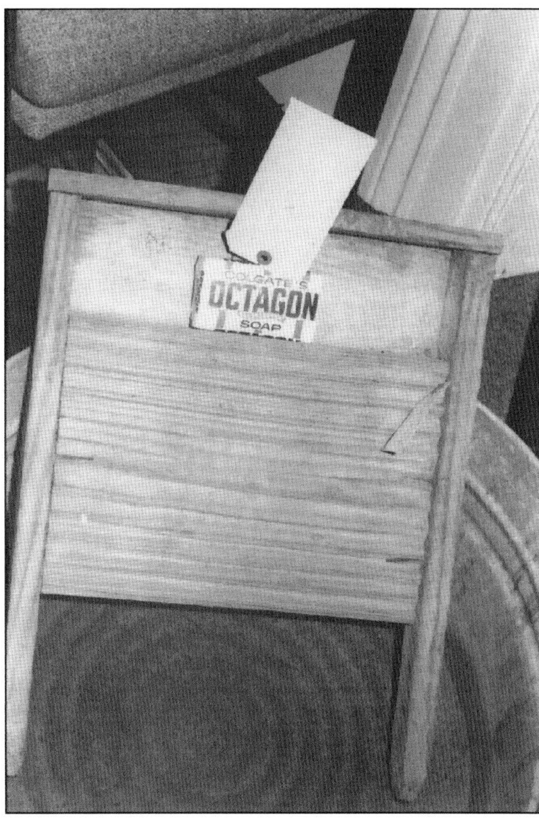

This is a photograph of a wash tub, a wash board, and Octagon soap. Many folks remember the "good ole days" when Momma washed clothes using these tools. When it came to washing out a child's mouth for saying a bad word, however, Palmolive soap was preferred. Octagon was lye soap and was bad for the mouth! (Courtesy of the Josie Dozier Collection.)

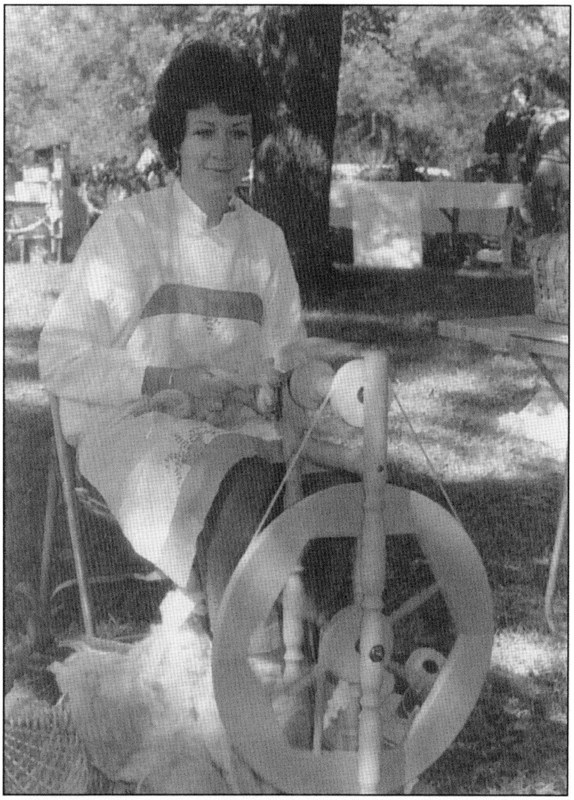

Here is a picture of a lady and a spinning wheel. This smaller version of the spinning wheel was usually used with flax. It could also be more easily carried by its user when going to a neighbor's cabin to sit and spin and socialize. (Courtesy of the Josie Dozier Collection.)

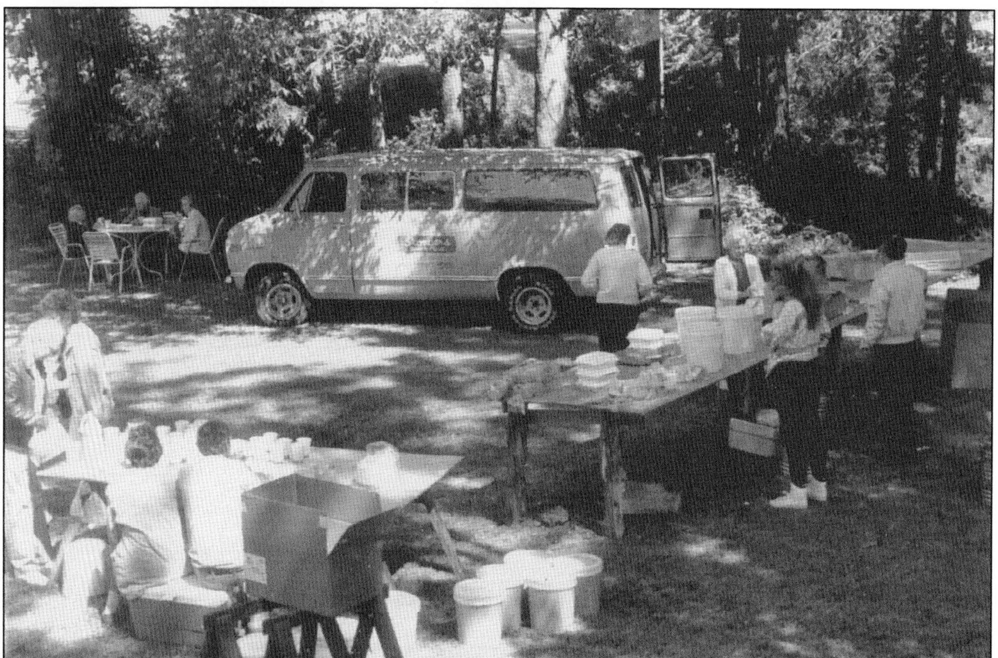

There was "dinner on the grounds" at the bicentennial celebration in 1976. (Courtesy of the Josie Dozier Collection.)

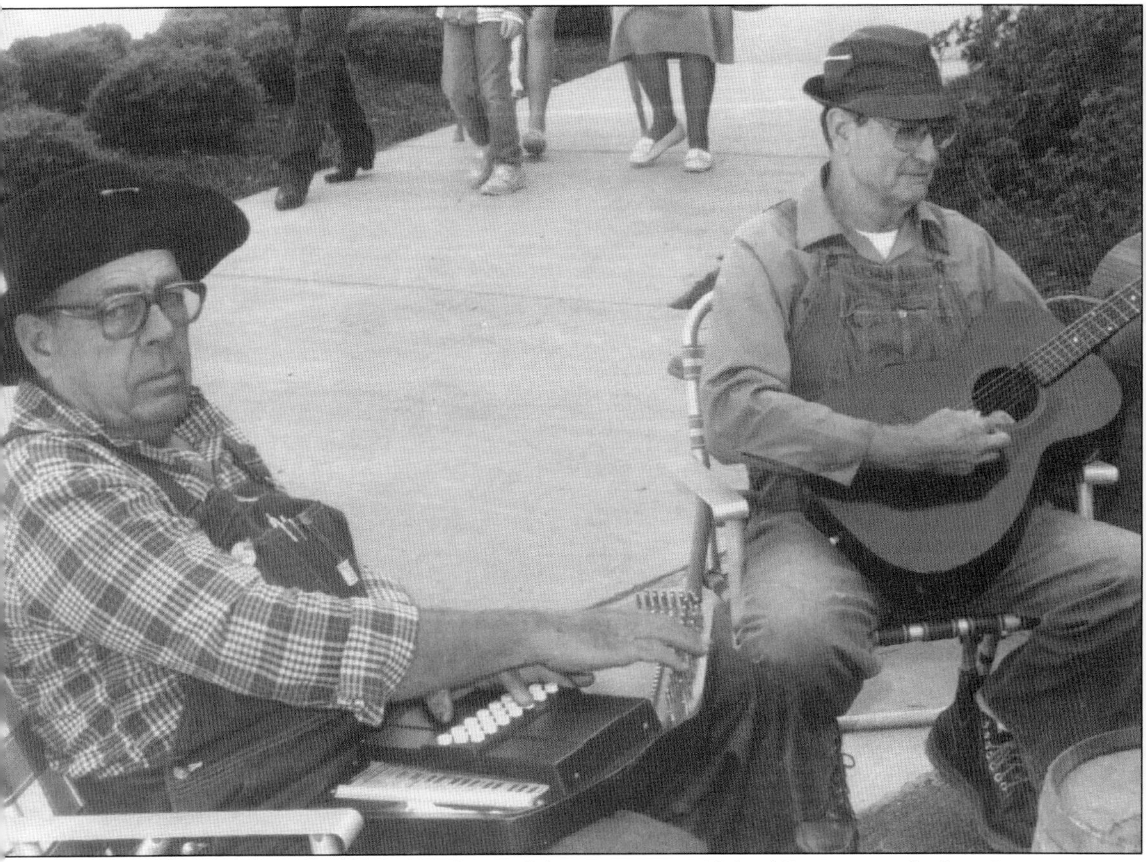

Pictured here are musicians at the celebration in 1976. (Courtesy of the Josie Dozier Collection.)

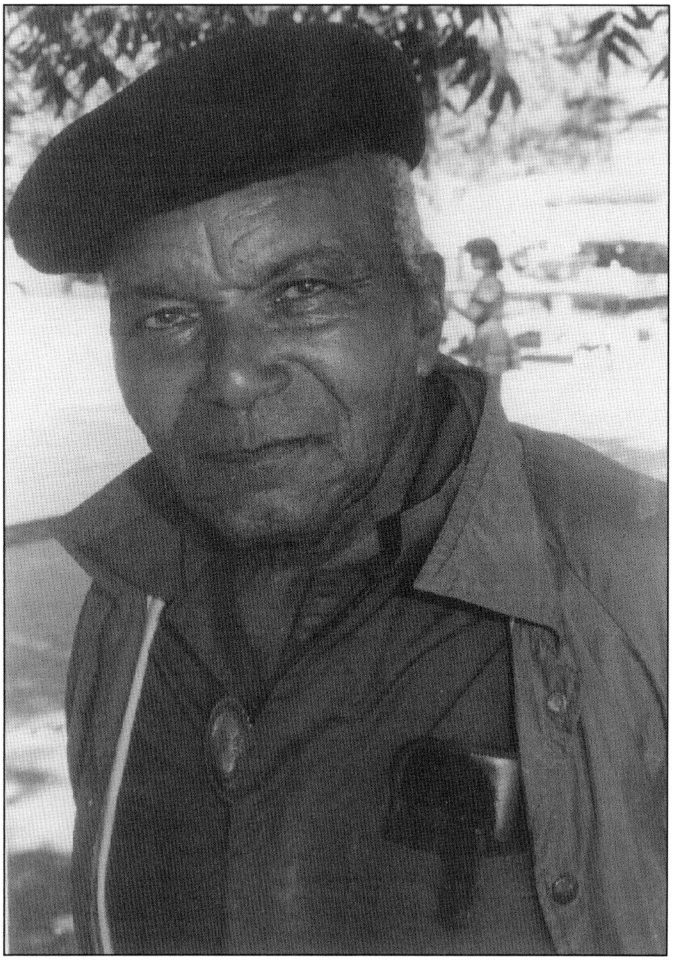

The bicentennial celebration honored everyone, regardless of ethnic background, because all helped to build the community and the nation we enjoy today. (Courtesy of the Josie Dozier Collection.)

Five

CHURCHES AND SCHOOLS

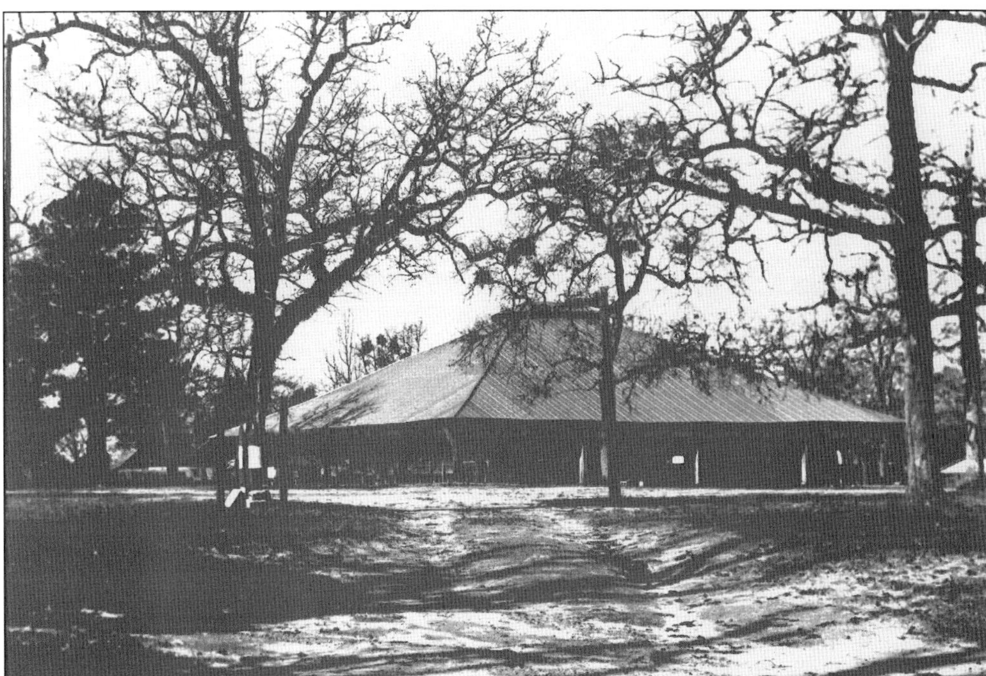

This tabernacle, or brush arbor, was the central meeting place for Methodists at the White Oak Campmeeting site. Built in 1873, it is still actively used by the United Methodist denomination. (Courtesy of the Josie Dozier Collection.)

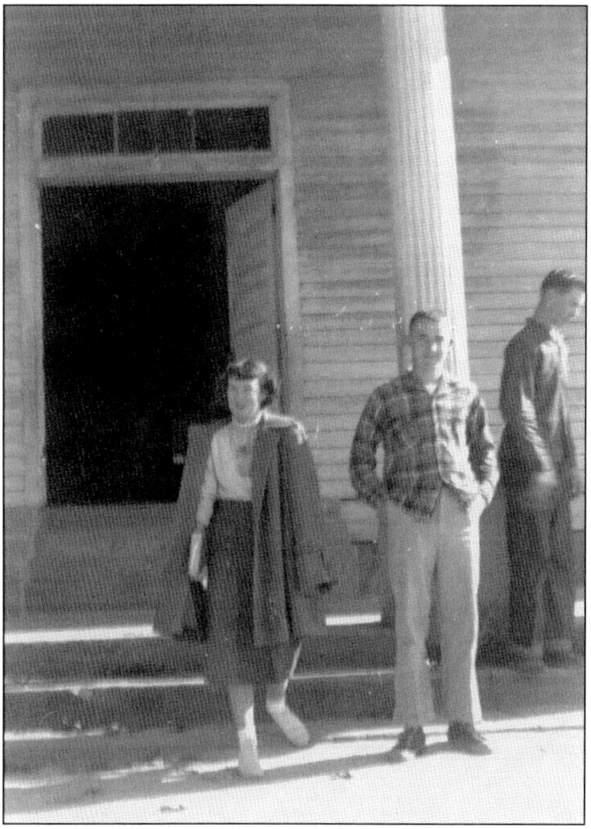

In front of the old Leah School in Leah, Georgia are Betty Smith, Sam Crawford Jr., and J.C. May. (Courtesy of Judy Sanderlin.)

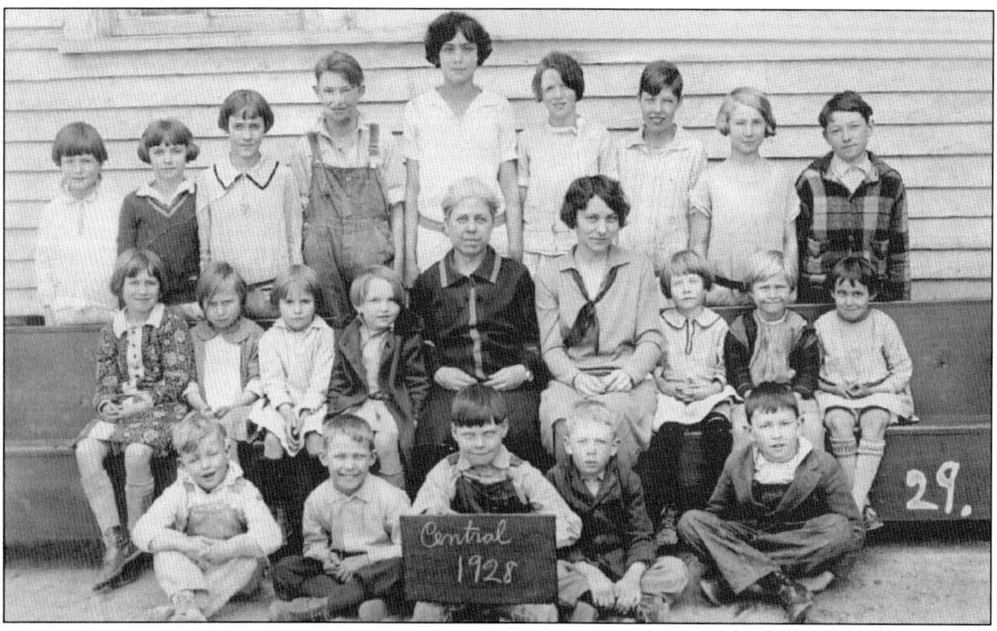

This is the Central School #29 Class of 1928. (Courtesy of Judy Sanderlin.)

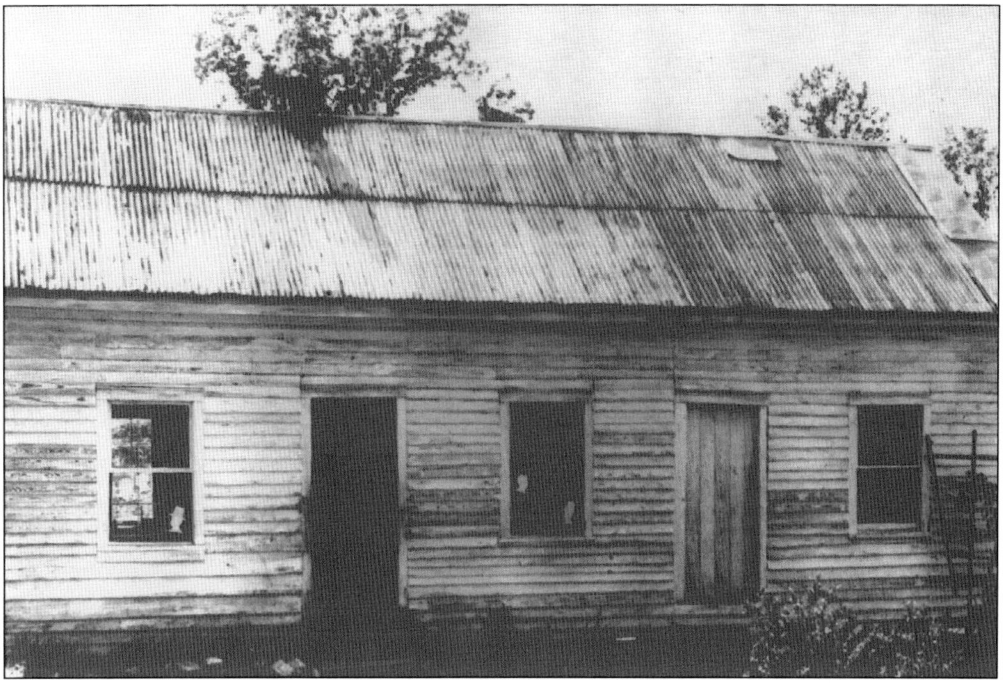

Mt. Moriah School for Negroes is pictured in this *c.* 1930 photograph. (Courtesy of Josie Dozier Collection.)

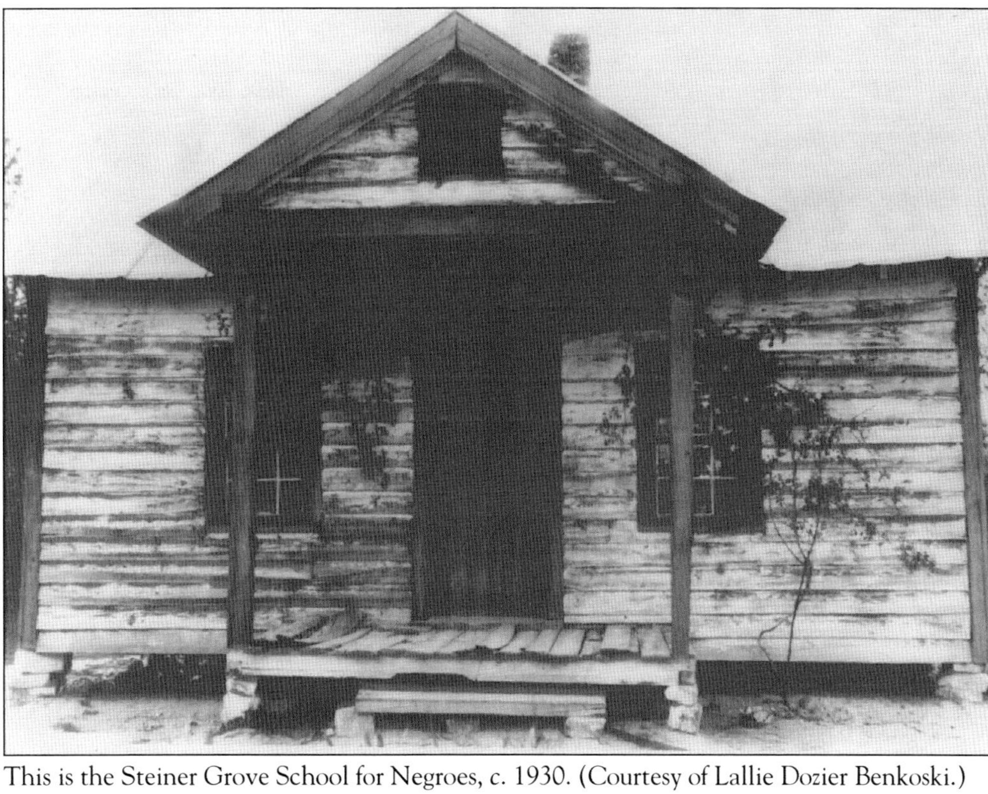

This is the Steiner Grove School for Negroes, c. 1930. (Courtesy of Lallie Dozier Benkoski.)

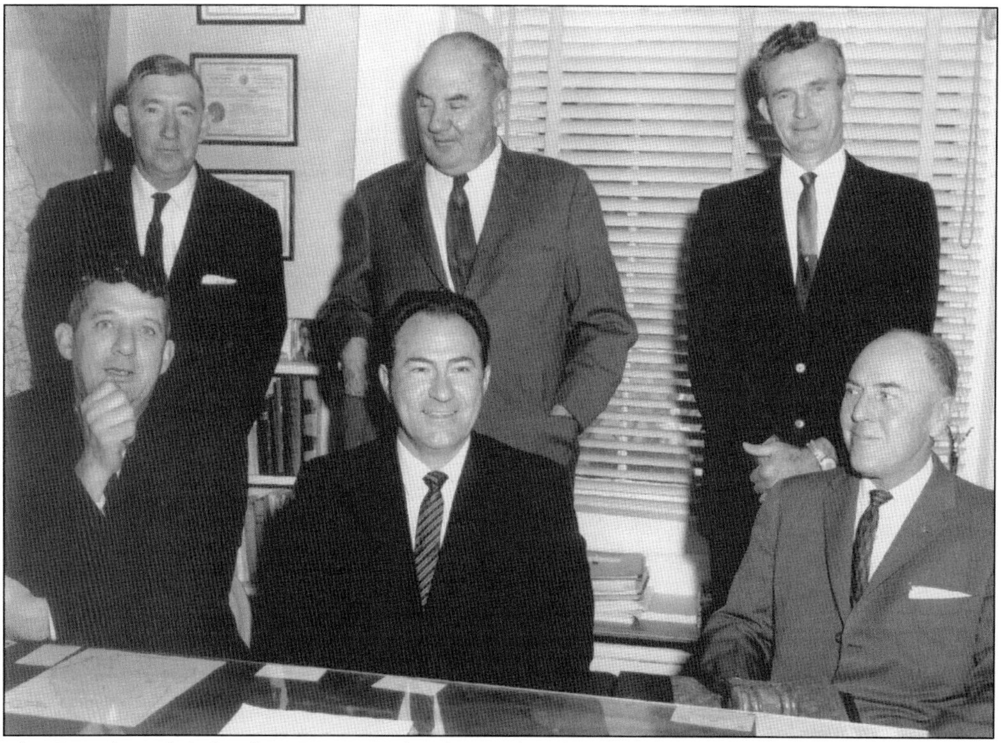

The first elected Columbia County School Board with John Pierce Blanchard are, from left to right, as follows: (seated) Otis Huffman, J.P. Blanchard Sr., and Ed Clary; (standing) John M. Price, Jack Eubank, and Claude Fuller. (Courtesy of Pat Blanchard.)

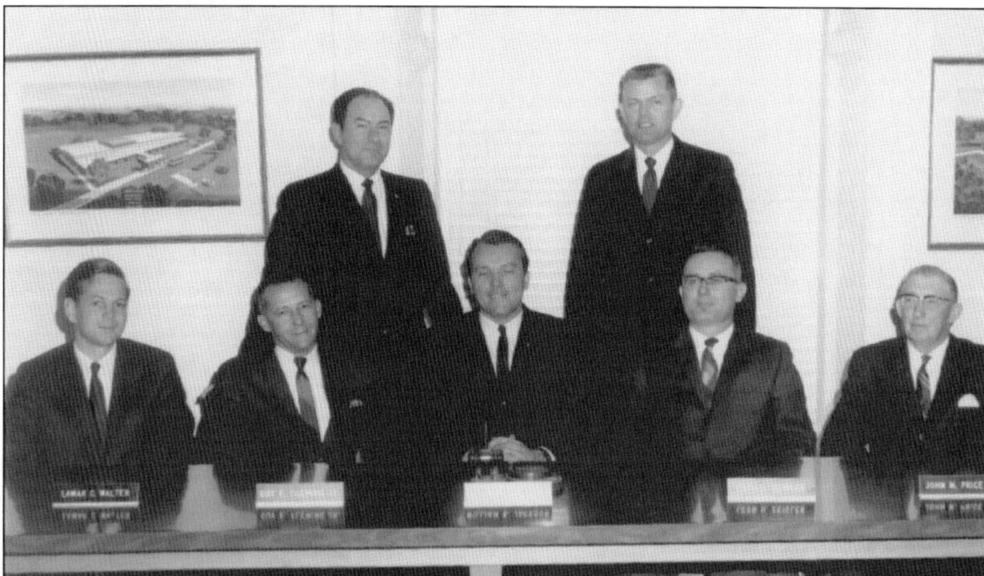

The last appointed school board, pictured with Superintendent Pierce, are, from left to right, as follows: (seated) Lamar C. Walter, Guy E. Fleming Jr., William S. Jackson, Leon H. Zeigler, and John M. Price Jr.; (standing) John Pierce Blanchard and Norris Long, the assistant superintendent. (Courtesy of Pat Blanchard.)

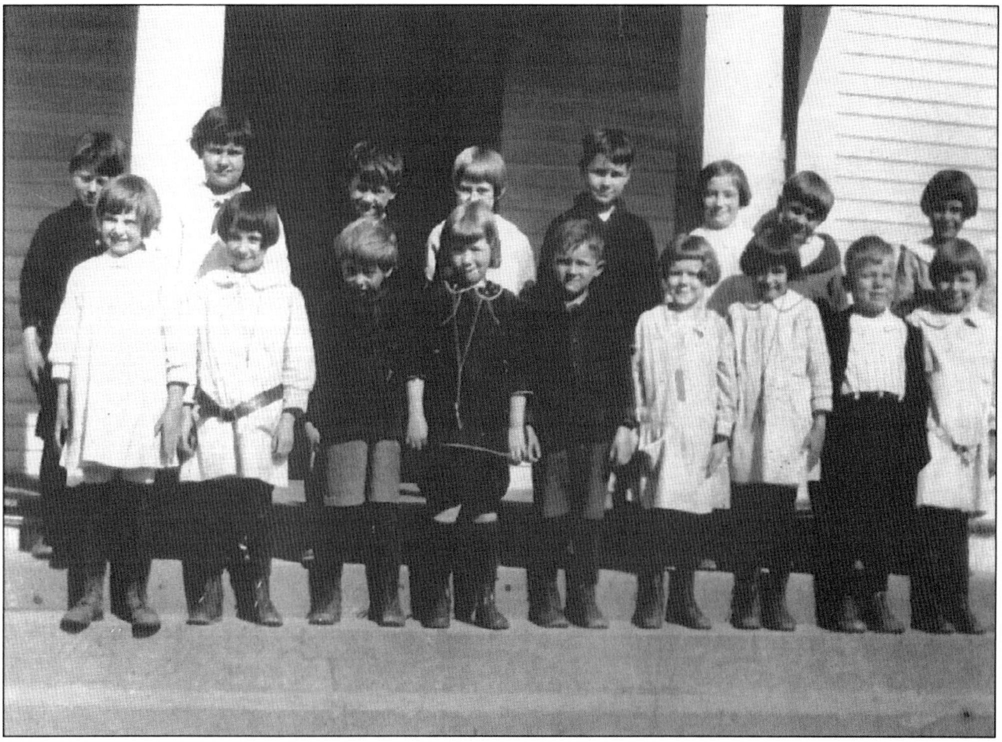

Pictured here are schoolchildren on the steps of Winfield High School, *c.* 1940. (Courtesy of Lallie Dozier Benkoski.)

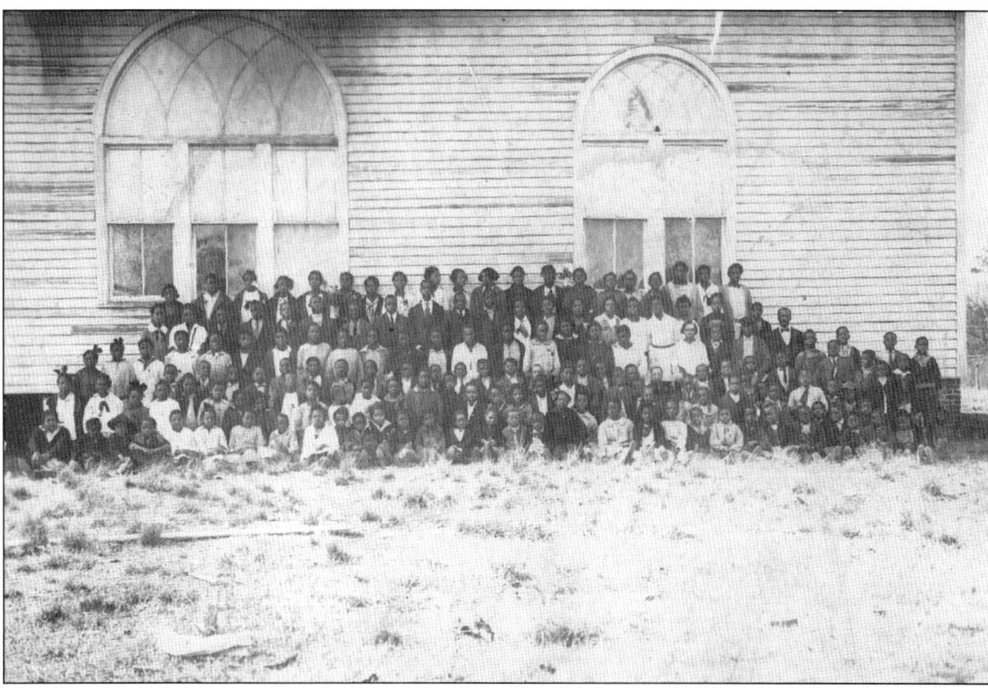

Students of Pollard Academy in Harlem, Georgia are seen in this *c.* 1930 photograph. (Courtesy of Mrs. Mary Sanders.)

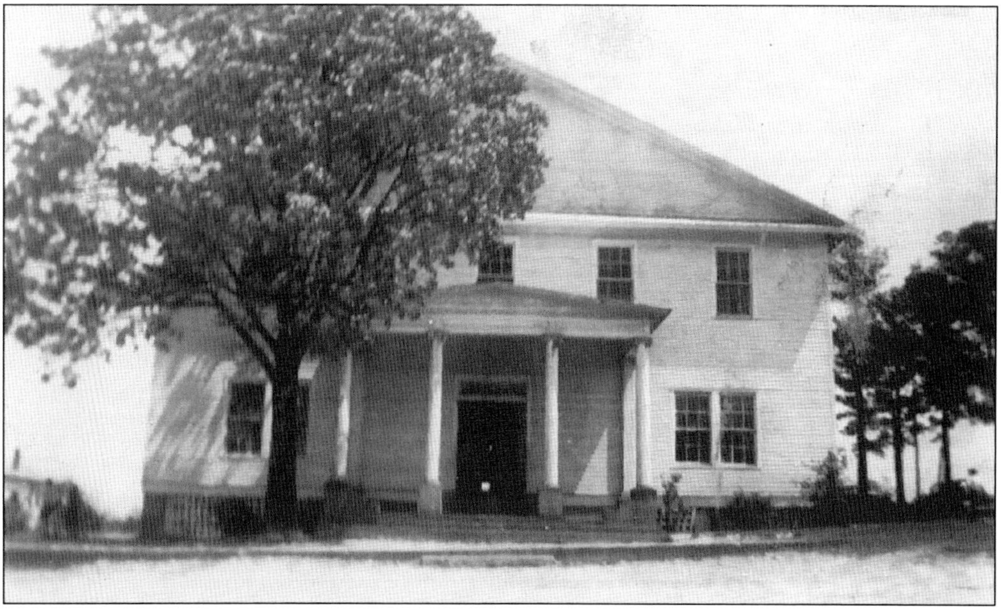

Old Citizen's Academy in Leah, Georgia, seen here *c.* 1930, was a very historic school near Little River. It was begun by a Dr. Bush in the 1790s; Dr. Bush was actually David Bushnell, the father of submarine warfare and a Revolutionary War veteran. (Courtesy of Lallie Dozier Benkoski.)

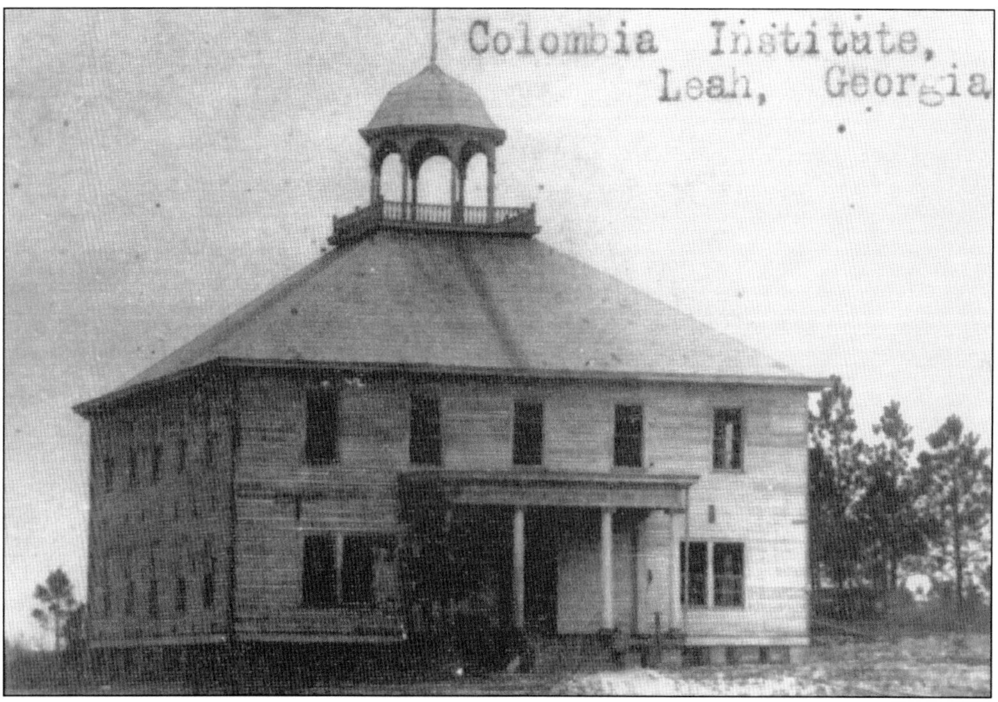

This postcard shows Columbia Institute in Leah. (Courtesy of Edith Reese.)

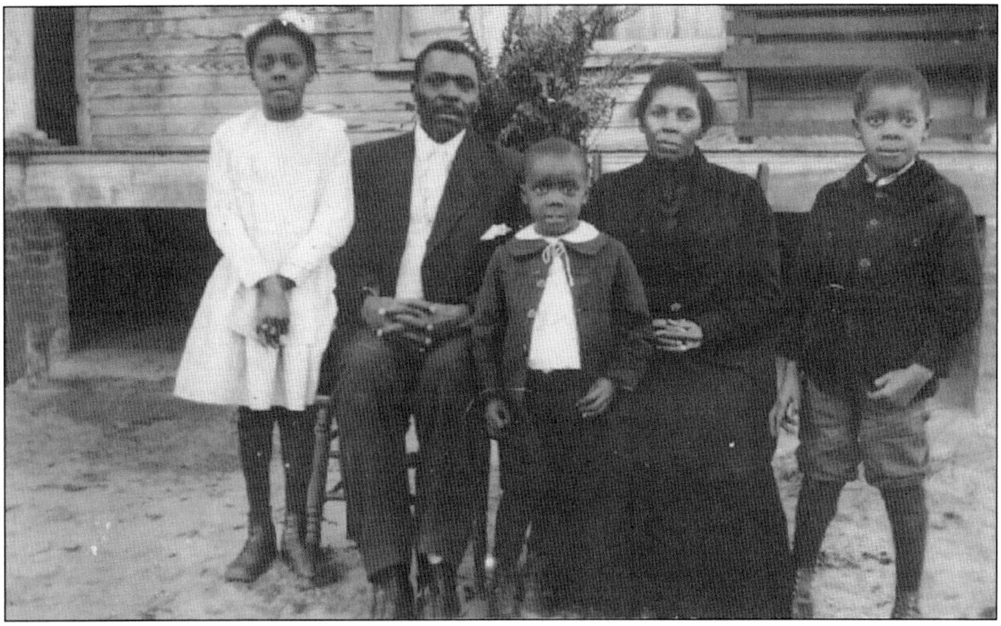

Mary Sanders, wearing a white dress, is pictured here with her parents and brothers (wearing knickers). Sanders, now retired, was a leading educator in the county. (Courtesy of Mrs. Mary Sanders.)

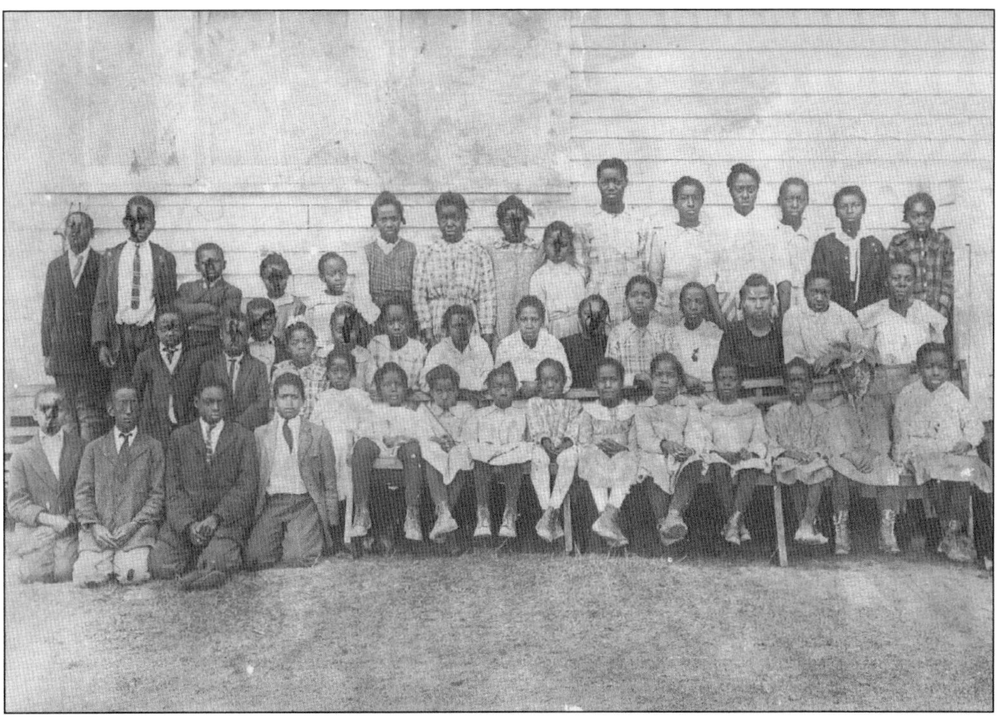

The graduating class of Pollard's Academy, *c.* 1940, pose with Mr. G.B. White, their teacher, in coats and ties. (Courtesy of Mrs. Mary Sanders.)

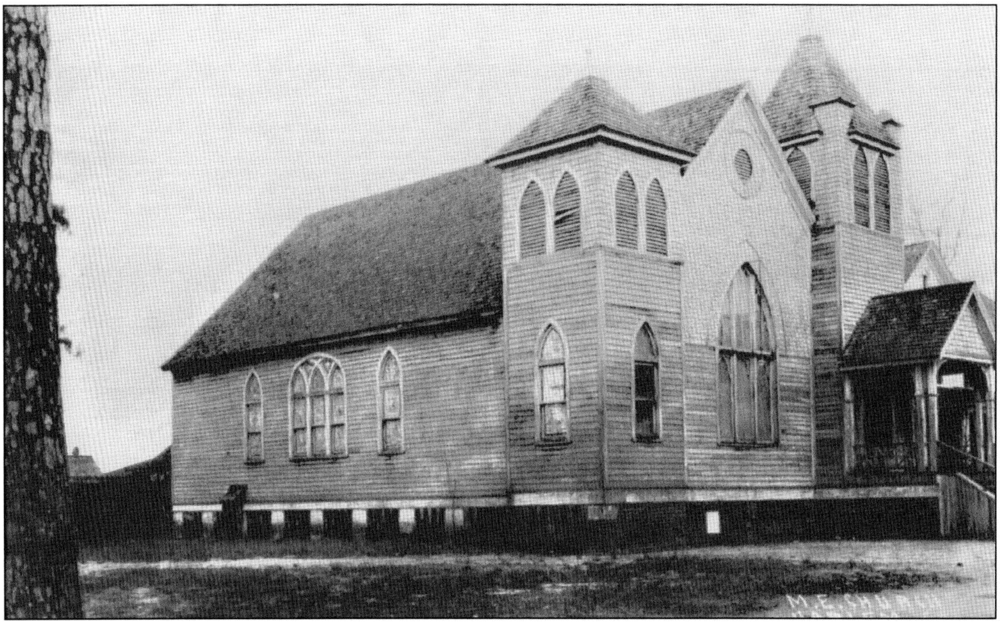

Pictured here is Harlem Methodist Church, *c.* 1900. This beautiful old structure with its unique architecture has since been replaced. (Courtesy of G.J. Smith.)

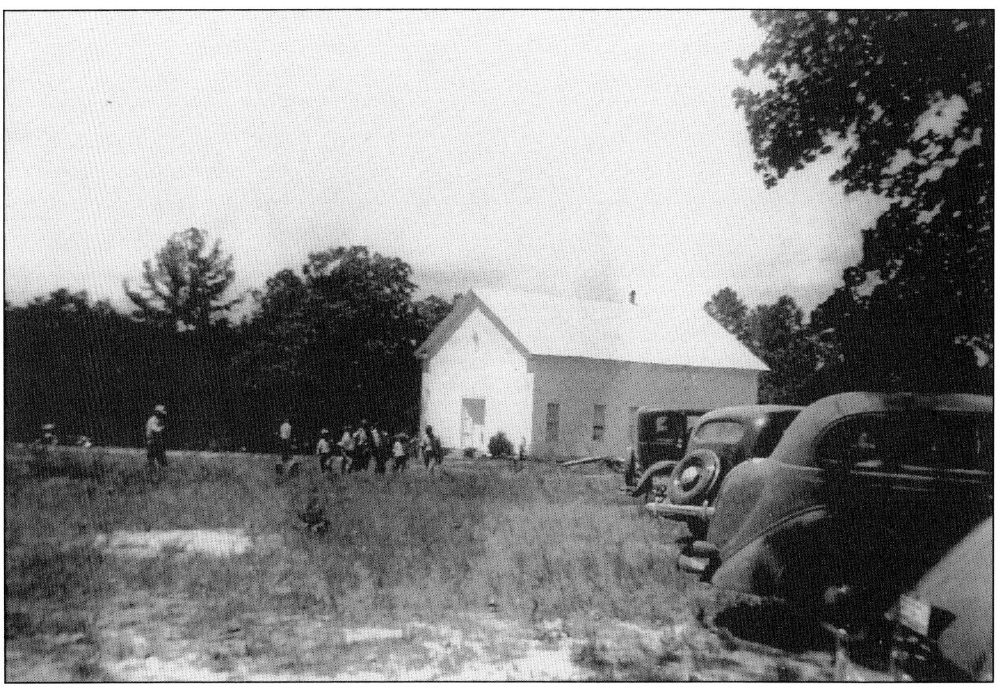

This is White Oak Methodist Church in 1930. (Courtesy Berma Ansley Gibson.)

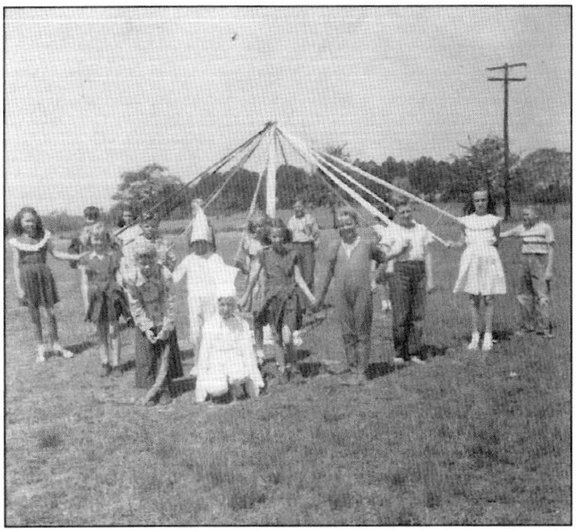

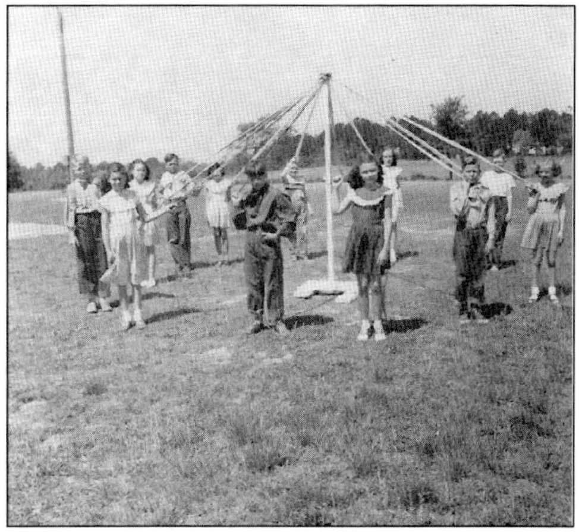

Pictured here are fifth grade pupils and a May Pole at Old Evans School in 1950–1951. (Courtesy of Elizabeth L. Johnson.)

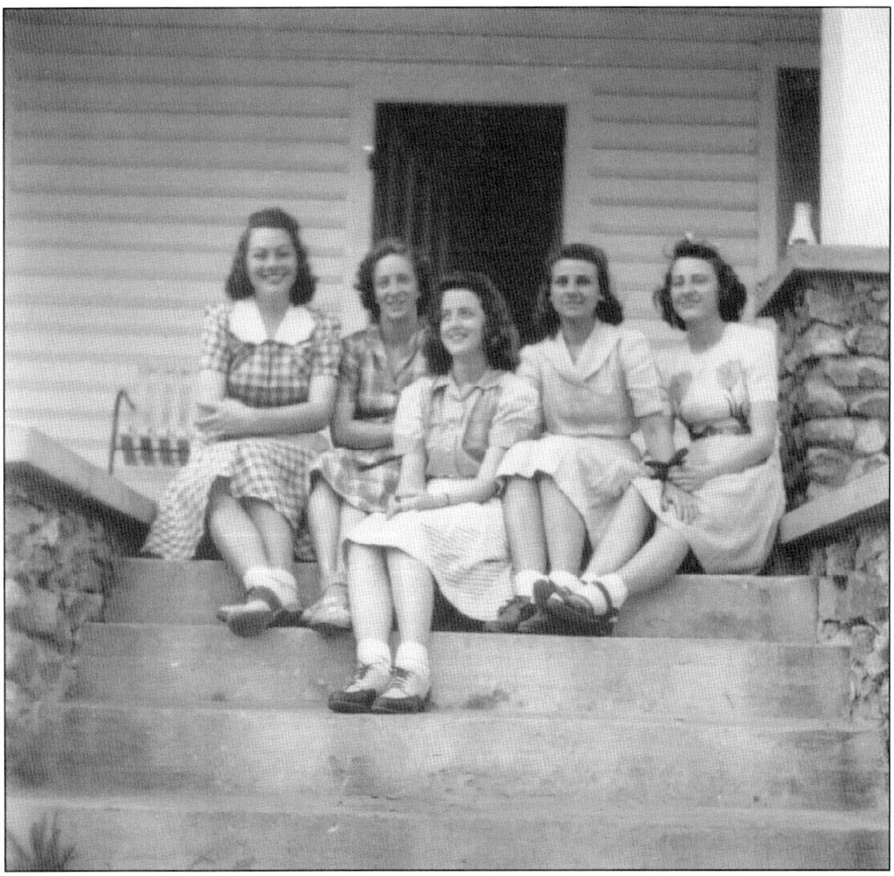

The teachers' cottage was also known as "The Dormitory" at Old Evans School. This picture was taken around 1940. (Courtesy of Elizabeth L. Johnson.)

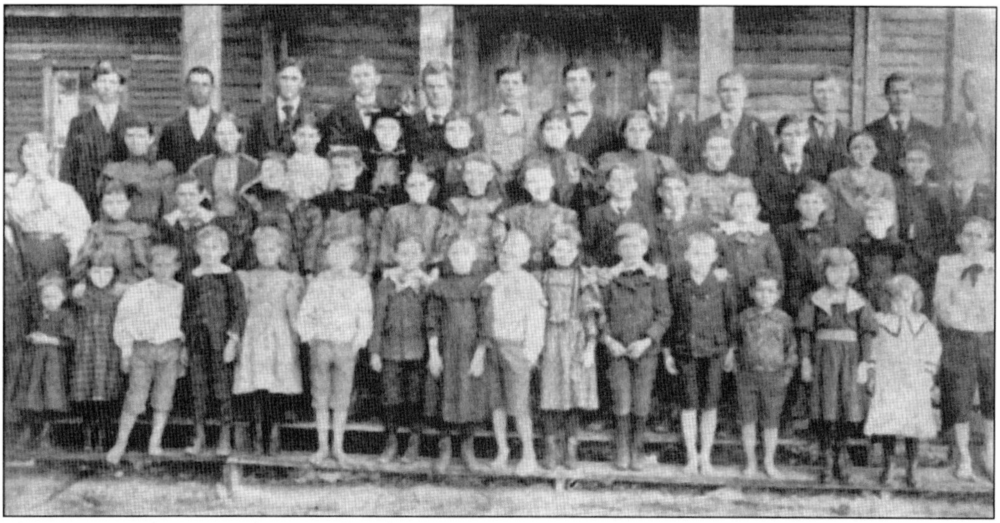

This picture shows graduation day for all the grades at Ellis School in 1897. "Done up" in their very finest, these youths are justly proud of their accomplishments. (Courtesy of Edna Ruth Paschal.)

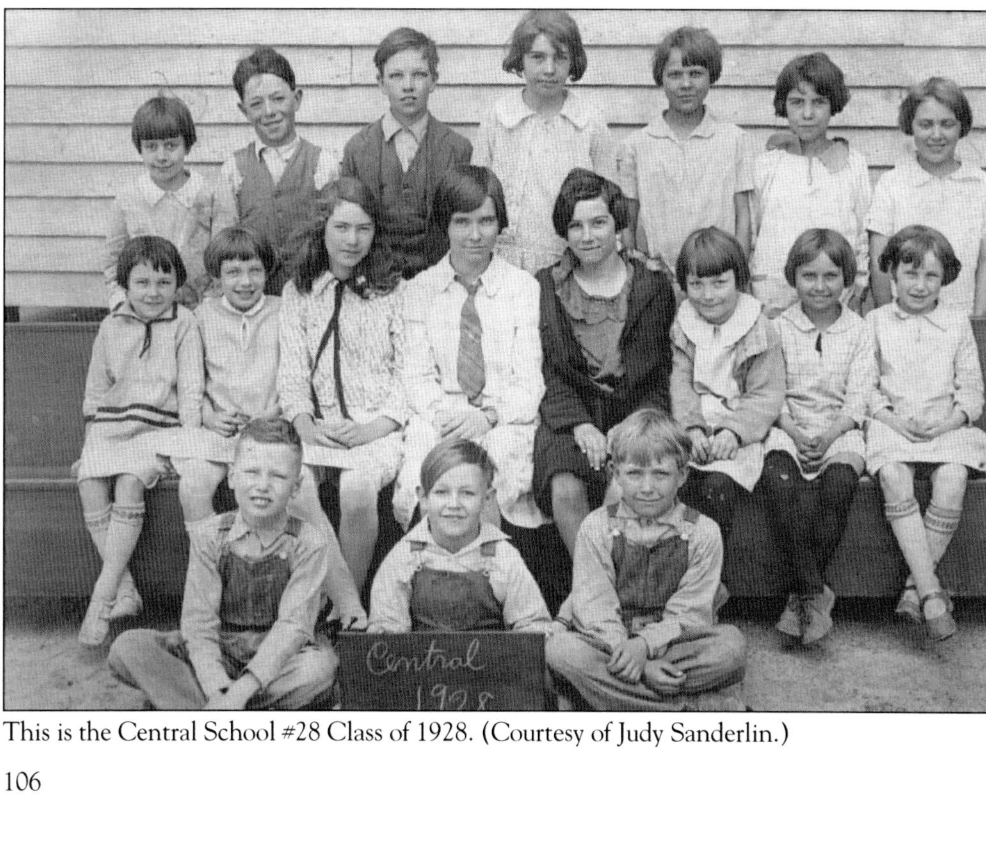

This is the Central School #28 Class of 1928. (Courtesy of Judy Sanderlin.)

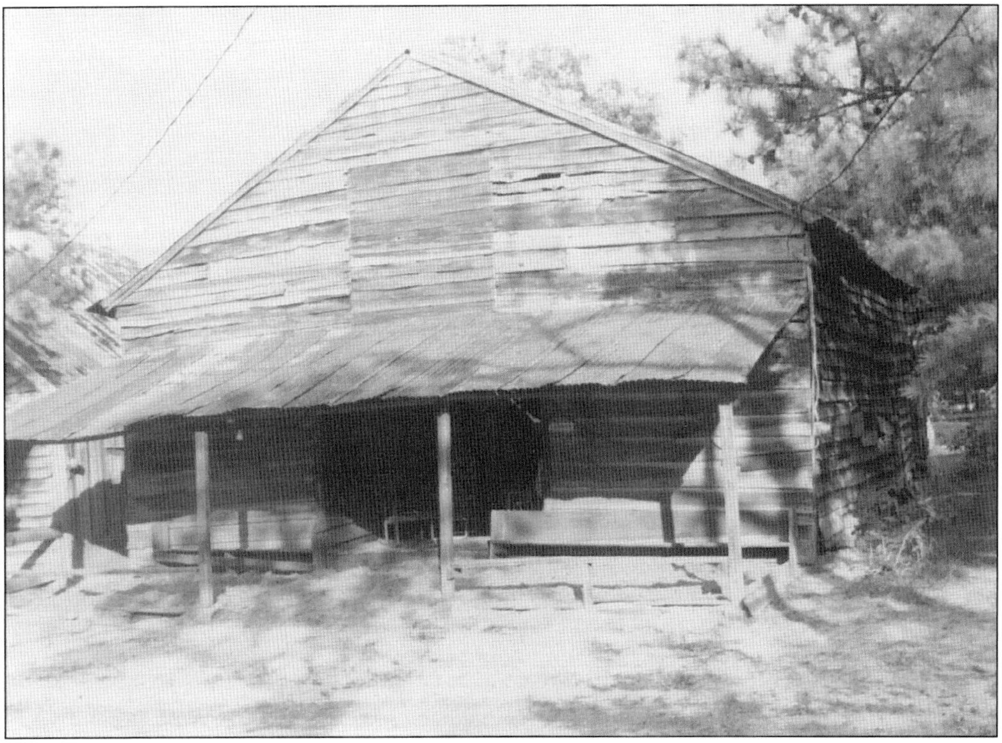

The Lamkin Tent at the White Oak Campmeeting site, shown above, is typical of the traditional camp meetings in the Methodist Church. People would "camp" during the "protracted meetings," or revivals, which lasted two or more weeks. (Courtesy of Elizabeth L. Johnson.)

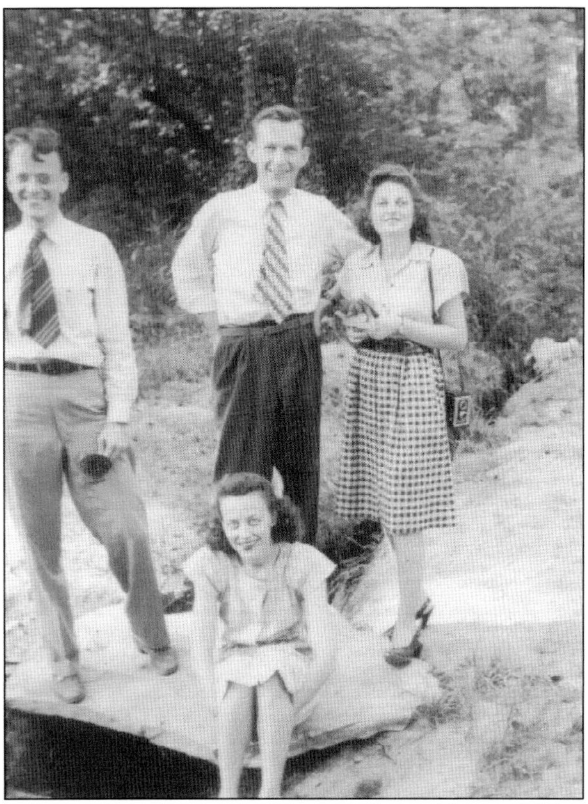

This picture, taken at a natural spring at the White Oak Campground, includes J.R. Johnson, Ramsey B. Davis, Hilda Lamkin Davis, and Evelyn Lamkin Bridges. (Courtesy of Elizabeth L. Johnson.)

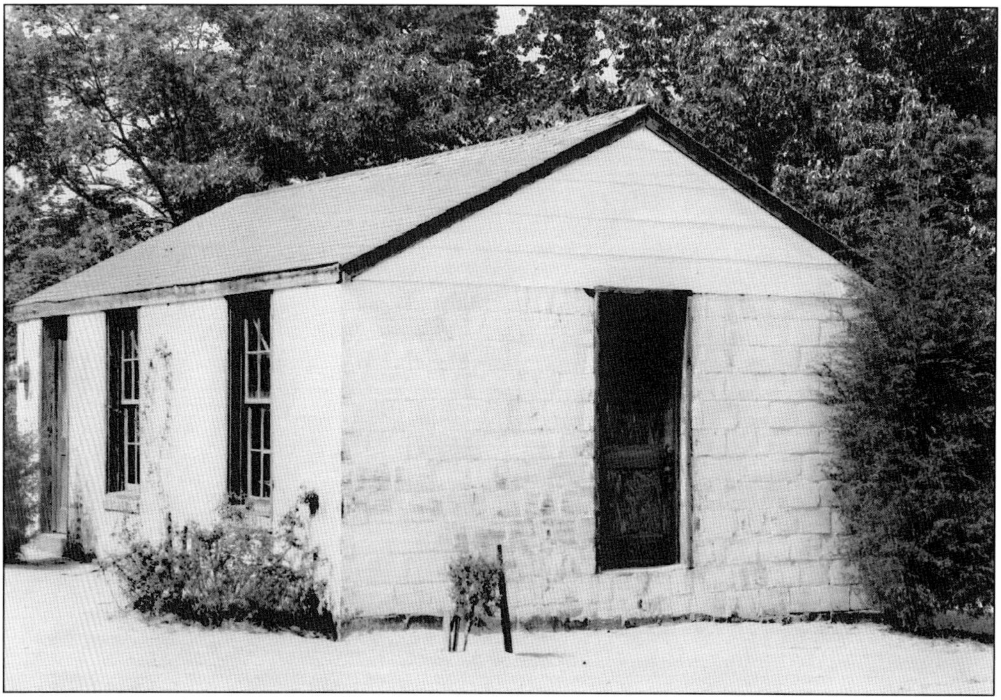

Steiner Grove School was one of the schools for African Americans in the 1950s. (Courtesy of Elma Jean Lazenby.)

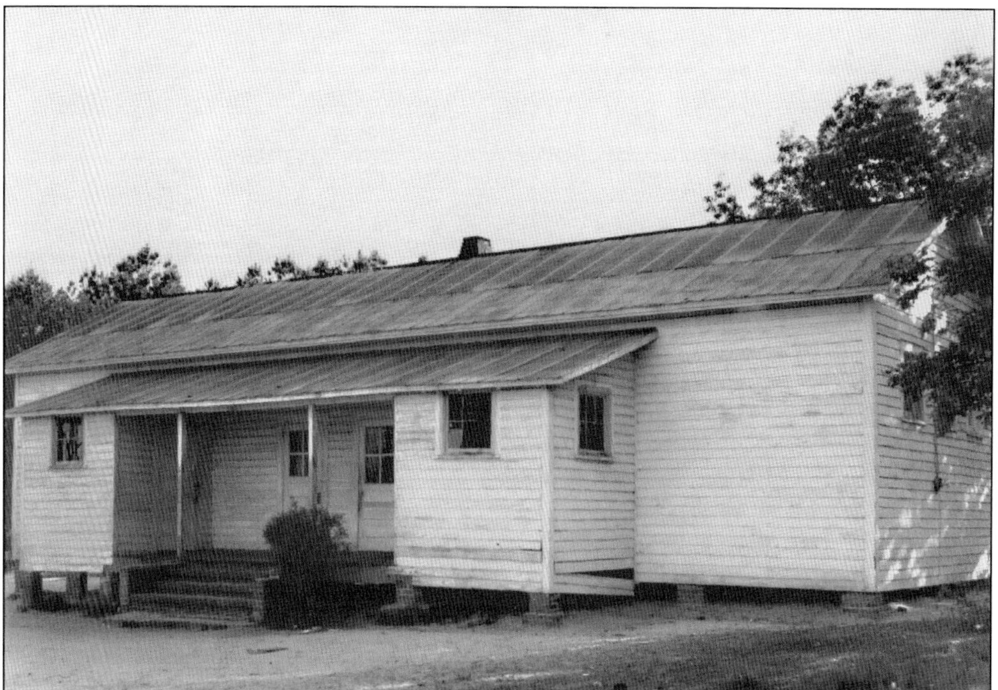

Oakely Grove School was another African-American school of the 1950s. (Courtesy of Elma Jean Lazenby.)

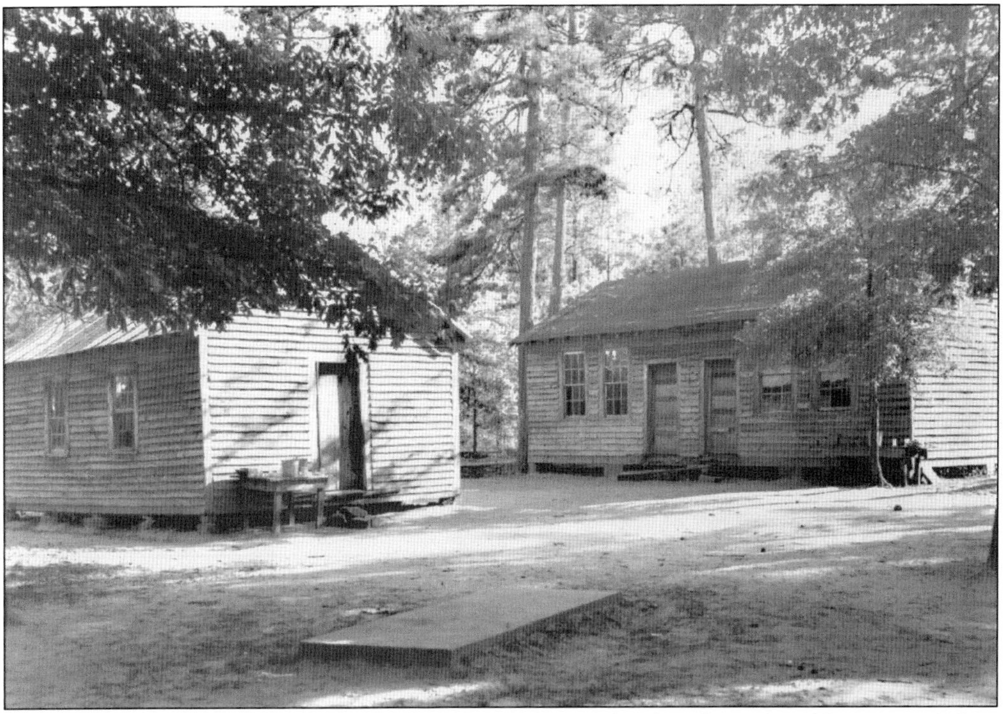

Galilee School, at right, was also an African-American school in the 1950s. (Courtesy of Elma Jean Lazenby.)

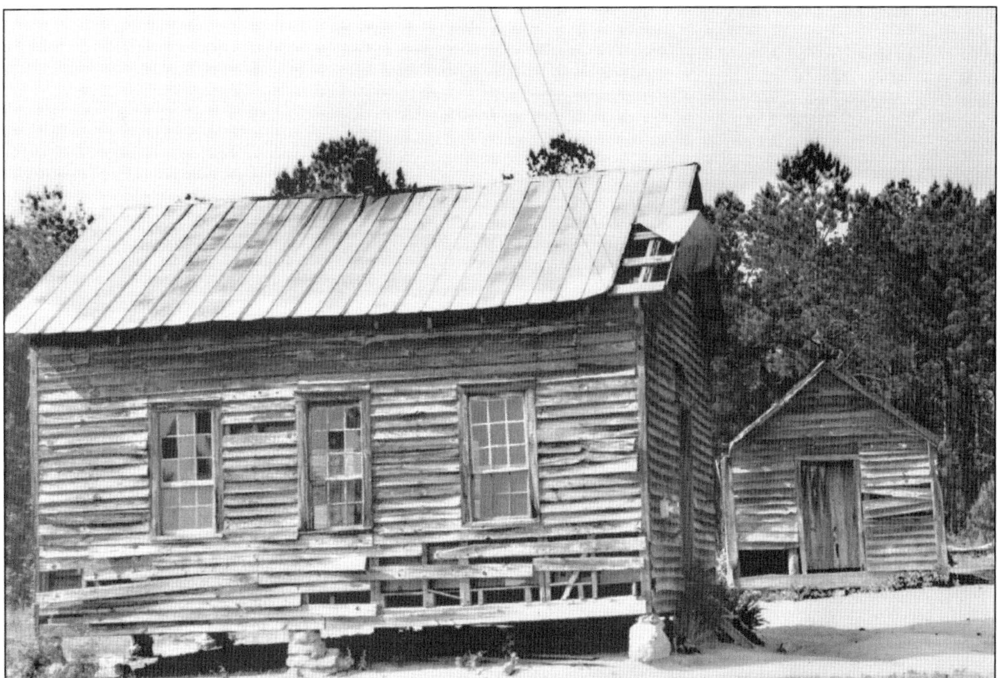

Another African-American school was Popular Springs School. (Courtesy of Elma Jean Lazenby.)

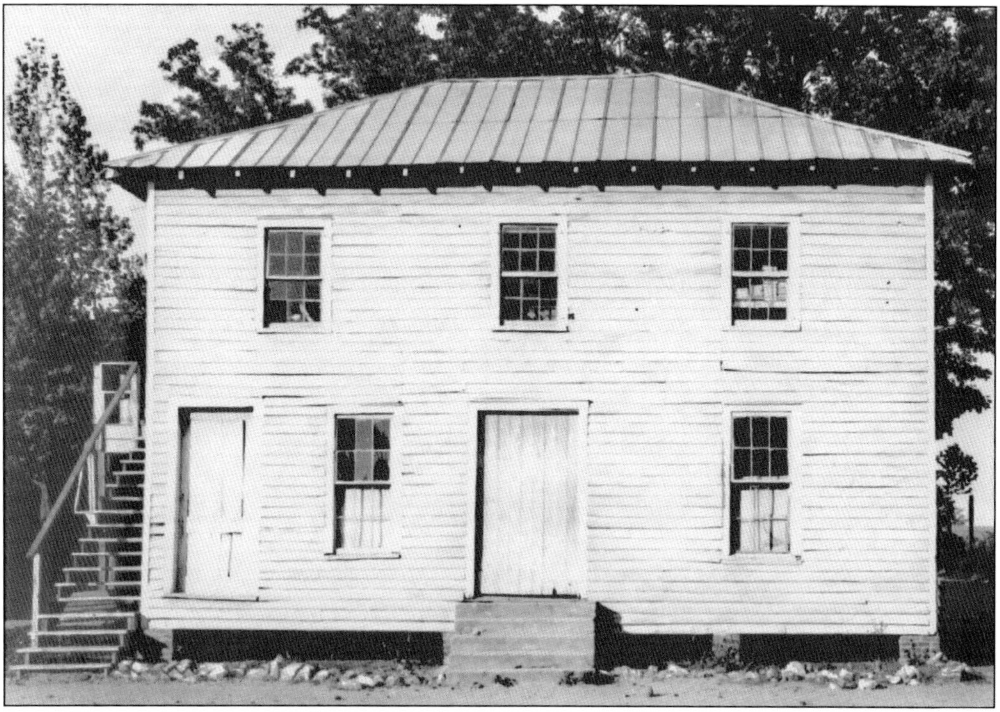

Gospel Water Branch School, a school for African Americans in the 1950s, is shown here. (Courtesy of Elma Jean Lazenby.)

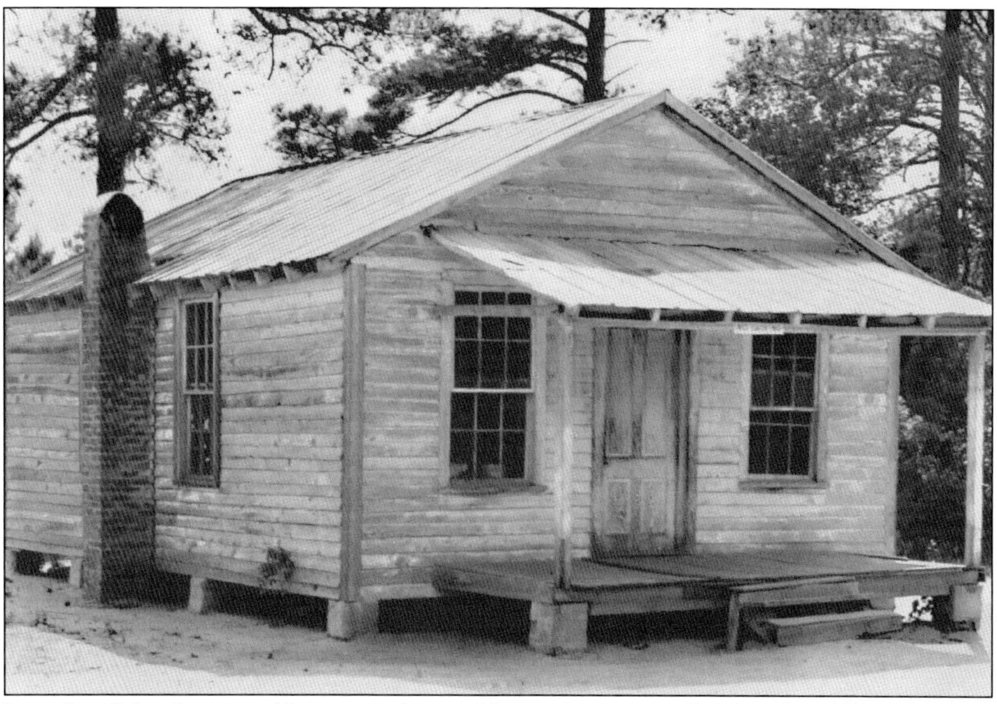

Jerusalem School, pictured here, was also an African-American school in the 1950s. (Courtesy of Elma Jean Lazenby.)

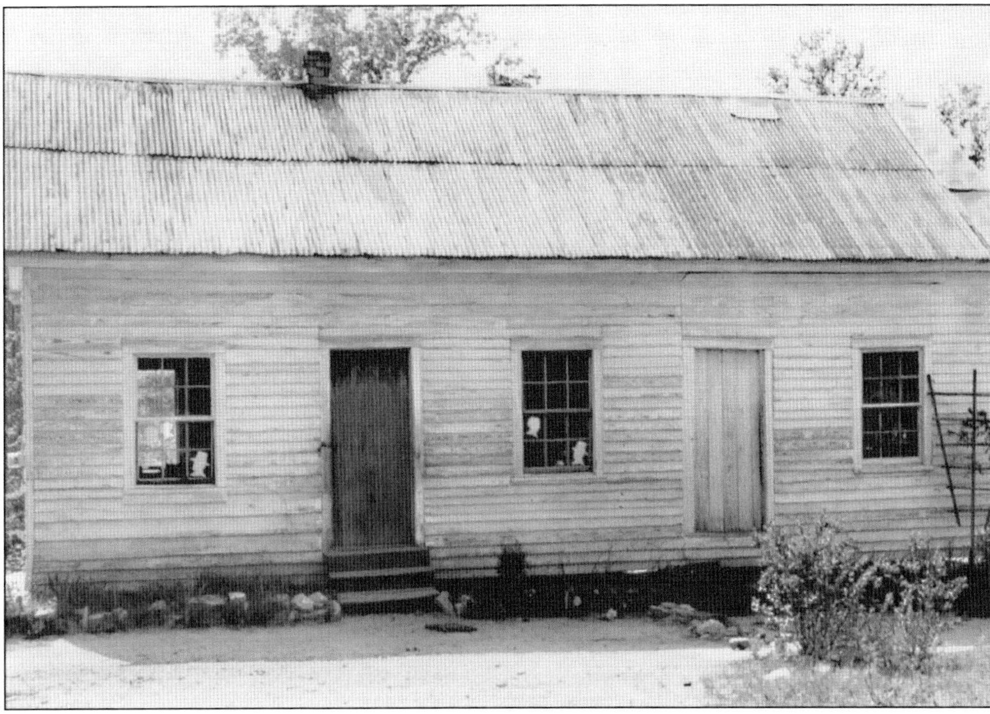

Pictured here is a school for African Americans in the 1950s called Lamkin Grove School. (Courtesy of Elma Jean Lazenby.)

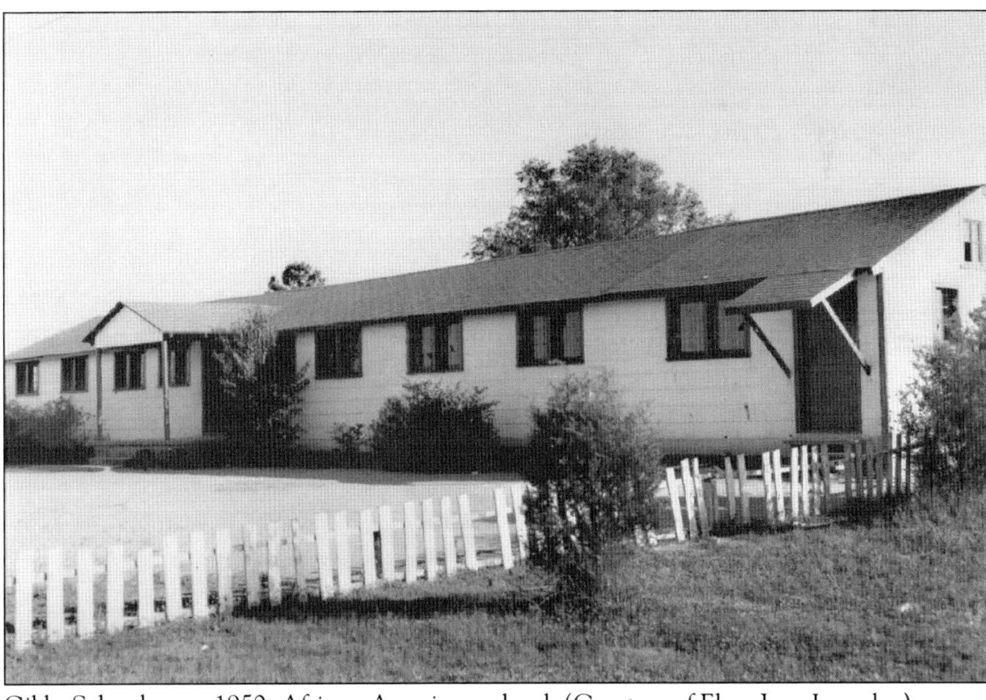

Gibbs School was a 1950s African-American school. (Courtesy of Elma Jean Lazenby.)

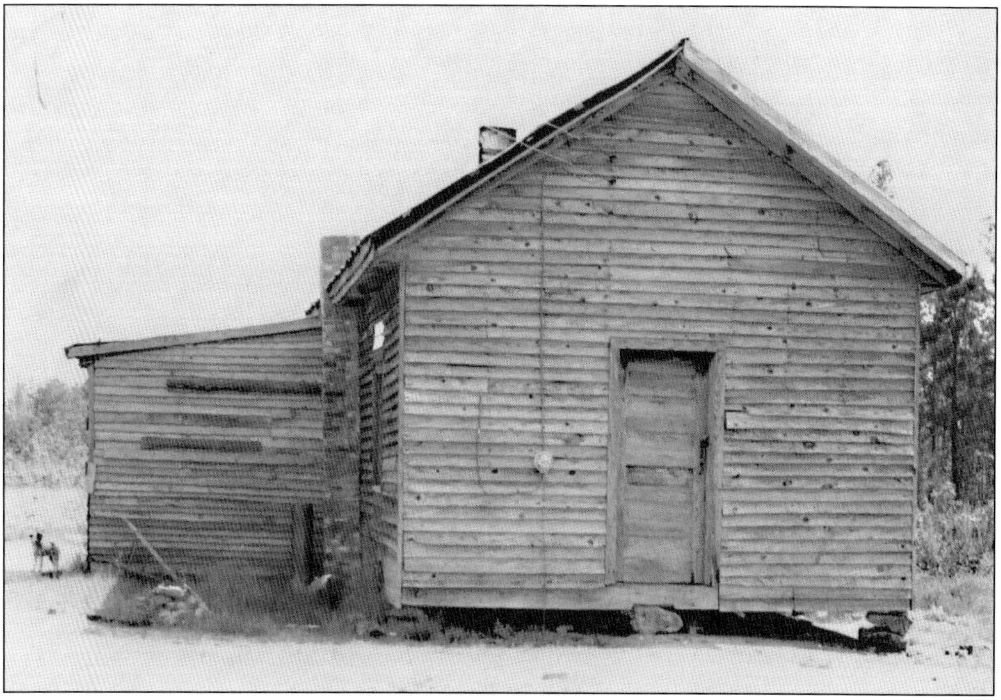

Clary Grove School was a facility for African-American students. (Courtesy of Elma Jean Lazenby.)

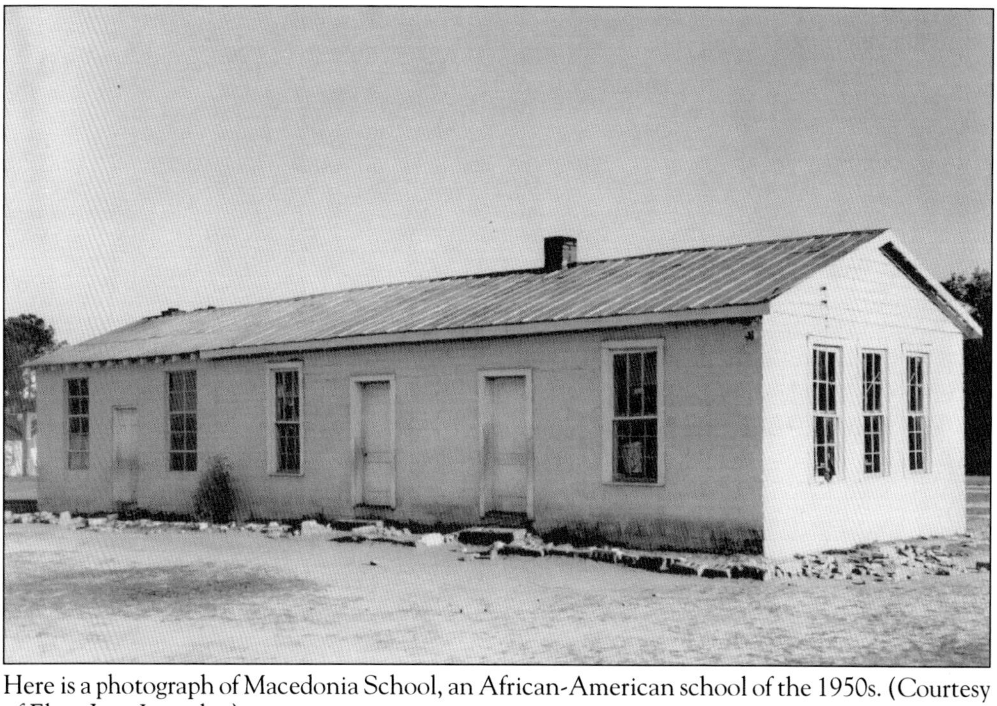

Here is a photograph of Macedonia School, an African-American school of the 1950s. (Courtesy of Elma Jean Lazenby.)

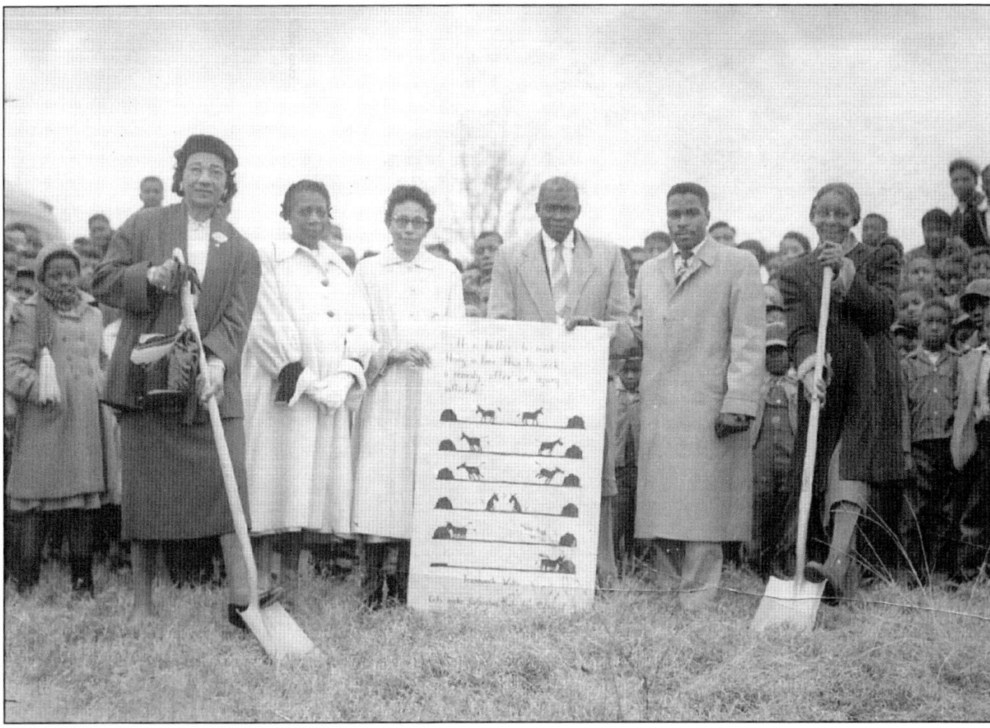
The first county secondary school for African Americans was Blanchard High School. Pictured here is the ground-breaking ceremony for the building. (Courtesy of Elma Jean Lazenby.)

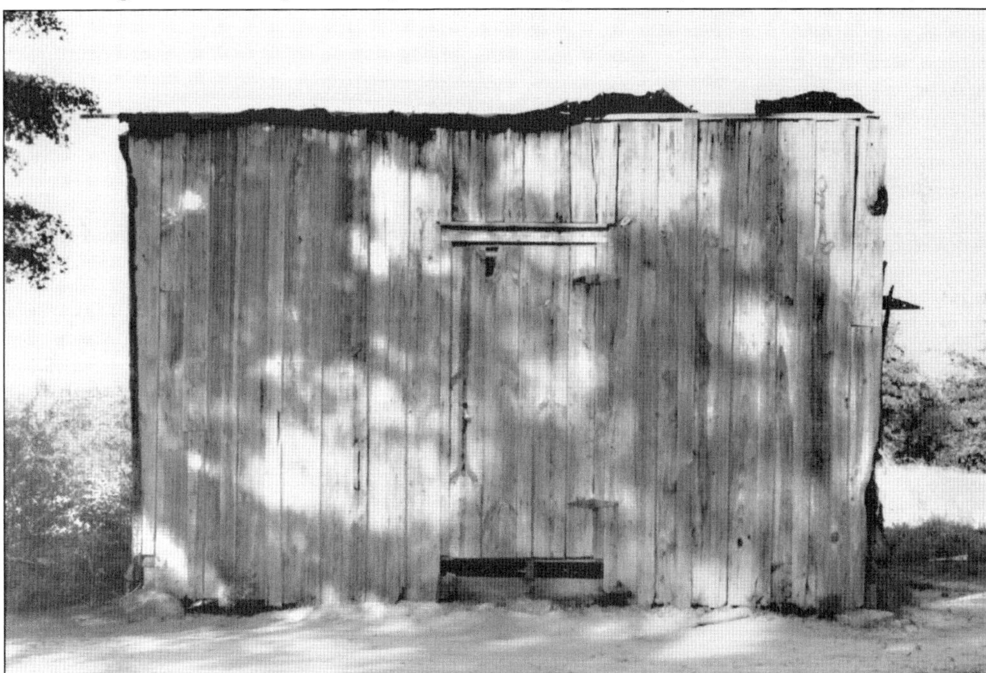
Pictured is the lunchroom of the Allen Grove School for African Americans, *c.* 1930s. (Courtesy of Elma Jean Lazenby.)

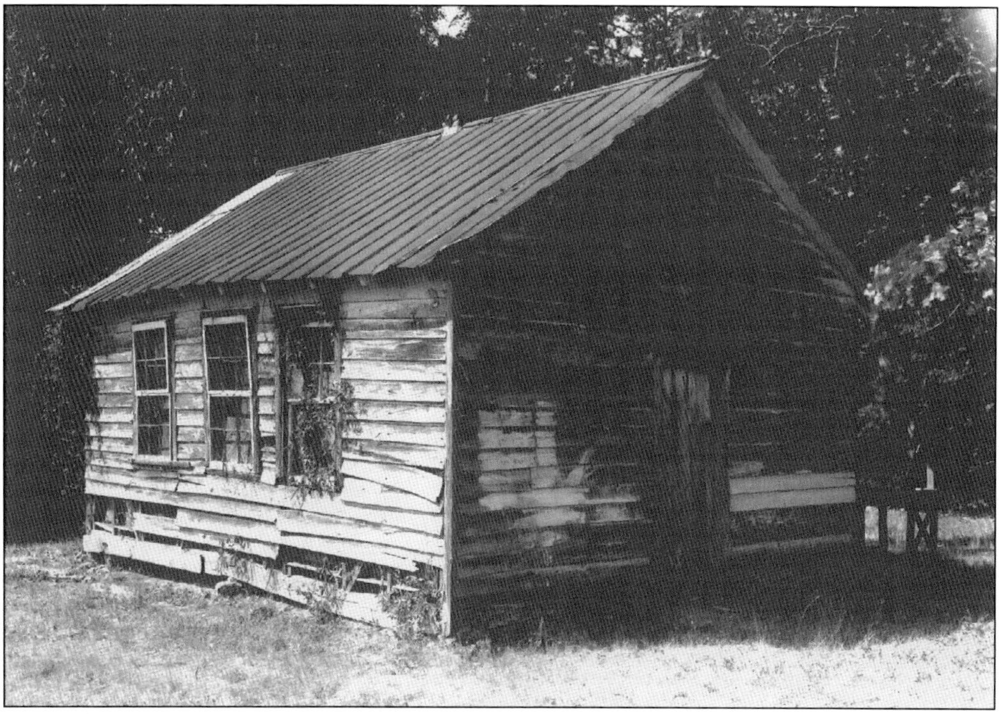

Pictured here in 1950 is the Walnut Grove School in Phinizy, Georgia. It was moved to Appling, where it is currently being renovated. (Courtesy of Lallie Dozier Benkoski.)

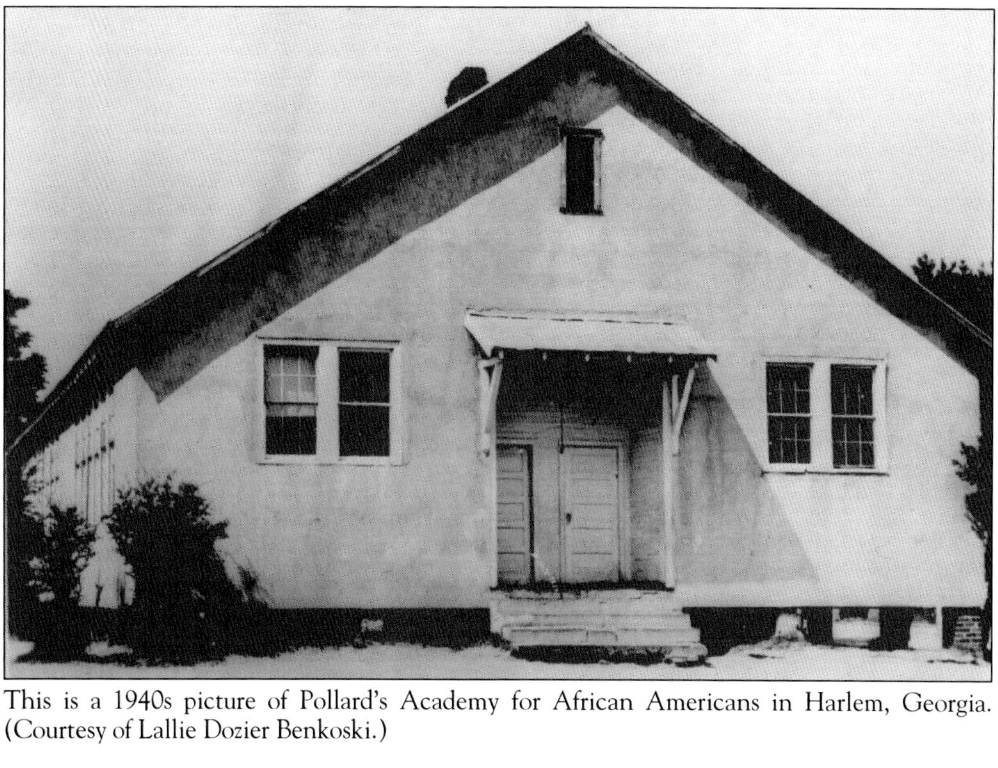

This is a 1940s picture of Pollard's Academy for African Americans in Harlem, Georgia. (Courtesy of Lallie Dozier Benkoski.)

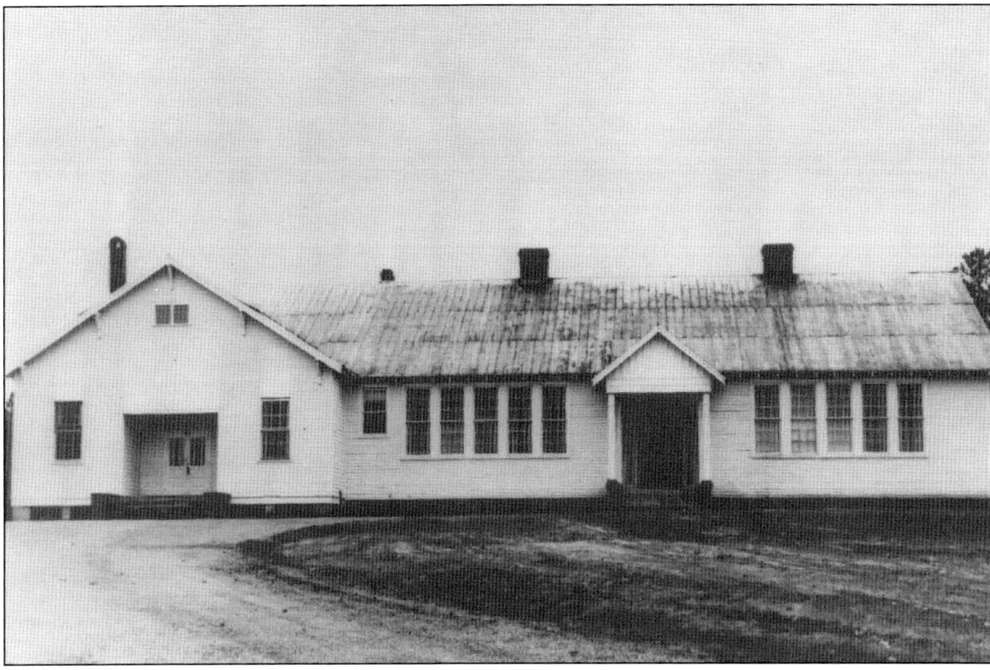

Appling Elementary School for white students, pictured here around 1900, was razed in the 1950s. (Courtesy of Lallie Dozier Benkoski.)

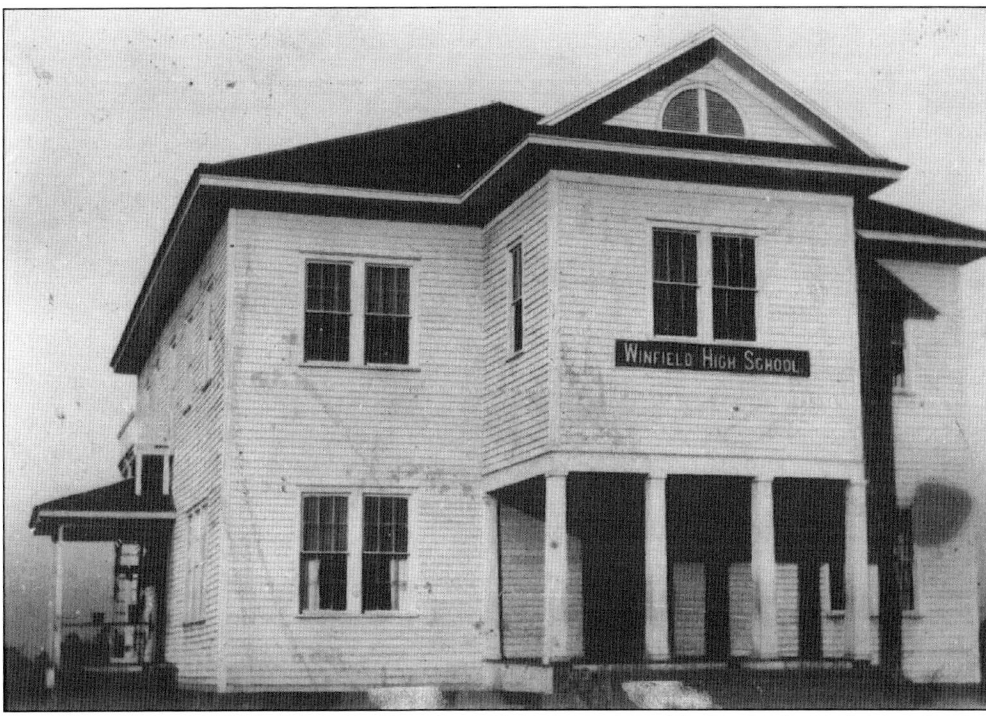

Winfield High School was torn down in the 1950s. It is pictured here as it looked around 1900. (Courtesy of Lallie Dozier Benkoski.)

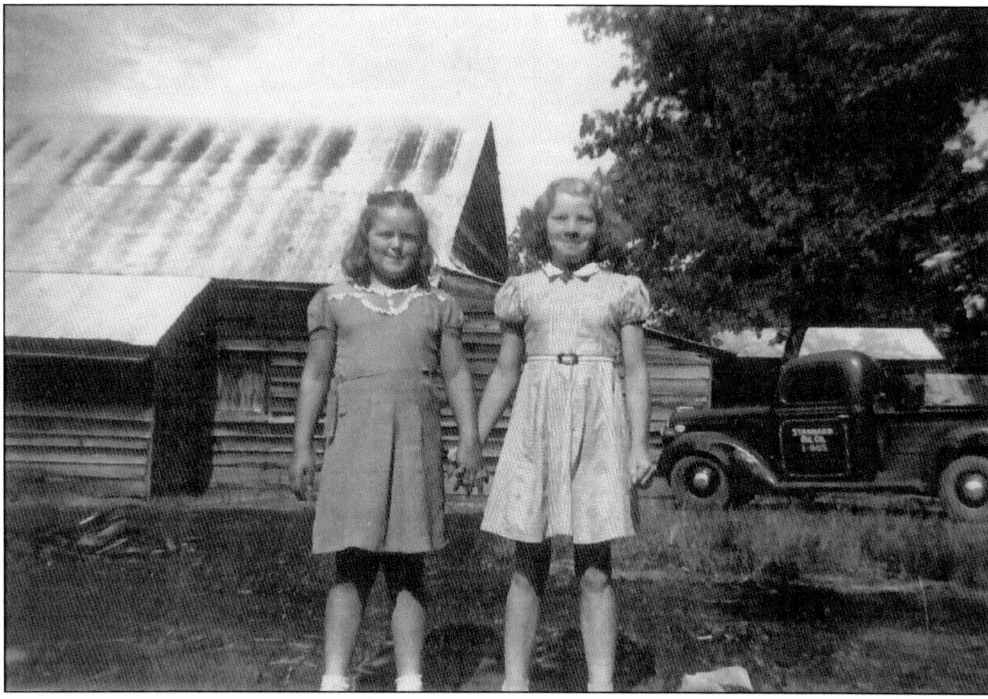

A Standard Oil truck is shown at the White Oak Campmeeting. The girls are unidentified. (Courtesy of Beth Ansley Gibson.)

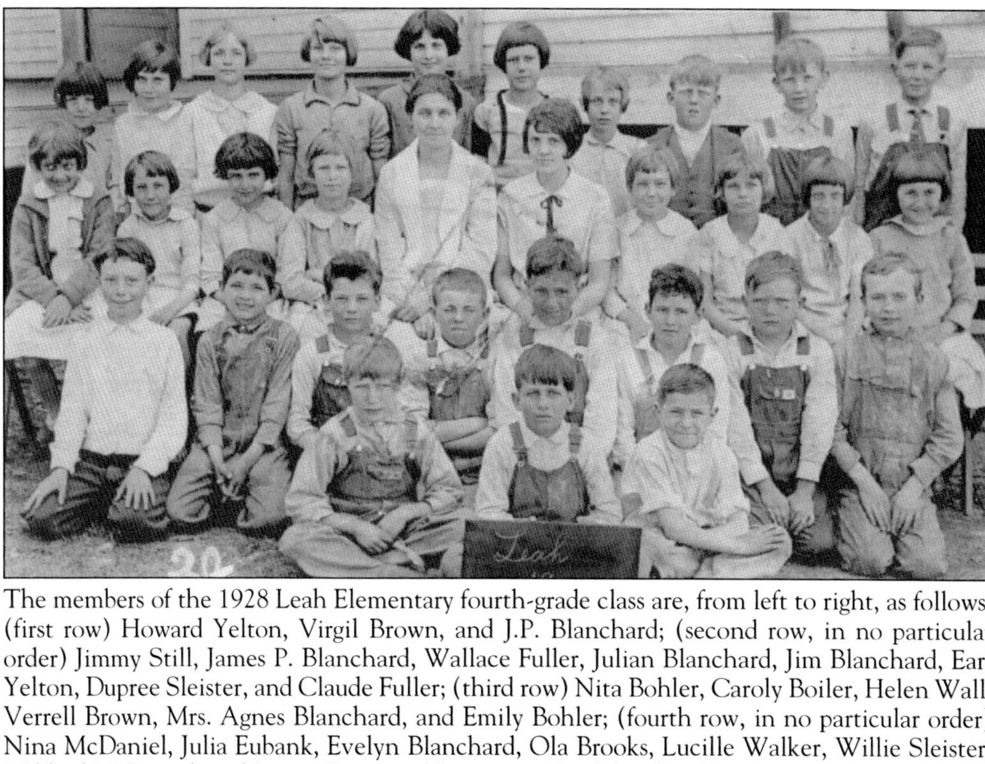

The members of the 1928 Leah Elementary fourth-grade class are, from left to right, as follows: (first row) Howard Yelton, Virgil Brown, and J.P. Blanchard; (second row, in no particular order) Jimmy Still, James P. Blanchard, Wallace Fuller, Julian Blanchard, Jim Blanchard, Earl Yelton, Dupree Sleister, and Claude Fuller; (third row) Nita Bohler, Caroly Boiler, Helen Wall, Verrell Brown, Mrs. Agnes Blanchard, and Emily Bohler; (fourth row, in no particular order) Nina McDaniel, Julia Eubank, Evelyn Blanchard, Ola Brooks, Lucille Walker, Willie Sleister, Mildred McDaniel, and Junior Connor. (Courtesy of Pat Blanchard.)

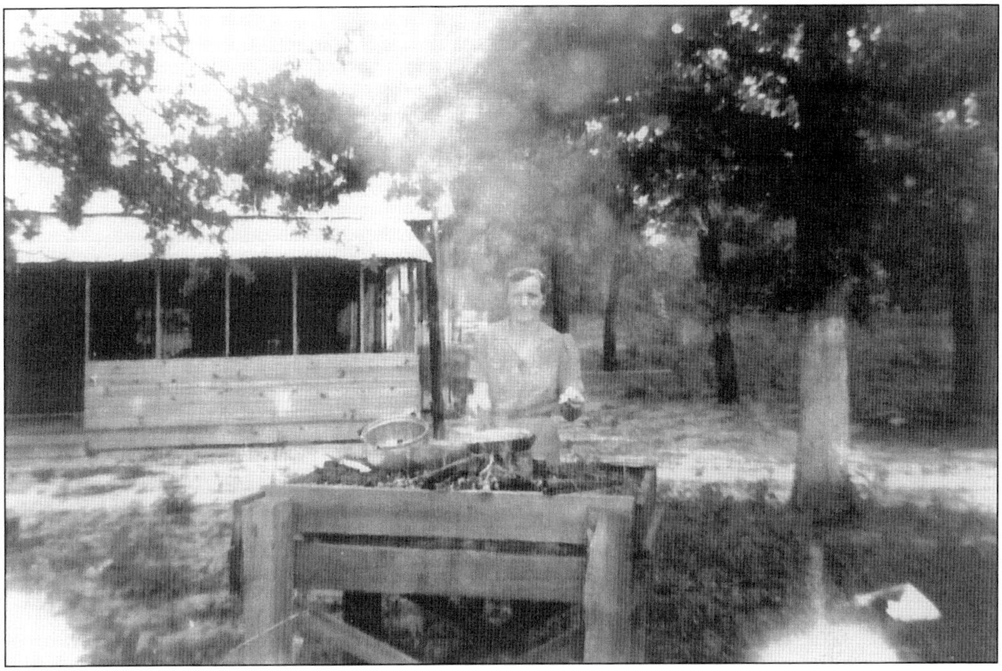

This firebox was used for lighting at night at the White Oak Campmeeting in the 1930s. (Courtesy of Berma Ansley Gibson.)

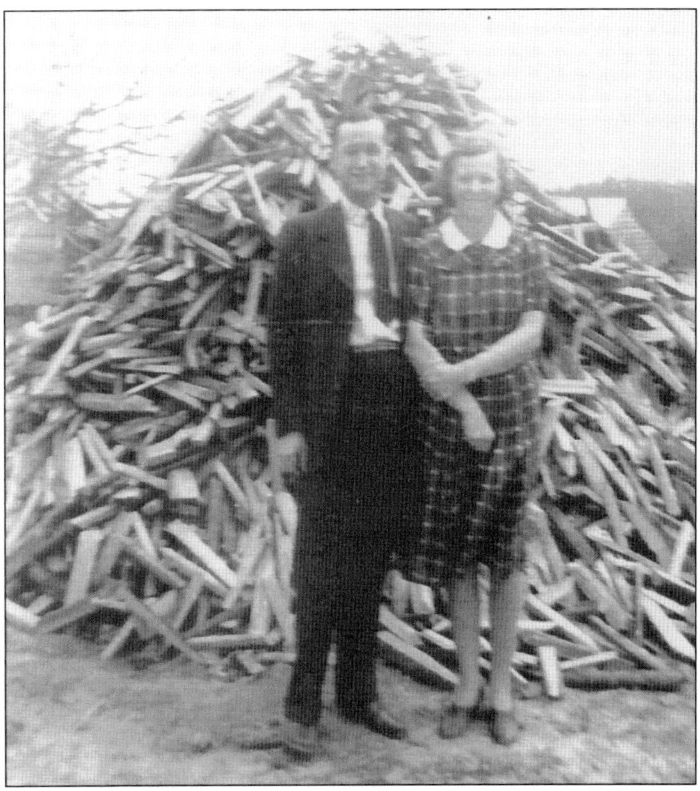

The cordwood stacked here was used to light the firebox (seen above) at the White Oak Campmeeting in 1930. Fran and Rosalie Guye stand in front of the pile. (Courtesy of Berma Ansley Gibson.)

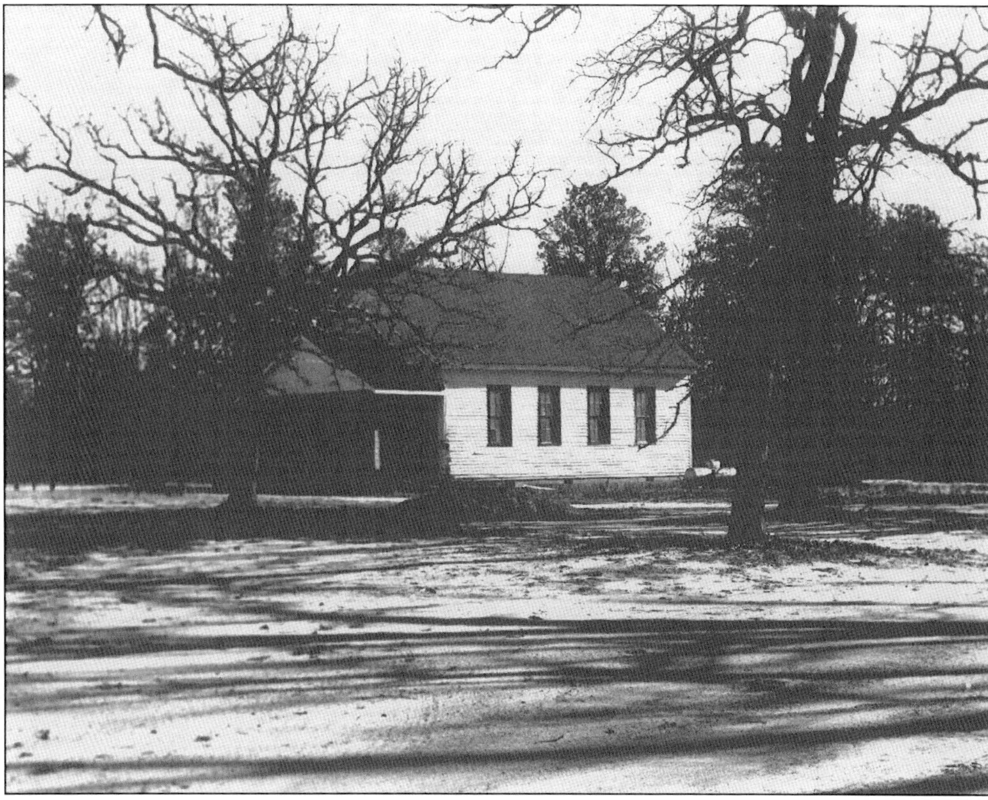

This is the Jones Chapel C.M.E. Church near the White Oak community. The Christian Methodist Episcopal denomination was begun in 1870. (Courtesy of Lallie Dozier Benkoski.)

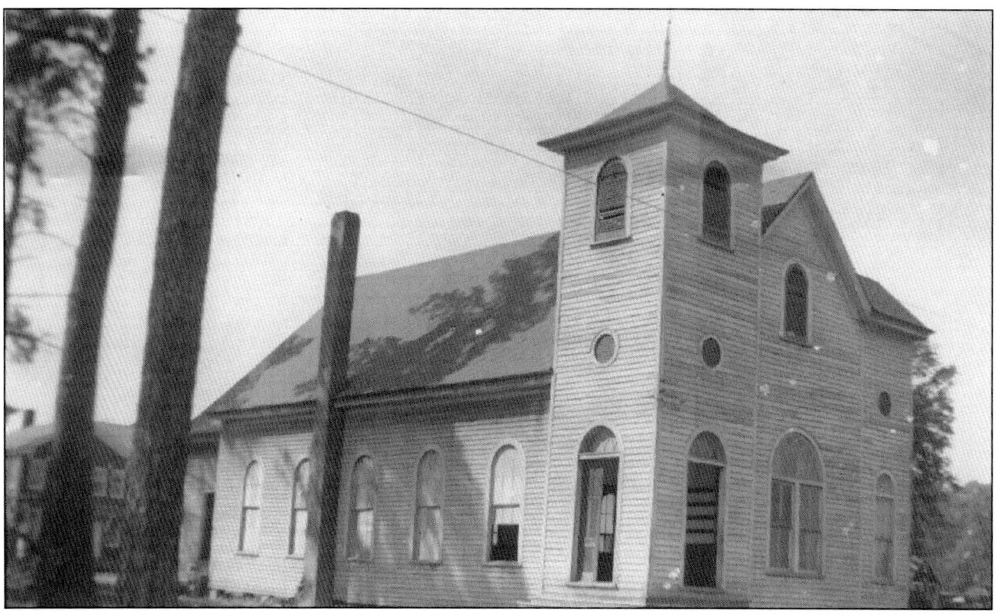

Here is the Appling Baptist Church, *c.* 1950. (Courtesy of Lallie Dozier Benkoski.)

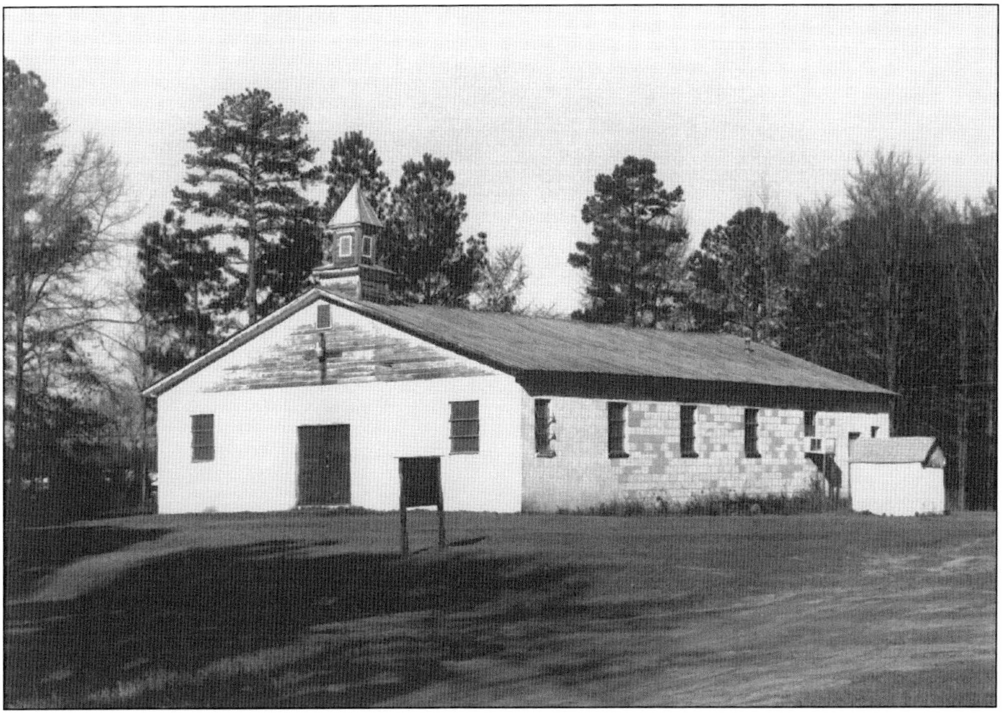

Here is the African-American Appling Baptist Church on White Oak Road. (Courtesy of Lallie Dozier Benkoski.)

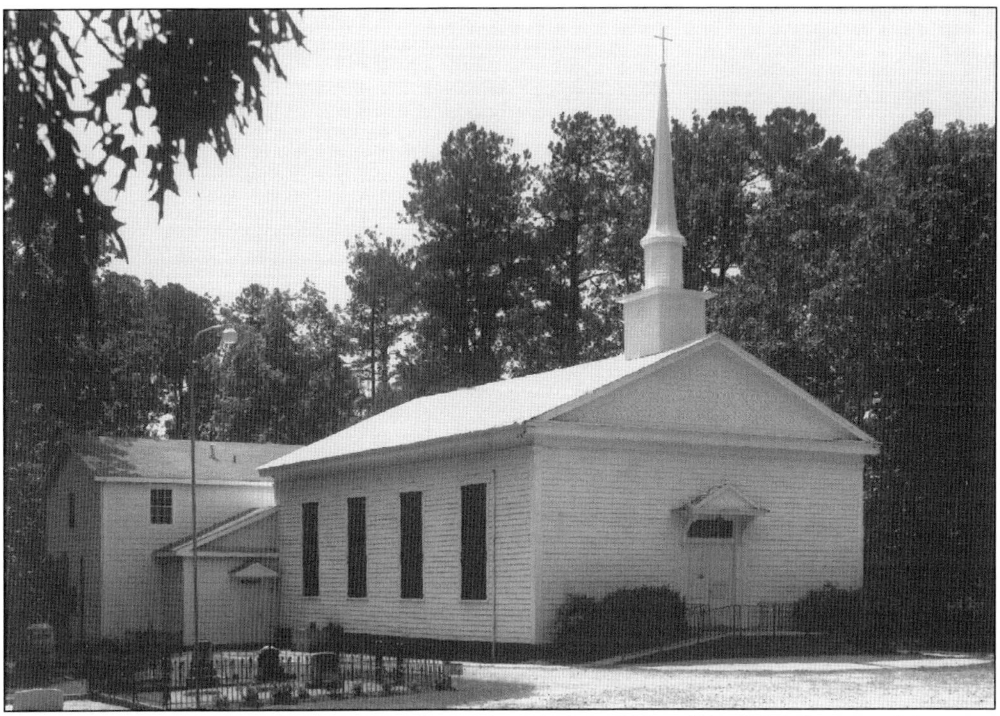

Dunn Chapel United Methodist Church was founded *c.* 1838 in Winfield, Georgia. (Courtesy of Lallie Dozier Benkoski.)

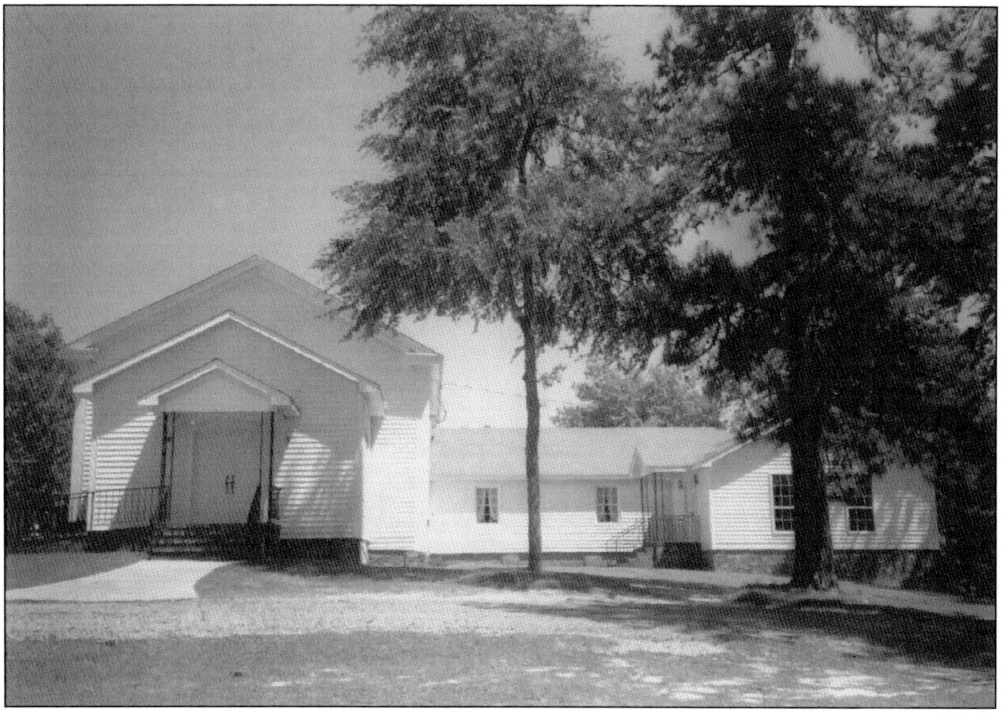

This is the White Oak United Methodist Church today. (Courtesy of Carla Grimaud.)

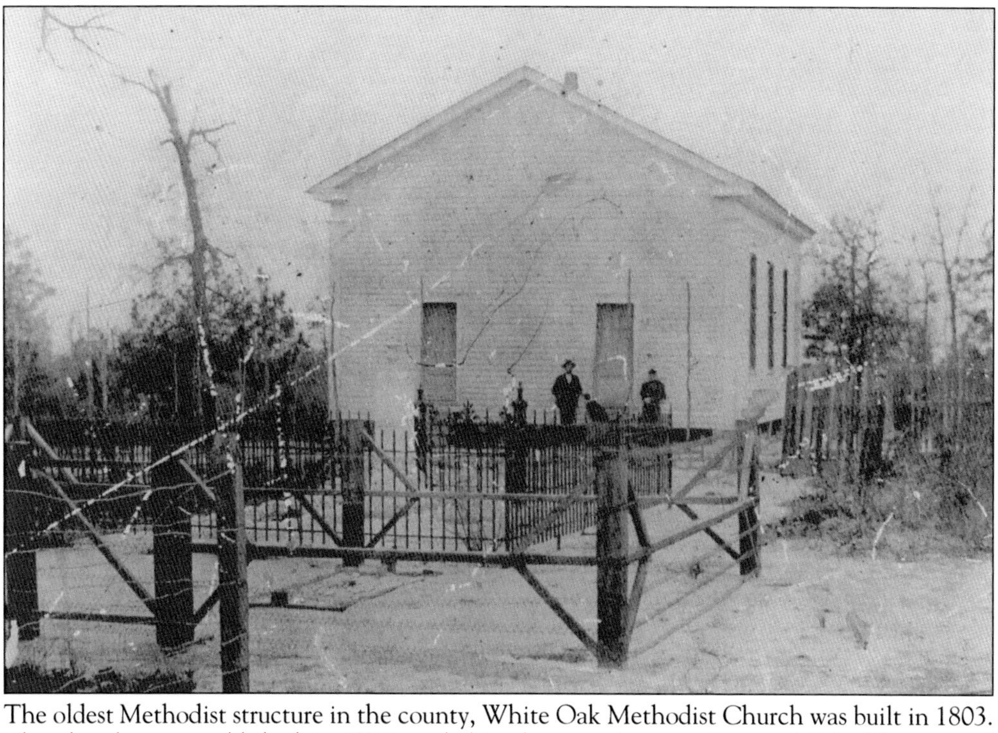

The oldest Methodist structure in the county, White Oak Methodist Church was built in 1803. The church was established in 1792, and this photograph was taken in 1903. (Courtesy of Carla Grimaud.)

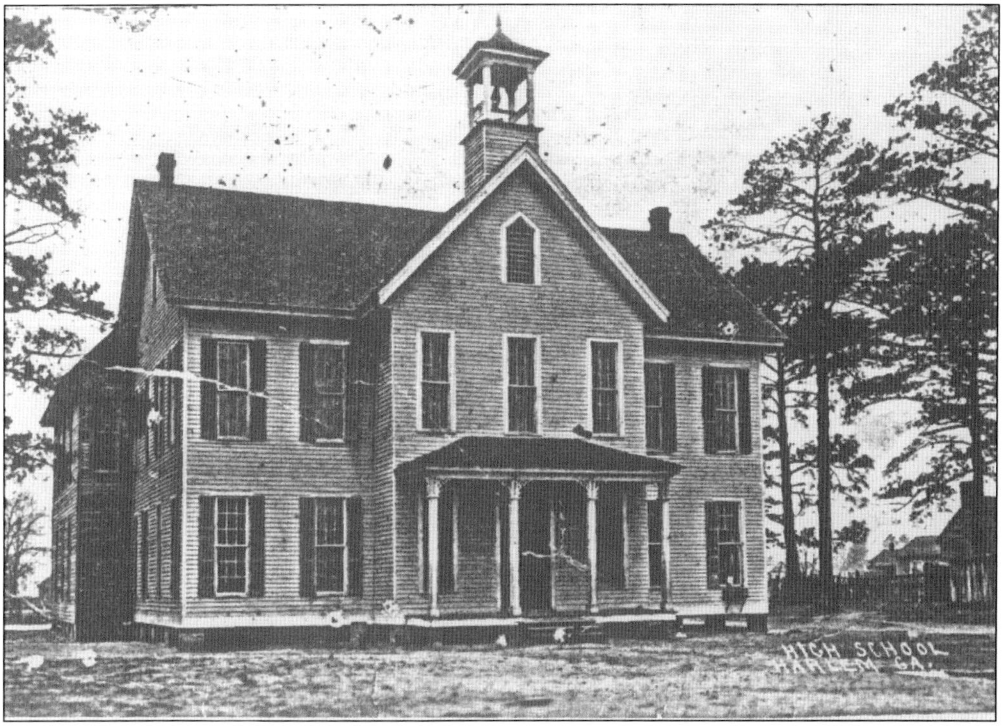

Pictured is a high school in Harlem, Georgia, *c.* 1900. (Courtesy of Lallie Dozier Benkoski.)

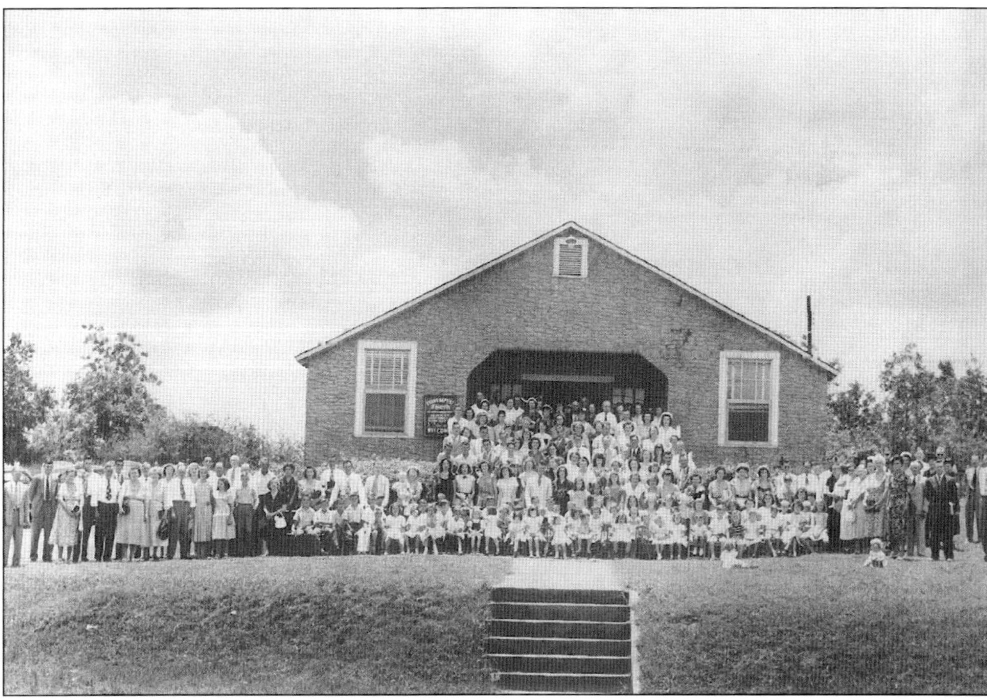

Old Evans Baptist Church in Evans, Georgia is pictured here. (Courtesy of Dan Marshall.)

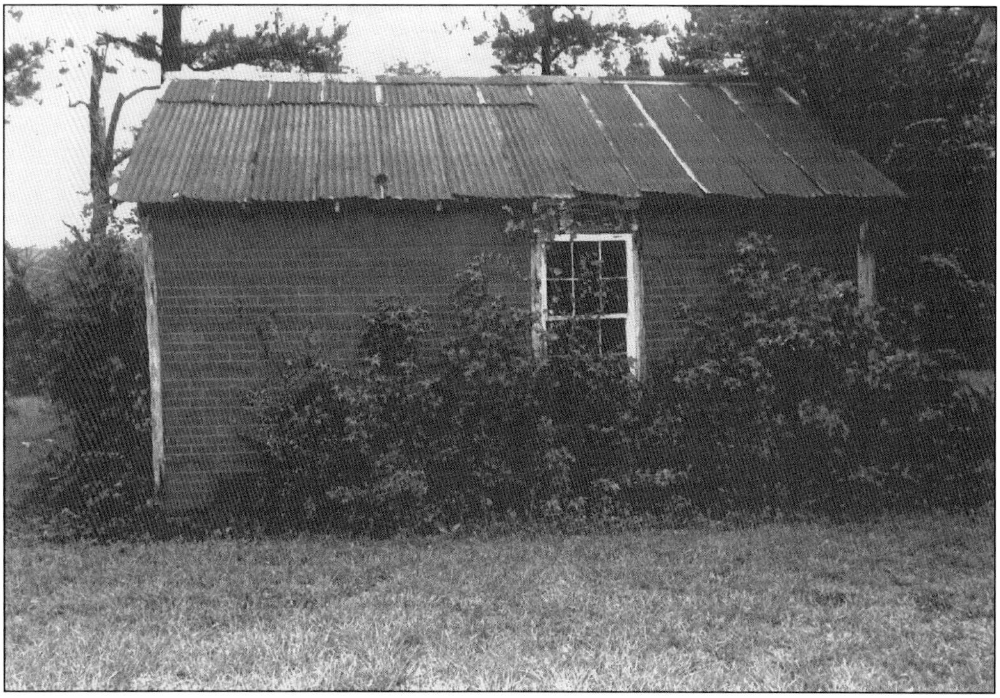

This c. 1950 photograph shows Mount Enon School for African Americans in Evans, Georgia. (Courtesy of Lallie Dozier Benkoski.)

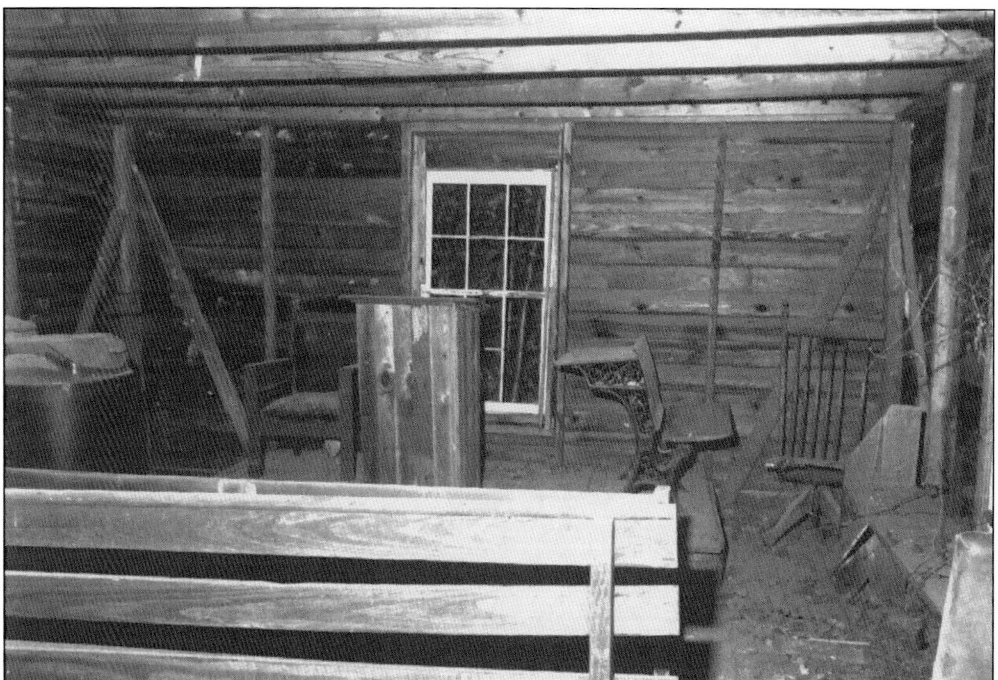

This photograph shows the interior of the old Mount Enon School. (Courtesy of Lallie Dozier Benkoski.)

The White Oak Campmeeting water tank is seen here in 1930. The rustic nature of the old site is preserved today. The preaching, singing, and fellowship are a very old and significant aspect of the county's past. (Courtesy of Berma Ansley Gibson.)

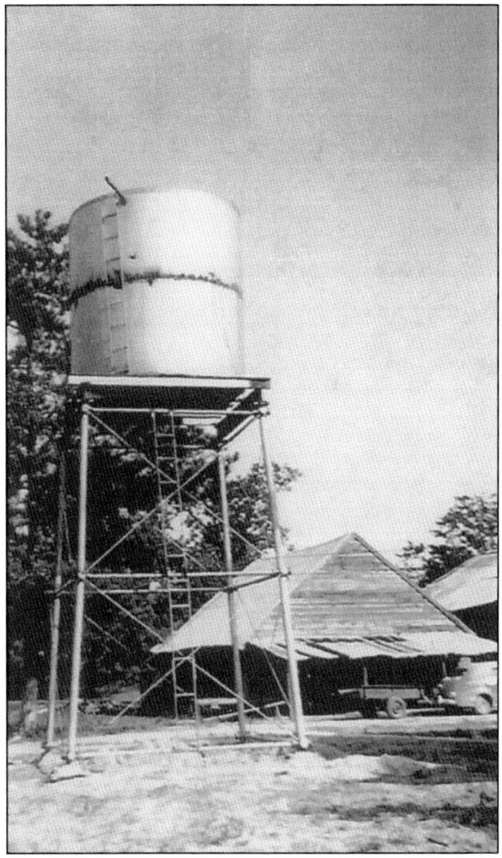

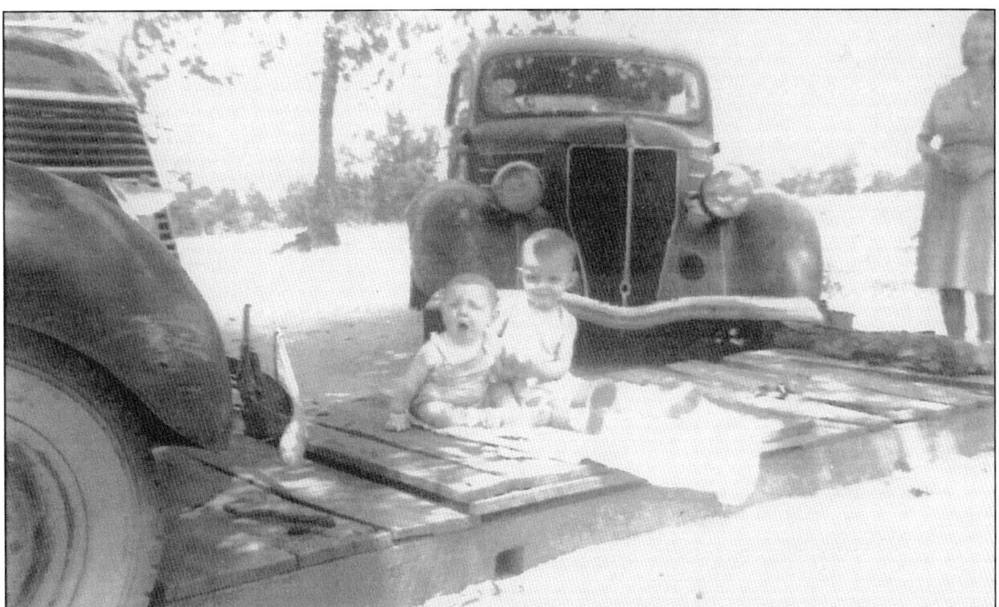

Pictured here are an unidentified lady and children at the White Oak Campmeeting in 1930. (Courtesy of Berma Ansley Gibson.)

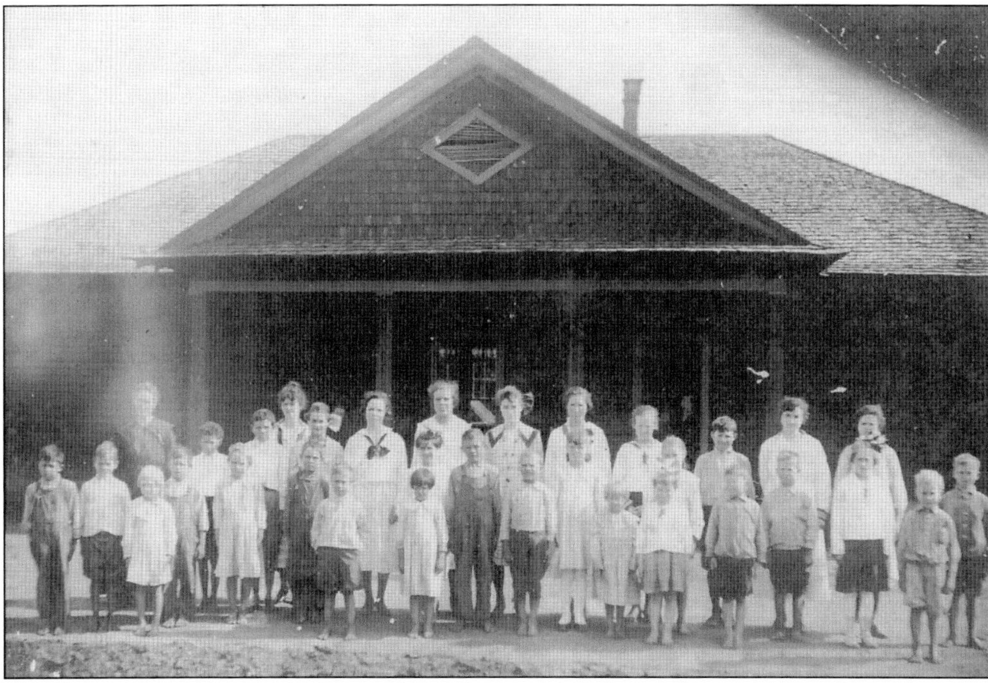

This early 1900 photograph shows old Callaway School on White Oak Road. (Courtesy of Lane Morris.)

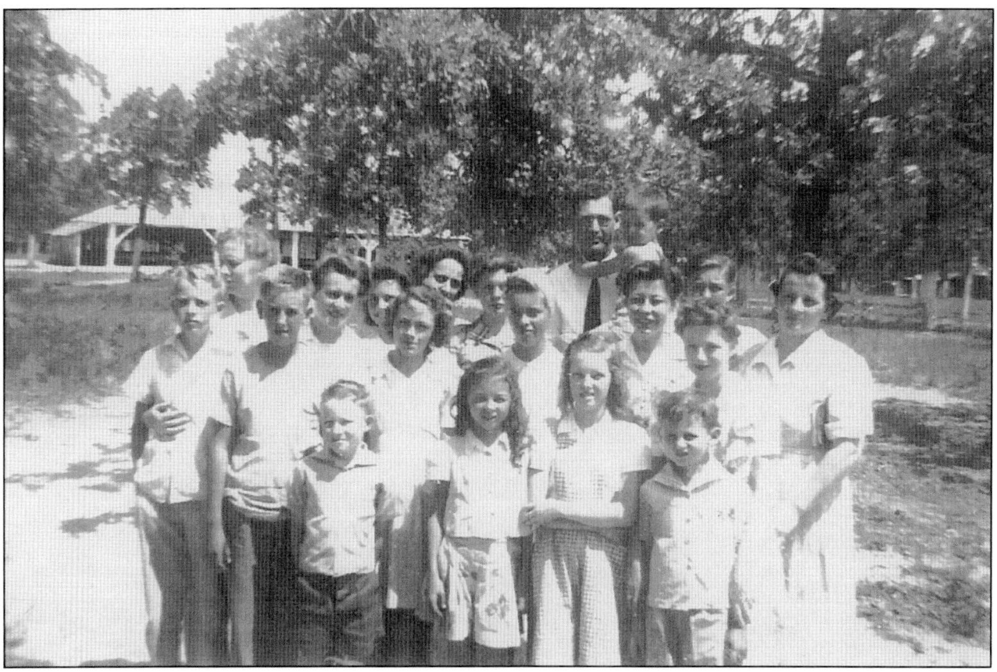

This is the White Oak Campmeeting youth group in 1930. (Courtesy of Berma Ansley Gibson.)

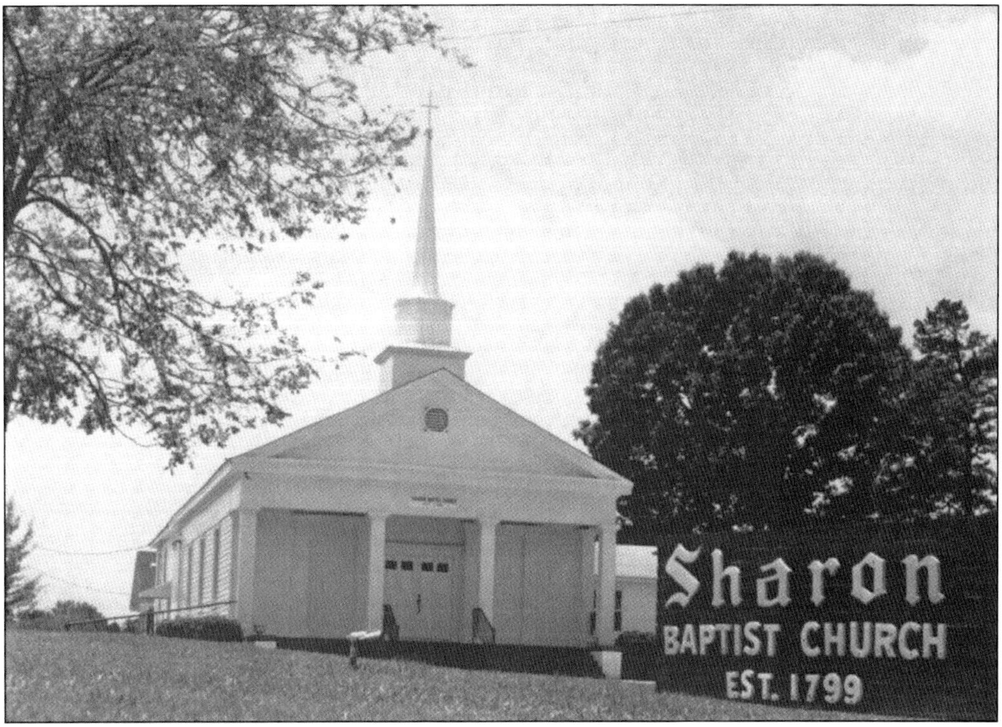

Sharon Baptist Church in Winfield, Georgia was founded by Abraham Marshall in 1779. (Courtesy of Lallie Dozier Benkoski.)

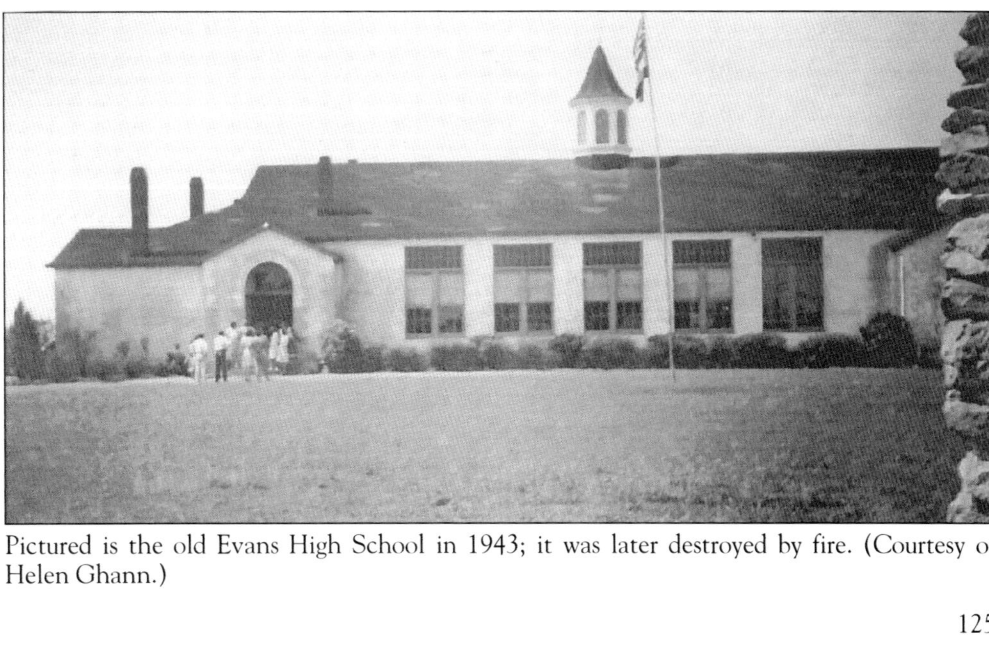
Pictured is the old Evans High School in 1943; it was later destroyed by fire. (Courtesy of Helen Ghann.)

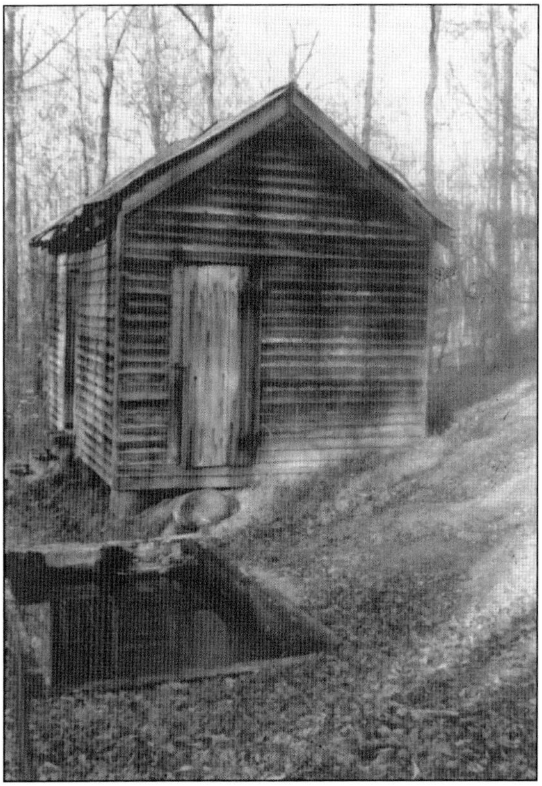

The baptismal pool and dressing rooms at Kiokee Baptist Church are seen here. (Courtesy of Kiokee Baptist Church.)

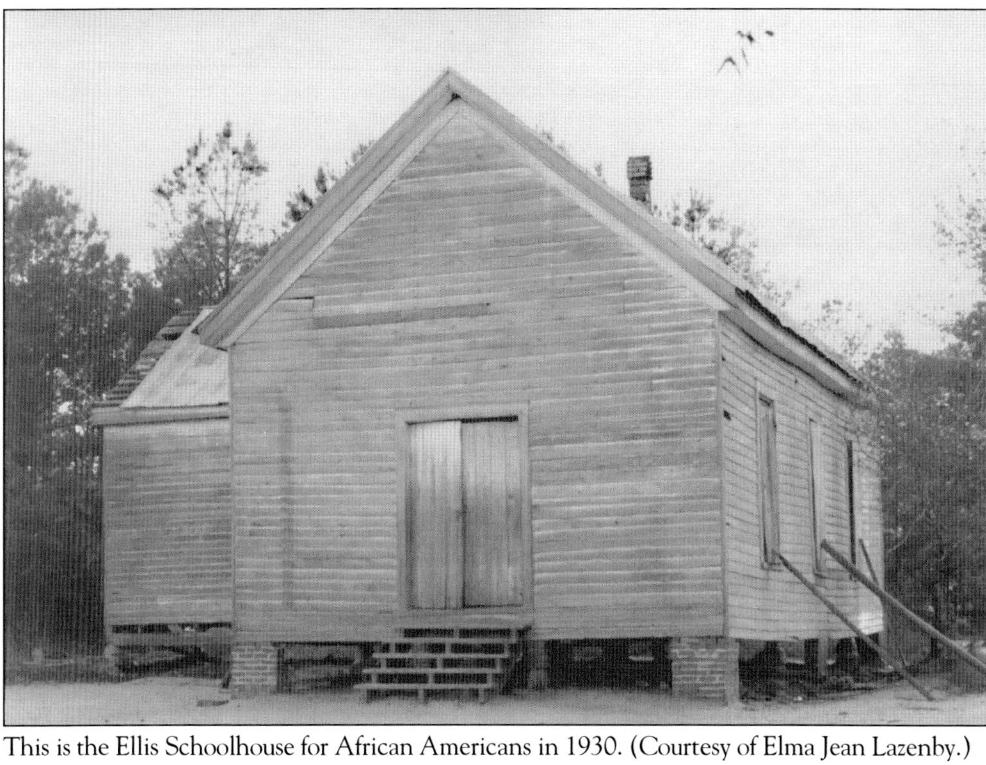

This is the Ellis Schoolhouse for African Americans in 1930. (Courtesy of Elma Jean Lazenby.)

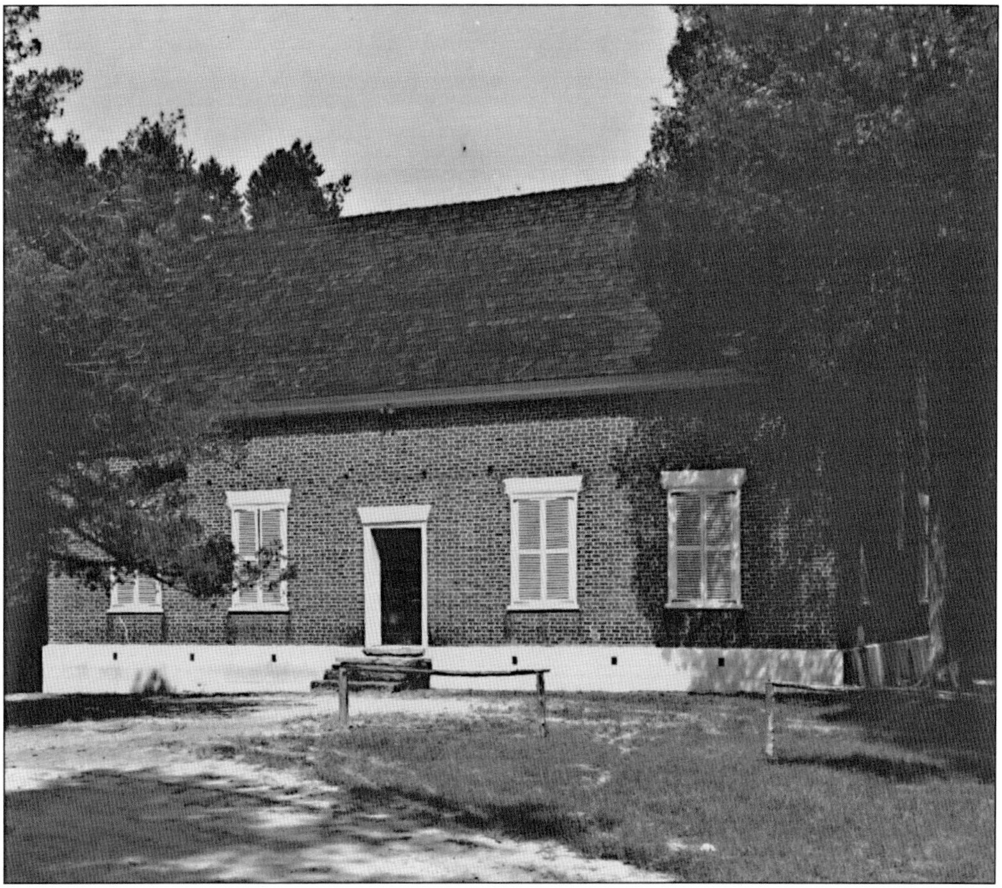

Pictured here is Kiokee Baptist Church. The oldest Baptist church in the state of Georgia, Kiokee Church was founded by Daniel Marshall in 1772 and produced some of the greatest preachers in the state's history.

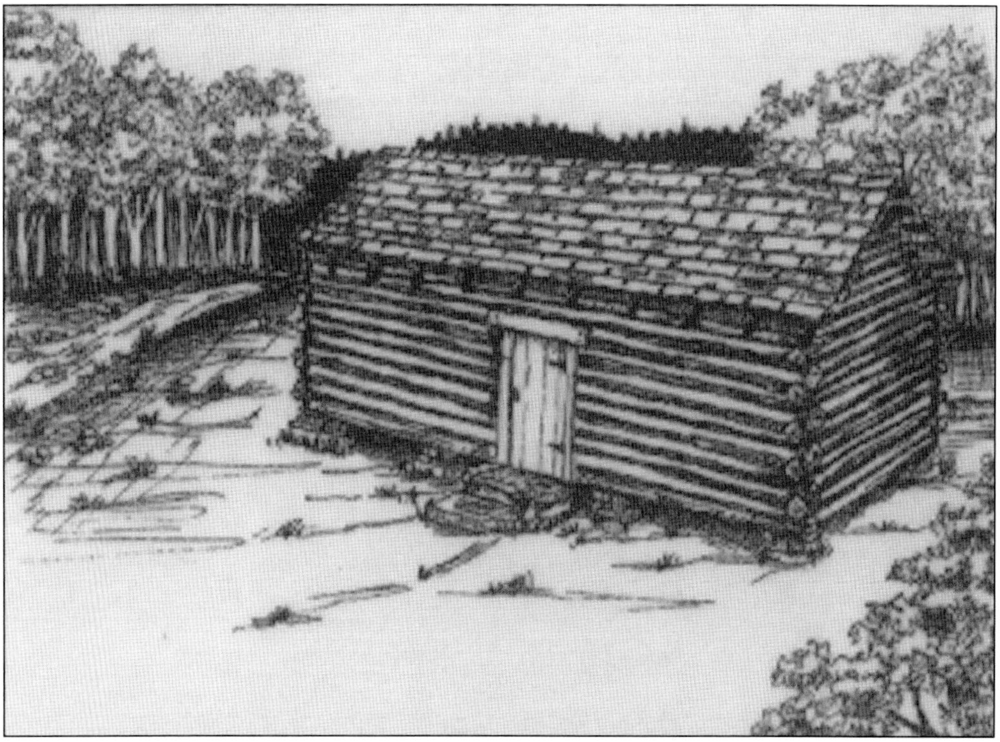

Abilene Baptist Church was founded in 1774, and this is an artist's rendering of the way the church may have looked in the beginning—a rustic, but typical log meetinghouse in the middle of the wilderness. (Courtesy of Abilene Baptist Church.)

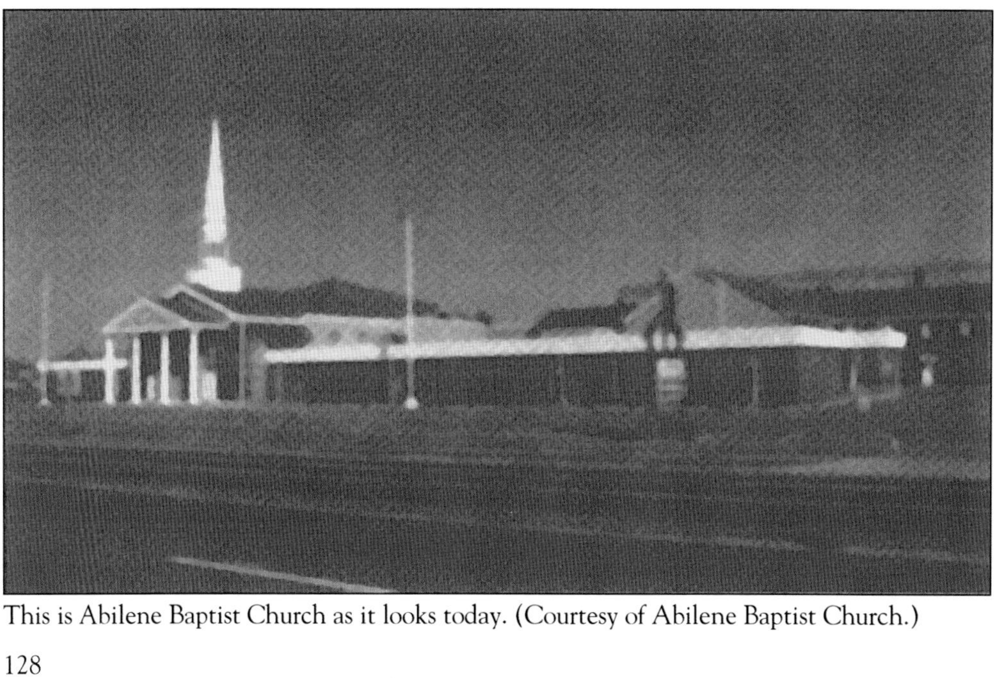

This is Abilene Baptist Church as it looks today. (Courtesy of Abilene Baptist Church.)